THE WAY OF THE WARRIOR-TRADER

THE WAY OF THE WARRIOR-TRADER

The Financial Risk-Taker's
Guide to
Samurai Courage,
Confidence and Discipline

Dr. Richard D. McCall, Shihan

McGraw-Hill
New York San Francisco Washington, D.C. Auckland Bogotá
Caracas Lisbon London Madrid Mexico City Milan
Montreal New Dehli San Juan Singapore
Sydney Tokyo Toronto

Library of Congress Cataloging-in-Publication Data

McCall, Richard.
    The way of the warrior-trader : the financial risk-taker's guide
to Samurai courage, confidence, and discipline / by Richard McCall.
        p.   cm.
    Includes index.
    ISBN 0–7863–1163–0
    1. Investments—Psychological aspects. 2. Stocks. I. Title.
HG4521.M39 1997
332.6'01'—dc21   96–40909

McGraw-Hill

A Division of The McGraw·Hill Companies

5 6 7 8 9 0 DOC/DOC 0 1

ISBN 0-7863-1163-0

Printed and bound by R. R. Donnelly & Sons Company.

This publication is designed to provide accurate and authoritative information
in regard to the subject matter covered. It is sold with the understanding that
neither the author or the publisher is engaged in rendering legal, accounting, or
other professional service. If legal advice or other expert assistance is required,
the services of a competent professional person should be sought.

*—From a Declaration of Principles jointly adopted by a Committee
of the American Bar Association and a Committee of Publishers.*

McGraw-Hill books are available at special quantity discounts to use as
premiums and sales promotions, or for use in corporate training programs. For
more information, please write to the Director of Special Sales, McGraw-Hill,
Professional Publishing, Two Penn Plaza, New York, NY 10121-2298.
Or contact your local bookstore.

Dedication

To my loving wife, Lyndee, the most supportive soul-mate a man could ever hope to have by his side, and to my two incredible sons, Benjamin and Timothy, through whom my life has been enriched and made enjoyable beyond words.

Additionally, to traders everywhere who have come to recognize that the mastery of self is the only true Way to trading success!

Acknowledgments

I wish to acknowledge several outstanding people and organizations without whom this book could not have been possible.

A very special thanks to Rick Knox and the entire CQG, Inc., organization, and Tom Joseph and the Trading Techniques, Inc., organization for introducing me to the special needs of financial traders. My thanks also to John Gambino of Merrill Lynch, Tim Slater of Dow-Jones Telerate, and Glen Larson of Genesis Financial Data, Inc., for believing in my work and for their respective roles in exposing that work to the international trading community.

To the many outstanding and professionally dedicated men and women who have attended my *Zen-Mind*™ *Challenge* retreats, my thanks for the word-of-mouth support and promotion in their respective corners of the globe.

And to the entire McGraw-Hill organization, my heartfelt thanks for their assistance with this manuscript, and for recognizing the potential benefit this information has to offer to traders everywhere.

CONTENTS

PART THREE

A *SENSEI'S* WELCOME AND INTRODUCTION

The relationship between a teacher of the Japanese martial disciplines (the *sensei*) and his personal student (the *sempai*) has traditionally been a very intimate one. That is why I am pleased to welcome you to this journey into the realm of personal warriorship, particularly trader-warriorship. It is also why I am inclined to begin our relationship with this special introduction. Please note from the onset that the operative words in the last sentence were *relationship* and *introduction*. It would not be proper to proceed with presenting this potentially transformational information and warrior wisdom without first establishing a sense of rapport with you. It is my hope that as the journey unfolds we might share a uniquely special "connection" with each other, even if it is one of a kind of "correspondence" nature.

I think you would probably agree that any mutually beneficial relationship is first built upon a sense of trust and a reasonable degree of unilateral disclosure. Experience has taught me that in order for the student to listen to (and ultimately learn and apply) what is being presented with a receptive mind, it is imperative that he possess some degree of insight into what his teacher's experience base is and has been. Likewise, the teacher should have a fairly good understanding of his student's unique needs and his expectations from their relationship and mutual efforts. Since you have gone to the trouble and expense of purchasing this book, I feel relatively comfortable making one or more assumptions about you and your motives. Any of these assumptions would indicate to me what *your* hopes and expectations might be of our relationship.

First, you may have identified with the term *warrior-trader* in the title, in which case you are probably some type of market trader or would like to be. The word *warrior* may have reflected your own past experiences with or observations about trading, through which you deduced that it is a truly unique and challenging kind of warfare. Hopefully this awareness is leading you to seek out a higher understanding of (1) what the Way of warriorship really is and (2) how to cultivate a warrior's mentality within yourself for the overall improvement of your psyche as well as your trading performance.

Another possibility is that you identified with the term *risk-taker* in the subtitle. In this case you are probably one of those special individuals who have chosen to regularly put their own hard-earned money on the line (and at risk) in any one of a number of financial "war games." You might be a commodity or stock trader or a real estate investor, or you might buy failing businesses and turn them around. Maybe you rejuvenate old cars for resale, or perhaps it's even something as uniquely exotic as playing professional blackjack or poker.

Whatever the case may be, it was probably the word *risk* that stood out in your mind. Although you are willing to take risks with your money, you may be looking for a better way to handle or regulate the inevitable emotional ramifications that risk-taking engenders, especially when the risk-taking results in a demoralizing defeat. You may also be looking for a better Way of stabilizing your behavioral discipline and "purifying" your business intuition in high-stakes situations.

Perhaps it was one or more of the words *courage, confidence,* or *discipline* in the subtitle that got your attention. In this case you have probably learned from experience how scary and unnerving it can be sometimes to "pull the trigger" on a trade. No matter how much you've paper-traded your trading method, you've no doubt come to realize it's just not the same when there is real money on the line. It is likely that you would like to understand how to develop the confidence and discipline to make live trading seem more like your paper-trading!

So these are some of the things I feel I know about you and about your possible expectations from this information and our relationship. Regardless of which of these issues may have motivated you to pick up this book and to undertake this journey with me, you can rest assured that you will not be disappointed. It may even be possible that we will surpass your greatest expectations and wishes for yourself and our relationship. It is exciting to note that even the fewest of steps in the direction of the true Way of the warrior can prove to be transformational, and I am honored to share this journey and relationship with you. And for the sake of the mutual disclosure I alluded to earlier and hopefully the deepening of our rapport, I would like to present a brief overview of my experiences, where I'm coming from with material, and my personal motives for writing this book for you.

To begin with, I've always been something of an adventurer, possessing an inner need to look deeply into things. I am told that I am an Aquarian in the truest sense of the word. From my earliest childhood up to now, I have always been fascinated with how people thought and acted and how the universe and its laws (what the *samurai* called the *kyokushin*) worked its physical and spiritual magic upon us. But perhaps more important to this story, I (like you, I suspect) have always been a little "different," with an almost stubborn need to be independent, to take the road less traveled, and to create my own wealth (or poverty) through my own independent efforts. In other words, I (like you again, I suspect) have always been a financial risk-taker at heart, something that my first wife and a myriad of creditors had a very hard time being comfortable with before I seemed to get the hang of it.

Sometimes it's hard to tell which came first, the chicken or the egg. Did I become different because of my early exposure to the Japanese martial disciplines and the metaphysical truths they bring to light, or did I gravitate toward those martial disciplines because of my different mentality and the rather unusual destiny paths it seems to lead me down? Who knows? And I guess it really doesn't matter since I am truly happy about where I am and the countless learning experiences I have had, both positive and negative. Thankfully, with the passing of the years and the eventual transformation of so-called knowledge into understanding, there has also come a bit of wisdom—wisdom about life, the nature of risk, and risk-taking.

At this point in my life I live what the Japanese would call a *shibumi* lifestyle, which means a kind of comfortable, unpretentious simplicity, which was probably the result of many years of Zen practice and the sense of detachment from materialism it promotes. I have finally learned that it is the inner spirit of a person that truly makes his home, his car, or the clothes he wears appear attractive or special, rather than the other way around, as so many people are led to believe. I am remarried to a truly wonderful and supportive soul mate, and share my life with her and my two teenage sons, all of whom are fellow *yudansha* (senior black belts) in our *dojo*. All three of these special people seem to exhibit and embody a true understanding and appreciation of the value of calculated risk-taking in life and the inescapable importance of living and thinking the martial Way.

For the past quarter of a century I have been the *shihan* of the *Bushinkai Dojo,* where I regularly practice and teach the traditional martial disciplines and philosophies of the Japanese *samurai,* including *Budo-Zen.* It is a responsibility I have always taken quite seriously and to which I have devoted a major percentage of my life force, soul passion, and personal finances. Other than the occasional fleeting moments when the rent was past due and the current student population was a little slow in rendering their monthly financial support, I have never regretted maintaining this very special training environment for those whose destinies called them to learn and then live the true *Budo* (the *samurai's* "martial Way").

The term *shihan* means headmaster or master instructor. A *dojo* is a formal training hall of any traditional Way of personal growth, refinement, or enlightenment. However, the term is usually associated with the classical "martial Ways" of historical Japan, as in this case. The name *Bushinkai* literally means the society (*kai*) of mental (*shin*) warriorship (*bu*), which gives you a hint as to the slant my curriculum has taken from the very beginning. It would seem that even long before I pursued a formal education in human behavior and received my doctorate in applied psychology, I was always something of an amateur psychologist and innovator. I seem to remember being constantly "advised" by some inner voice as to how the philosophies and methods of the *samurai* could serve this or that situation or occupation. Perhaps the ghost of some ancient *samurai* warrior has been listening and looking over my shoulder from the beginning. Who can say? But wherever that inner voice may have come from, I am nonetheless appreciative of and indebted to it!

So, for better or for worse, I guess I see "warriorship" in everything, and perhaps one day you will too. But I do know that in the course of 15 years of professional consulting, I have personally seen the *samurai* Way bring success for countless clients in a wide variety of situations and applications, where the usual psychological mumbo jumbo and rhetoric had failed. These would include, for example, psychological crisis intervention, phobia management, marital discord, collegiate and professional sports performance, business management, sales and service enhancement, and, for an occasional movie star, help with suffering from career burnout.

I'm quite certain that over the many years my family, close friends, and perhaps even the occasional student at the *dojo* have at times grown weary of hearing me point out the "warrior perspective" in every adversarial or challenging situation that may have presented its ugly head. However, considering the positive outcome of most of these situations where they ultimately *did* apply a warrior mentality, I have more often than not felt justified in having voiced the distinction. I just feel it is unfortunate that when most people think of the words *warrior* or *warriorship* they tend to think of physical combat or conflicts. While on the surface this may appear to be true, *warfare* may best be defined as *any* situation that results in conflict or struggle—whether it be internal or external. This broadened definition brings about a heightened awareness of the need for and applicability of personal warriorship in every aspect of human existence.

Like it or not, it would seem to me that we are *all* warriors by either default or design. And until a short while ago I believed that a study of *samurai* insights and wisdom would prove of *equal* value and benefit to just about everyone, regardless of their profession. But that was before synchronicity and fate decided to give me a polite shove into a new world and down a challenging new path, one that would once again expand my scope of how important warriorship can be in today's fast-paced competitive world! Interestingly, it was that shove that has ultimately brought you and me together as well!

I was first introduced to the business of "professional" financial risk-taking late in 1992, when a polite, soft-spoken gentleman contacted me in regard to a "unique problem" associated with his occupation that he wished to work on. Upon meeting with him in person, he proceeded to explain to me that he was a futures and commodities trader, a professional field that I admittedly knew little about at the time. After taking the time to patiently convey to me as many facets of trading as were possible in a single sitting, he was able to paint a clear picture of the problem as he perceived it.

Even though he had been trading and making other high-risk investments for many years with reasonable success, he had only done so on a part-time basis. He had also developed and thoroughly "paper-traded" a new system he believed to be potentially profitable. However, when it came down to the real risk and "pulling the trigger" he just didn't have it all together. Additionally, he was strongly motivated to commit to trading full-time and to break the ties to his alternative employment obligations.

My new trader/investor friend further explained that he had read with great interest and enthusiasm such "warrior psychology" books as *The Art of War* by Sun Tsu and *The Book of Five Rings* by Miyamoto Musashi. Although he enjoyed reading these classical works, their deeper inner meaning was somehow not coming to life for him or his trading. Having heard from friends about my being a combination occupational psychologist, *samurai* historian, and master martial artist, he had hoped that in some way I might serve as a kind of interpreter of these warrior insights and wisdom. Recognizing that the *samurai* of feudal-era Japan was probably history's most accomplished "professional risk-taker," he further hoped that I would in some way be able to teach him to emulate the mentality, methods, and living philosophy of this elite warrior.

That meeting led to the development of an outstanding in-residence retreat training program which we called the *Misogi Challenge* (which has since evolved into the *Zen-Mind™ Challenge*). *Misogi* is a Japanese word that literally means "to forge and purify the warrior's mind/spirit into a Zen-mind," which, of course, was the ultimate objective of the program. My trader friend brought in a handful of special associates (all serious traders of various types) to participate in this experimental program with him. I can honestly say that the results of this three-day program were, at the very least, astounding. My new warrior-trader *sempai*—all of whom (I came to realize later) were some of the most respected traders in the world—returned to their various corners of the globe with a new-found focus and an understanding not only of themselves but of the Way of trading and investing as well.

The only improvement that seemed to be needed in the training approach I had used was uncovered several weeks later as I conducted follow-up surveys with each of the original participants. Each enthusiastically agreed that the retreat and the *samurai* mentality they had been exposed to (and were now practicing) were the most empowering experiences and information they had ever known. However, they each seemed to also indicate that they wished they had perhaps done some preparatory reading on warrior psychology in advance of actually experiencing the various warrior "challenges" I confronted them with during the course of the program. This way they might have been more initially receptive to and appreciative of what they were experiencing, and would perhaps have consumed less mental energy and valuable time overcoming the usual novice learning curve.

Having always been a proponent of accelerated learni
input to heart and began providing future retreat attendees
sortment of books to read in advance of their training with
for this assortment was that there simply wasn't any one b
all the important aspects of warriorship clearly and conc
written in an easily understandable vernacular. Additionally, ...
books I had to use for this purpose admittedly contained a considerable
amount of literary fluff that tended to obscure the important truths.

These two problems resulted in attendees showing up not having invested the time necessary to weed through the books to find the points I was
hoping to expose them to. Those that did manage to read the combination
of books often arrived with an array of confused questions resulting from
the rather abstract way much warrior philosophy is often written or presented. Thus, it became evident to me that there was a genuine need for a
kind of handbook on this very important and valuable subject for profes-
sionals just like yourself, a book that clearly detailed the inner workings of
the *samurai* warrior's mentality and his time-tested methodology for acquiring the same.

As a result of all this, as you've probably deduced, the seeds for this
book began to germinate in my imagination along with the motives and impetus to bring the project to life . . . and then ultimately bring it to *you!* Since
I laid the first words to paper, I have held no misguided notions of becoming rich or famous as a result of this work. What I do intend, however, is to
fulfill your needs and expectations of me by providing you with a clear-cut
look into the mind and the method of history's most accomplished professional risk-taker—the *samurai*. And somewhere along the Way, I am also
hopeful that you will catch a glint of personal enlightenment as well. How
much enlightenment or benefit you derive will ultimately be up to you, of
course, since no matter what you learn or experience, it is still you, and you
alone, at the helm of your destiny.

And as for me, being responsible for my own destiny as well, I have intuitively chosen to take yet another potentially rewarding financial risk in my
life. I have let go of the financial security of my former behavioral consulting practice and my university teaching positions in order to dedicate my
full-time energies to personally taking warrior-trader candidates like yourself on the very journey we are about to embark upon. So in a real sense, for

for worse, we are in this together. The following chapters represent
t of my nearly three decades of study, observations, and experiences
the realm of the warrior-traditions of Japan and the true Way of the
samurai. I cannot claim to have all the answers, but I have experienced an incredible number of simple yet dynamic truths, most of which will be
brought to light herein.

For ease of reference and to hopefully facilitate a more immediate inte-
gration of this warrior wisdom into your financial risk-taking endeavors, I
have arranged this book into three sections.

Part One, "*The* Samurai's *Psychology of Existence,*" is intended to help you understand and then begin to emulate the warrior's point of view about himself, his philosophy and manner of existence, and the truly unique Way he
approached thinking and mentality in general.

Part Two, "*The* Samurai's *Psychology of Engagement,*" addresses the overall
structure of the warrior's tactical thinking and philosophy, and breaks them
down into an easily understandable blueprint that you can apply to any con-
frontational situation in life, especially trading.

Part Three, "*The* Samurai's *Psychology of Recovery,*" will provide invaluable warrior philosophy and wisdom regarding emotional rejuvenation after the inevitable setback or loss we must all experience occasionally in high-risk investing situations.

As you go about reading this book, absorbing its valuable information,
and then attempting to apply its transformational wisdom to your own situation, please remember something I try to impress on every new student at
my *dojo.* It is important to recognize that as you learn any new skill or psychological approach to doing anything, you will inevitably evolve through
four distinct phases of progress, none of which can be side-stepped! Just knowing
where you are within the four phases can often be of great assistance to you
in moving on to the next level.

The first phase is *unconscious incompetence,* which refers to the point wherein
you begin the learning curve. Unconscious incompetence implies that you
are thinking or performing inefficiently, but with no knowledge whatsoever
that you're doing so in a faulty or incorrect way. Usually, at this phase the
only thing you would notice is the frustration and aggravation of not getting the results you want and need from your efforts.

The second phase of learning is what I call *conscious incompetence*. After I describe the correct or more effective way of doing something, you will predictably become more aware of your mistakes and how you tend to make them. This should lead you to an all-important impetus toward conscious self-correction, and then hopefully move you toward the third phase of the learning curve!

With awareness of your errors on the increase, you will then have the opportunity to consciously (and sometimes awkwardly) make the necessary corrections or adjustments in your thinking or behavior. This third phase is known as the *conscious competence* phase. At this point, providing that you understand the correct or more effective way of handling a situation, you can do so when you consciously think about it! With enough intentional conscious repetition of the prescribed approach, it will hopefully result in what educational psychologists call neuropsychological entrainment. When this occurs, you will be well on your way to the final and most important phase of our student–teacher relationship.

The fourth phase—and the ultimate hope of any teacher for his student—is *unconscious competence*. At this point the appropriate warrior philosophy, psychology, and behaviors you will have been practicing will become fully committed to your unconscious right brain, from which all emotional control, intuition, and higher automatic behavior originate. It is at that time that the teacher of the warrior Ways can remove himself from the equation and can enjoy the incredible satisfaction of watching the wisdom and knowledge he passed along working for his student.

Now before we begin our study, let me make a couple of comments about the chapter design I have employed in this work.

It is my genuine desire to provide you with as many different possible perspectives concerning this valuable information. To better facilitate your learning curve and to afford you a better grasp of the essence and applicability of this information, each chapter will open with a true story that holds historical or personal significance to me. My personal students like to refer to these fascinating historical stories and personal anecdotes from my warrior experiences as "true tales of the *Budo*," a title I have chosen to use for your stories as well. These opening "True Tales of the *Budo*" will provide you with real-life glimpses of how the contents of each chapter apply to the historical *samurai* or to contemporary practitioners (such as myself), of the "hard-core" Japanese martial disciplines.

Concluding each chapter you will find (and hopefully enjoy) what I call "True Tales of the Warrior-Trader." These brief closing commentaries will provide you with some degree of insight as to how the information and/or concepts in that chapter benefited an actual professional trader I've trained or consulted with. Over the years I have collected the comments and feedback from hundreds of my warrior-trader *sempai*, and I have drawn extensively from that collection in presenting each closing chapter's real-life anecdotes. Hopefully you will be able to closely identify with some of these experiences of your peers and then perhaps gain a better understanding of how the warrior Way can help a trader's attitude, performance, and life in general!

So, as our traditional *sensei–sempai* relationship officially begins, let me reaffirm that the information I am about to pass along to you, and the deeper truth and wisdom contained therein, have enabled me, like our *samurai* predecessors, to confidently prosper or fail and occasionally even live or die by my own decisions and actions. Hopefully they will empower you to do the same. It has often been said that when the student is ready, the teacher will appear. If your time has now come and you are ready, then I am honored to serve in some small way as your teacher! And with this in mind I am inclined to shout the *samurai* battle cry, *Hajime* (Let the engagement begin!).

THE WAY OF THE
WARRIOR-TRADER

PART ONE

The Samurai's Psychology of Existence

CHAPTER I

Understanding the Warrior's Way

TRUE TALES OF THE BUDO

Tanemura Kenshi stood stoically before the five-inch-thick column of wetted straw, waiting to draw his blade. After a few moments of setting his mind and preparing his spirit for the task at hand, he suddenly drew his razor-sharp katana *from its scabbard. In less than a blink of an eye, his 42 inches of cold, hardened steel cut the straw column into two pieces with flawless surgical precision. There was no doubt in the minds of the observers that, if this had been an actual human torso, it would have been cleanly severed from shoulder to hip.*

Master Tanemura was presenting a training session in tamishi-giri batto-jutsu, *test-cutting with a "live" blade, to a select handful of* sempai, *each of whom was seeking a certificate of proficiency from the reputed swordsman. After comparing what he had just seen to his own less-than-perfect cuts, one* sempai *cautiously asked, "*Sensei, *is it not possible that your cuts are superior to ours because you are armed with a superior blade with a superior edge?" The master, without so much as a look at the inquiring student, placed a large melon on top of a chest-high pedestal and then proceeded to pick up a length of the coarse string used to bind the bundles of wet straw for cutting.*

Stepping back into the hasso-gamai *stance, Tanemura Kenshi slowly and dramatically raised his hands to the right side of his head as if holding an imaginary sword, now represented by the string that drooped behind his shoulder, and prepared to strike! Suddenly, in a blur of lightning-quick efficiency and with a deafening* kiai *that shook the observers to the bases of their feet, he stepped forward in a seemingly effortless cutting motion. After a moment of stunned stillness, the* sempai *looked with disbelief at the target. What had moments ago been a large, whole melon was now clearly "decapitated" with the same surgical precision as if it had been cut with a top-quality sword!*

With an intensity and a wisdom in his eyes that seemed to span the ages, the master turned to his pupils and simply said, "Remember this invaluable truth! In all matters of warfare, all methods, techniques, or armament are secondary *to inner spirit and mentality! Only by following the true Way of the warrior can he be assured that his weaponry will not fail him in battle!"*

A Look at the True Way of the Warrior

Inasmuch as any journey must start at the beginning, to begin this journey is to come to understand and appreciate the Way of the *samurai* warrior. By now you have probably noticed my emphasis and capitalization of Way. This is because the Way serves as the very foundation of everything else presented in this book. The Japanese word for Way is *Do* (pronounced "dough"), and refers to "a life path, occupation, or discipline that results in the refinement of the followers' spirit, character, and inner composure." In another words, it means that regardless of the task, discipline, or behavior that is undertaken, it is literally transformed by the practitioner into an art form. Then, reciprocally, the art form transforms the practitioner into a work of art as well.

Although *Do* (plural and singular forms are the same) can be found in many facets of Japanese culture, they are most noticeable within the realm of its martial disciplines. *Judo, kendo, aikido, kyudo, iaido,* and *karate-do* are all examples of highly refined martial disciplines that date back as far as the *samurai* era. Although the objective (e.g., self-defense or fitness) of learning and practicing one or more of these martial disciplines might at first seem obvious, a deeper analysis of the training motives of its more serious practitioners would reveal that rather esthetic outcomes (such as self-control, inner strength, mental and spiritual discipline, and/or personal enlightenment) are being pursued.

The Art of Becoming Art

The point I want to make here is simple yet important. You must first understand that before you can elevate your personal performance in any area, your performance must first be viewed as an art form, and that the pure objective of practicing this art is the refinement of your inner spirit and discipline and ultimately the unconditional enjoyment and appreciation of having done it as well as is currently possible. This pulls you away from the distraction of watching or wishing for the desired outcome (such as profits) and puts your attention fully on the flawless execution of the act itself (such as trading)! This is what is referred to as the *Zen Way of performance*, a subject that I will delve much deeper into later.

You must first understand that before you can elevate your personal performance in any area, it must first be viewed as an art form. . .

As I mentioned earlier, *Do* are not limited simply to the Japanese culture or their traditional martial disciplines. To be sure, it is a universal principle that can potentially be found within almost any activity, regardless of how mundane or frivolous it may at first seem. If you will just take the time to look with new eyes at the world around you and the various pastimes and occupations people engage in, many different (yet similar) *Do* will appear—sometimes in the least-expected places.

Some Everyday Examples of the Way

My mother-in law Dottie has always had a knack for hand-making very special commemorative gift baskets and decorations. She seems to be able to dream up something unique for literally any occasion. As you would expect with any product where special talent and workmanship are evident, word-of-mouth advertising has placed her and her creations in fairly high demand.

Seeing how hard she worked at this and the relatively little amount of money she seemed to make doing it, I once rendered a little of my famous free advice about ways to streamline her operation, perhaps train an able co-manufacturer, and thus increase her net profits. The look of surprise in her eyes and the comment that followed produced instant enlightenment (and, admittedly, a bit of shame) in me. She politely said, "Sweetie, the real reward in this for me is kind of getting 'in touch' with the recipient of my basket and then creating something that comes from deep within me that I know will make that person feel special and appreciated! Plus, making these baskets makes me feel young, so the way I see it, the more baskets I create with my own mind and hands, the younger I'll be!" It was at that instant I recognized basket-making to be her true Way.

And there are many other examples of *Do* I can cite right here in my immediate family, as I am sure there are in yours. My wife Lyndee runs a large women's apparel store where she dedicates an incredible amount of energy to teaching her employees the Way of quality customer service and to developing in them a sense of pride in the appearance of the place where they work. My older son Ben, an avid basketball enthusiast, spends countless hours practicing free-throws, outside shots, and ball-handling to the point where the game has become a form of "moving art" to him. And my younger son Tim, a promising cross-country runner, presents an inspirational example of the Way of a warrior-athlete, getting up before dawn five days a week to execute his grueling five-mile run across hilly terrain.

Is It the Way or Obsession?

Perhaps you might wonder, What qualifies these various endeavors as examples of a *Do* or true Way? Maybe these are just examples of obsessive or compulsive behavior rather than something of a higher order. My response to your query would be that it depends on what truly motivates the individual at his deepest gut level to perform the behavior. It is generally not a true Way if a person is driven to do such things out of some inexplicable need within his mind, or if he is motivated by pure ego gratification or the potential acquisition of some down-the-line reward he hopes to attain after the fact. If, on the other hand, the performer is motivated by the sheer sense of inner gratification, centeredness, and vitality that can result from having totally applied himself to the best of his current ability, then he has indeed practiced the true Way I am discussing.

Common sense naturally tells me that Lyndee obviously wants to ultimately make her store as profitable as possible and to be recognized as a top-producing manager by the company she serves. But I know it is the satisfaction she feels when she rings up a satisfied customer, or the pride she feels when the store is as neat as a pin, that motivates her to practice and share with her employees the tenets of "higher-order" store management.

I'm reasonably sure that in the long run, Ben would like to be a star basketball player (and, I sometimes secretly suspect, the next Michael Jordan), and to enjoy the usual accolades that such a status engenders. But when I look closely, the pure bliss of simply playing the game well for the game's sake shines through in his eyes.

And as for Tim, there is no doubt in my mind that he looks forward to one day receiving first-place medals at his many track meets and possibly receiving a full athletic scholarship in track. But there is also little doubt that what gratifies him most is simply entering into his daily training log that he executed his prescribed workout and that he successfully met his pace criteria for that day or at least got as close to them as was humanly possible. So it is fair to say that Tim has, like Dottie, Lyndee, and Ben have done with theirs, transformed his activity into a true art form, and it is equally fair to assess that their respective art forms have inevitably transformed them in the process as well.

Inner Spirit, Not Outer Trappings

By viewing your performance as an art form, you will also tend to downplay the importance of the tools or system being utilized in the course of the performance.

Now let's look at another major advantage to approaching personal performance from the perspective of the Way of the warrior. By viewing your performance as an art form, you will also tend to downplay the importance of the tools or system being utilized in the course of the performance. As Tanemura Kenshi told his small group of students in the opening segment of this chapter, "In all matters of warfare, all methods, techniques, or armament are secondary to inner spirit and mentality! Only by following the true Way of the warrior can he be assured that his weaponry will not fail him in battle!"

Development of the internal side of people would appear to be something of a lost cause in the so-called modern world we live in. Advertising bombards society with a myriad of misguided notions leading the consuming public to believe that everything that empowers them is external to their being. It's the clothes or the fragrance that makes men or women attractive—the shoes that make them run faster or jump higher—the kind of car they drive or the kind of wine they drink that makes them sophisticated. The list could go on and on, and unfortunately it probably will.

But for our purposes here, it is important to recognize that this fallacy is not limited to just the simple, superficial issues I've just mentioned. Regrettably, such shallow thinking tends to foster other possibly more hazardous beliefs as well. One of the most common notions (one embraced by many market traders) is that if you only had the "right hardware" or the "right software" or the "right (you fill in the blank)," you could make a fortune in this or that market. This is probably the result of our sometimes overtechnological and mostly automated lifestyle. Our sophisticated digital world tends to deceive us into believing that we can do or have anything we want with a simple touch of a button. Not only that, but we are also led to believe that we can have it right now, without delay!

The Fruitless Search for the Holy Grail

Another important thing I have learned in the course of interacting with and training hundreds of professional traders is that, at one point or another, nearly all of them looked for or believed in the so-called holy grail—that perfect investment scheme or trading system that would make them money no matter what they did.

Of course experience tells us that this holy grail cannot exist. The closest thing to it is attentiveness to current market conditions and the near-flawless execution of a reasonably sound investment or trading methodology. The true Way of the warrior dictates that we should simply execute the system of our choice with consistency and accuracy, deriving pure and immediate gratification simply from having done so. Only in this way can we be assured of profits in the long run, which of course is the ultimate objective of having assumed the risk of investing our money or resources in the first place.

We must never forget that on this side of that instant-success or instant-wealth button you may have been wanting to push, there is a human finger required, a finger that is directed and managed by a human mind with all its fragile complexities and variables. It is only through the patient, disciplinary refinement of your inner spirit and mental processes that you can be assured that your external armament will serve you without fail in the heat of the battle.

You can begin right now by making it a point to become more aware of the Way of the warrior being demonstrated by people around you. Allow everything you do, particularly financial risk-taking, to be gradually transformed into a disciplined art form, one that will genuinely reflect the Way of the warrior taking shape within you! If the idea and importance of transforming your trading behavior into a precise art form comes at all as a shock or surprise to you, then you have just graduated from the *unconscious incompetence* phase to the *conscious incompetence* phase. If so, then congratulations! You can begin now to change your perspective of your investing philosophy and performance wherever it is needed. In this way you will start laying down a firm foundation upon which we can build an indestructible fortress of *samurai* courage, confidence, discipline, and inner strength.

If the idea and importance of transforming your trading behavior into a precise art form comes at all as a shock or surprise to you, then you have just graduated from the unconscious incompetence *phase to the* conscious incompetence *phase.*

If, on the other hand, you already recognized and valued the fact that trading behavior must become an art form—a true Way—then it is appropriate that I applaud your existing warrior intuition and spirit! But in either case I am excited about your warrior-trader potential as we move on to the pivotal issue of day-to-day personal motivation!

True Tales of the Warrior-Trader

I was admittedly surprised that B.H. of Tucson, Arizona, had requested a consultation with me. In the initial fact-finding phase of our time together, it quickly became clear that he was not only a good, consistent commodity trader, but maybe even what most of us would call a great trader. B.H. specialized in trading precious metals, currencies, and three specific agricultural futures, and had been at it for about 15 years.

Even though B.H. had built a good life for him, his wife, and their two children, it seemed that he had always been very uncomfortable introducing himself to new acquaintances and associates as being a market trader. Somewhere in his past he had absorbed from the mumblings and low-key criticisms of his conservative parents and siblings that playing the markets in some way reflected the actions and obsessions of a fool and a dreamer and—worse yet—one who thought he could strike it rich without having to work at a real job.

One problem that these almost unconscious attitudes seemed to create for B.H. was that of dealing with a series of drawdowns appropriately. Naturally, any investor will feel badly in those times when plans or investments don't pan out the way he hoped. But the typical "you win some and you lose some" philosophy didn't alleviate the depression and despondency B.H. felt in such situations. Rather, he found himself believing and subscribing to the opinions of his detractors and subsequently losing confidence not only in his abilities, but in his chosen profession as well. Naturally this wreaked havoc on his performance from time to time—and that was what he sought to consult with me about.

B.H. indicated that he really had a knack for finances as well as for pattern and trend recognition, and that commodity trading was the only way he had ever found to fully use and integrate these talents. Upon hearing this, combined with my knowledge of his previous success with trading, I immediately recognized trading to be his true Way to fulfillment and satisfaction, and I proceeded to tell him so in no uncertain terms! I also pointed out that no one can select our life purpose or identify our soul passion for us. Only he could do that for himself—and it was obvious to me that he already had! He had simply fallen prey to seeking the acceptance and respect of others over his own personal satisfaction and sense of purpose and fulfillment.

After a couple of months of studying the samurai's Way of looking at life and occupation, B.H. fortunately came to see successful trading (with the eyes of a true warrior-investor) for what it is—hard work requiring considerable talent, skill, patience, and discipline. In fact, B.H. has since told me that he has come to see and describe his trading (and the considerable income he derives from doing it) to his critics as "an honorable, artistic expression of his talents and intellect—a true Way of making a living worthy of the respect of even the legendary samurai!"

I am pleased and proud to say that B.H., as have countless others like him, has discovered that the Way of the warrior-investor is perhaps the road less traveled—but it is their road nonetheless!

CHAPTER 2

The Way of Warrior Motivation

TRUE TALES OF THE BUDO

The samurai's Way encouraged a sense of detachment and independence from material possessions in order that their lives and service to their masters would be unencumbered. There were, nonetheless, three things of irreplaceable value to the Bushi (the warrior class) of feudal Japan: their family lineage, their swords (which were crafted for them at the time of their birth), and their purpose of existence, which was to serve the master or lord whom their father had served.

One of the most famous stories in Japanese history is that of lord Soma and one of his relatively unknown samurai retainers. By his own admission, Soma's most valued possession was the book of his family genealogy, which he kept in a special place in the center of his fine home. One day, as his karma would have it, Soma's home caught fire, the flames spreading furiously to engulf the entire structure. Fortunately everyone who had been inside managed to escape the inferno, but there had been no time to save any possessions whatsoever.

As he watched everything he owned being consumed by the blaze, Soma woefully commented to the group of samurai who stood with him, "There is nothing irreplaceable in there except my family genealogy. My only regret is that I was unable to retrieve it before I escaped!" One of the lower-rank samurai immediately volunteered to go into the flames and retrieve it. This drew quick looks of surprise from his fellow samurai inasmuch as he had never been of very much service to their master before. Soma responded, "No, it is far too late! The house is consumed by flames and you will be killed!" The samurai, disregarding his master's warning, ran quickly toward the house, saying, "I have known since my birth that my purpose in life was to someday be of service to you! Today is the day I will serve and die!" With that he disappeared into a wall of fire.

Soma and his other samurai waited anxiously, but the brave volunteer did not come out. Several hours later, after the flames had burned out and the embers had cooled enough for a search to take place, they began to sift through the rubble to find his body. They eventually found

10

it curled up, knees to chest, in a fetal position on the ground not far from where the genealogy had been kept. Upon turning over the samurai's *body, they were shocked to discover that his stomach had been cut open. Inside the gaping wound they were even more shocked to find the genealogy, bloody but unburned! To keep the flames from destroying the book, he had cut himself open and placed the book inside his belly. He had not only accepted his destiny with courageous action, but had also fulfilled his gut-level life purpose in the process. Since that day, this famous book has been know in Japanese lore as "the Blood Genealogy."*

Motivation and Life Purpose

The subject of motivation and life purpose has always been of great interest to me, both as a teacher of the Japanese martial disciplines and as a psychologist. What is it that makes one person in a given situation productive and happy, yet another person in exactly the same setting unproductive and dejected? Considering what you and I want to accomplish through our relationship and this study, this question should be of paramount importance to you as well, especially if you plan to follow the true Way of the warrior-trader!

In my 10 years of private clinical practice I had the opportunity to work with the issue of motivation quite a bit. Since I chose to specialize in occupationally related "performance enhancement psychology," it was to be expected that such terms as *job stress, career burnout,* and *emotional fatigue* would come up quite regularly. It was also evident with occupational specialties involving financial risk-taking that these problems, each of which can be a serious symptom of motivational anemia, came up with even greater frequency and intensity.

After consulting with over 3,000 clients and with the help of *samurai* warrior-wisdom, I have acquired what I believe to be a fairly accurate appraisal of (1) what motivation is, (2) the three "emotional carcinogens" that can destroy it, and (3) the "four pillars of warrior motivation" that can support an exciting, fulfilling, and productive career and life. I would like to address all three in order to give you a chance to honestly reflect on your own life and situation, particularly as they relate to your trading and/or other financial risk-taking you may regularly engage in.

The Nature of Motivation

First, let's briefly discuss what motivation appears to be. Funk & Wagnall's dictionary defines it as "a conscious need, drive or objective that incites a person to some action or behavior." This typically conventional definition tends to explain why so many people suffer from a lack of fulfilling and lasting motivation, and why so many of today's books, tapes, and so-called motivational seminars fall short of their objective. In essence, they generally tend to preach that all that is necessary for motivation to exist is a reasonably desirable "dangling carrot" to pursue. Experience has taught me that nothing could be farther from the truth.

In order to help you understand motivation from the warrior's point of view, at least initially, let me offer the expanded definition that would likely have come from a *samurai*. His definition of motivation would probably have been *"the end result of holding within your heart a balanced blend of passion, life purpose, a meaningful mission or target, and a genuine recognition of the fact that* now *may be the only chance to fulfill all three!"* As you can see, there is a great deal more implied in this definition than in Funk & Wagnall's, once again highlighting the difference between Eastern and Western philosophy and thought. The dictionary simply recognizes the importance of some external target or objective, whereas three of the four requisite conditions in the *samurai*'s version are internal, and even metaphysical in nature. Hmmm, maybe this is worth looking into after all!

The samurai's *definition of motivation: "The end result of holding within your heart a balanced blend of passion, life purpose, a meaningful mission or target, and a genuine recognition of the fact that* now *may be the only chance to fulfill all three!"*

I am confident that you would like to make financial risk-taking not only a profitable endeavor, but an emotionally fulfilling one as well. After all, who wants to become an emotionally burned-out shell as a result of financial risk-taking, unable to enjoy the "spoils of battle" after the fact? Not me, and not you either, I would hope. So before I set up the four pillars of warrior motivation for you, we need to next look at the three emotional carcinogens that incessantly seek to destroy them. They are *stress, anger,* and *fear!*

The Three Emotional Carcinogens

Emotional stress is a phenomenon of existence common to all members of the animal kingdom, including man. It has been around since the first thinking creatures swam in the primordial seas and will probably continue to exist until the end of time. It tends to play a role in everything we do and how and why we do it, so it is essential that financial risk-takers, like you and I, understand it as well as possible since knowledge of the "enemy" is always crucial to victory.

Go back with me, if you will, to a time when life was more primitive and simplistic for man. We are paying a visit to one of our early predecessors, and we arrive just as he is awakening in his cave dwelling. As he does, his needs and priorities are relatively simple: urinate, defecate, gather, and eat. So he steps outside and does what he has to do. Then he turns his attention to searching for food to eat now and possibly store for later. As our caveman friend goes about his business of finding suitable sustenance, his keen senses suddenly detect another creature's presence in his *immediate* vicinity—in fact, just overhead on a rocky perch. The huge, hungry predator above ferociously growls, bares its razor-sharp fangs, and prepares to gather *its* breakfast. As our friend looks into the savage eyes of his opponent, he is instantly aware that he has no choice but to implement one of the two basic options natural *evolution* has made available to him and physiologically and chemically prepared him for. He must either *attack* or *run!* It's that simple. Fortunately, he chooses to run, thereby not becoming a part of the natural food chain today.

The Primordial Battle Continues

As we return to present time, we look in on one of our caveman's considerably distant descendants. As his wake-up alarm goes off, he is just that—"alarmed" into wakefulness! Getting up and preparing for his day, his fundamental needs and priorities are essentially the same as his primitive ancestor's: urinate, defecate, eat, and gather. After doing what he has to and quickly choking down a not-so-delicious energy bar, he heads for his place of business downtown, the Chicago Mercantile Exchange. It is time to "gather"!

On this particular day he finds the S&P 500 is really moving, but it's doing so very erratically. This presents both danger and opportunity to our friend as he takes an early position, hoping to see a margin of profit develop. As he intently watches the changing prices cross the lighted quote board, it looks like the elongated, glowing pupils of some huge predatory cat preparing to attack. The multitude of trader and broker yells and screams seem to produce a ferocious growl that fills the frenzied arena. The price point suddenly begins to seriously drop and it becomes evident to our trader that he must liquidate his position immediately or see his trading account viciously "mauled." Even though tens of thousands of years have passed, nature still physically and chemically affords our friend the same two options as his ancestor: *attack* (usually in *anger*) or *run* (usually in *fear*)! In this case, by closing out his position as quickly as he was able, our friend chooses to run, motivated by his fear of losses. On the other hand, he could have just as easily become motivated by anger and chosen to attack by following his losing position with more money, thus making his situation worse.

The True Enemy Can Be Found Within

The points I want to make you aware of with these fictitious examples are simple and important. First, I want you to be aware that physically and biochemically we are still primitive beings inside, possessing primordial reflexes intended for self-protection in animalistic situations in an uncivilized world. Second, I want you to understand that we constantly strive to eliminate within a student of the warrior Way this potentially destructive "fight-or-flight" reflex, as behavioral scientists call it (and as you will learn to do in subsequent chapters). Third, I want to make certain you recognize that there is *no place* for emotional "reactiveness" in financial risk-taking—only for efficient, intelligent "warrior-responsiveness." And fourth, I want you to realize that it is an accumulation of *anger* and *fear* that is responsible for nearly all of modern man's emotional maladies, including the absence or deterioration of personal motivation!

Whereas primitive man simply let go of these emotional by-products of the fight-or-flight reflex once the danger had passed, modern man tends to hold on to them, destructively harboring and accumulating them within his subconscious mind. It is my hope that you will begin to recognize any accumulative anger or fear you hold within yourself, and see what roles or influences they may exert on your life or your professional performance. This way you can pave the way for the four pillars of warrior motivation to serve you, both personally and professionally. So with these points understood, let's move on.

... physically and biochemically we are still primitive beings inside, possessing primordial reflexes intended for self-protection in animalistic situations in an uncivilized world.

The Four Pillars of Warrior Motivation

As you may have deduced from the *samurai's* definition of motivation, the four pillars of warrior motivation are mortality awareness, life purpose, soul passion, and higher goals and objectives. Please keep in mind that each of the four is of equal value to the warrior's overall sense of fulfillment, each working in harmony and support of the other three. To picture this, I have always found it helpful to think of motivation as a tabletop and the four pillars as the legs of the table. If the table has four legs of equal length and strength, it will be quite stable and useful. If, on the other hand, the legs are of various lengths and strengths, it will be quite unstable, wobbly in fact (like a lot of people you probably know), and possibly of no value to anyone.

THE PILLAR OF MORTALITY AWARENESS

The first pillar of warrior motivation, awareness of mortality, refers to the importance of being ever mindful of the fact that, from the time of our birth, our days are numbered. In Western society the subject of death is practically taboo as a subject of social discussion or personal introspection. We tend to hide from the reality of its inevitability in every way we can. Even reading about it here may cause you some degree of discomfort, possibly tempting you to skim on to the next item on our agenda. But I encourage you not to do that and to give my message your most serious contemplation.

Perhaps a little exercise in honest introspection might be helpful for you here. If you will, take a moment to deeply and sincerely consider your answer to the following question: If you knew beyond any possible doubt that you would die *one week* from today, what would you change about yourself or do differently in the seven days that remain? And before you begin to formulate your answers, I will eliminate the issue of fear by further qualifying this question with two important presumptions. First, your death will be absolutely painless, and, second, you have absolutely no qualms about your status in the hereafter. Again I encourage you to approach this exercise with a serious attitude, since the answers you come up with could very well change your life for the better. But for now I'll assume that you will continue reading on before you actually give this question any reflective thought, so I will take this opportunity to comment on mortality awareness from the *samurai* perspective.

It has been estimated that on any given day the samurai had about a 50–50 chance of being killed. With such lousy odds as these you would think that motivation would have been a problem for these guys. But surprisingly, just the opposite was true.

It has been estimated that on any given day the *samurai* had about a 50–50 chance of being killed. With such lousy odds as these you would think that motivation would have been a problem for these guys. But surprisingly, just the opposite was true. There is absolutely no mention in the abundance of *samurai* literature about such maladies as career burnout, depression, whining, or complaining about their lot in life, or even any midlife crisis. In fact, midlife to them could have been about noon any day, if you get my drift.

Empowered by the Acceptance of Death   Although there were many psychological traits that contributed to the *samurai*'s indomitable spirit (all of which are covered in this book), the first and most noticeable was his recognition and acceptance of his probable "early" death. With the acceptance of his imminent death (a subject we will delve fully into in Chapter 6), the *samurai*, like the one who saved the "Blood Genealogy," found himself unencumbered by procrastination and was inexhaustively motivated to utilize each moment of every day to the fullest. It empowered him, first, to take the necessary risks at any cost to achieve his mission and fulfill his destiny, and, second, to recognize the role that his immortal spirit (meaning soul in this case) played in reinforcing his confidence, courage, and ability to succeed. That is certainly a state of mind all financial risk-takers could benefit from at times, don't you agree?

THE PILLAR OF LIFE PURPOSE

The second pillar of warrior motivation, life purpose, refers to something common to all people in all walks of life. As I speak of it, I'm not so much trying to tell you how to identify your life purpose as I am wanting you to come to believe that there is bound to be one, and to impress upon you the importance of looking for it if you need to. While the *samurai* was fortunate enough to be born into his life purpose and trained and conditioned from early childhood to fulfill it, all of humanity shares a primal need to find meaning, direction, and, more specifically, purpose for their existence. This can be as important to your overall motivational balance as sleeping is to your physical health.

Although I realize that possibly you have never given a second thought to the idea of even having such a thing as a life purpose, I can confidently assure you that deep down inside you somewhere there is an "inner warrior" that knows at the gut level what you are meant to do. Sometimes it communicates this truth to your conscious mind in the form of inner longings or certain talents you may display. Or you may even find clues within the scope of your hobbies or pastimes.

But wherever or however you might find this life purpose, you'll know it's the right one because of how good it feels at the very core of your being to simply acknowledge its existence. And even more convincing is the "life purpose motivation" you should feel within your gut every time you think or talk about the purpose you've determined, a feeling that would seemingly enable you to conquer the world or at least the markets. Hopefully you *will* find trading (or your favorite variety of financial risk-taking) to be an important part of fulfilling your true life purpose. But ultimately only one thing is absolutely certain, and that is that only *you* can be the true judge of your destiny path!

The Pillar of Soul Passion

The third pillar of warrior motivation, soul passion, could be described as a combination of overwhelming sensations such as joy, exhilaration, fulfillment, satisfaction, or inner-completeness. It is also inseparable from the second pillar we have just discussed. You will probably discover, as I have, that soul passion *always* exists within the experiencing of true life purpose. In many cases, experiencing soul passion can actually lead to the accidental discovery of that purpose. My sister-in-law Erin brings to mind a perfect example of such synchronicity.

I have known Erin for many years—in fact, exactly as long as I've known my wife Lyndee. The one thing that originally stood out in my mind about their family, besides their incredible warmth and hospitality toward *me*, was their obvious warmth and hospitality toward animals. In fact, I tended to joke with Lyndee about going over to the wild kingdom when we went to visit. Over a period of time I began to wonder how this wide assortment of "orphaned" creatures came to live with them. I ultimately discovered that it was Erin who had a major passion for wayward animals of any species, particularly if they seemed to be sick or injured in any way. Because of this deep-rooted sense of caring, she has probably made more trips to local veterinarians at all hours of the day and night than you and I have made to the local grocery store.

As you would suspect, all these visits have put Erin on a first-name basis with half the vets in town, which finally led one of them to inquire as to why she never became a veterinarian herself. When she responded that she hadn't thought herself to be smart enough to do it, the doctor asked if she would like to come to work for him as a veterinarian's assistant, thereby allowing her to at least work in the environment to see how she liked it. As her destiny would have it, this turned out to be a major turning point in her life, both professionally and personally, as she went on to obtain the necessary education (graduating with top honors) and certification to be a Veterinary Surgical Technician. Her soul passion had indicated and ultimately led her to find her true life purpose.

But for the sake of balance, I should also warn that just because someone experiences the exhilaration of soul passion in some area of her life, it does not *necessarily* mean she has pinpointed her "higher calling." For example, just because someone exhibits an apparent soul passion for fishing or duck hunting does not necessarily mean that her life purpose is to become a professional hunter or angler. Or if a person feels a sense of passion for another at what he thinks is the "soul level" and chooses to marry her, it certainly doesn't have to mean that his life purpose is to be the other's spouse. Hopefully you can grasp my point here without being confused because it is very important that you keep sight of the role and value these two interactive pillars of warrior motivation serve in making your life and career meaningful and fulfilling.

> *... just because someone experiences the exhilaration of soul passion in some area of her life, it does not* necessarily *mean she has pinpointed her "higher calling."*

THE PILLAR OF HIGHER GOALS AND OBJECTIVES

The fourth and final pillar of warrior motivation, higher goals and objectives, refers to something deeper and more important than just simple goal-setting. The operative word in this pillar is *higher*, the idea being that whatever you may choose to do, whether it be professional investing or anything else with a reasonably sound purpose, you should cultivate an inner drive to be the best at it that you can be.

An ancient Zen proverb says, *"When you walk, walk. When you sit, sit. But whatever you do, don't wobble!"* How many people do you know who "wobble" through their lives, bouncing endlessly from one activity or career path to another? Plenty, I'm sure, as do I. And the most noticeable characteristic common to these people is their seemingly short attention span and short-lived drive or motivation to improve their performance or themselves.

As a sidenote to the above, I have noticed a trend in recent years toward blaming the now-famous Attention Deficit Syndrome (ADS) for these problems. Personal observation has told me otherwise. Being a clinical professional myself, I will admit that there is such a condition as ADS, but, more often than not, it tends to serve as a great clinical excuse for a lack of character and discipline development in the patient. I can't tell you how many times I have had parents bring their adolescent children with emotional or behavioral problems attributed to ADS to my *dojo*, hoping that the rigors and psychological discipline of our martial training might render some assistance to them. Upon coming to know these kids, I am often quick to notice that they are selectively attention-deficit. It seems that when they want to apply themselves, they are able to do so to very high caliber. Anyone who knows video games (as do most of these kids) can attest that it's not easy to get to the ninth level of Zelda®, something they all seem to be able to do.

My point here, as we discuss the motivational pillar of higher goals and objectives, is to warn you to not fall prey to self-limiting or self-excusing labels or syndromes. Anyone is capable of pursuing and achieving greater things for himself, of being the best that he can be despite seemingly handicapped circumstances. In fact, it is sometimes the very existence of a physical or situational handicap that can inspire us to achieve higher goals, as I learned from my dad's example a number of years ago.

I and the rest of my family have always considered my dad to be intelligent and certainly mechanically inclined. Since he served in maintenance and support for the U.S. Air Force all of his adult life, I grew up believing that he could literally take a jet fighter apart from nose to tail and put it back together again single-handedly. I also knew, however, that economic circumstances had forced him to drop out of high school to join the service at an early age. I guess that's what prevented me from seeing him as "learned" in the traditional sense.

All of this changed suddenly for me, however, with the advent of the challenging game of Trivial Pursuit® in the early 1980s. Looking back, it seems as if we played this game nearly every week with my parents, and what truly amazed me was my dad's overwhelming victory tallies. He literally beat the socks off everyone, hands down. My curiosity piqued, I inquired as to how he came to know so much about literally everything. To this he simply replied, "Oh, I've done some reading on my own and taken some correspondence courses over the years." But a subsequent visit to his office at the base a few weeks later revealed the magnitude of truth behind his earlier statement.

The office, which I had not had occasion to visit since the late 1960s, was a literal shrine to his academic efforts. Every nook and cranny of wall and shelf space displayed certificates, diplomas, and various other accolades of his educational achievements, all of this coming as a total surprise to everyone including my mom, once I let his secret out of the bag. It was obvious to me that at some point years ago, my dad had made up his mind to overcome the stigma or "handicap" of being a high school dropout and to become as highly educated as possible, and in doing so he unconsciously chose to pursue "higher" goals and objectives purely for the sake of self-betterment. And because of the "higher" nature of his objectives, he never lacked the warrior motivation to see them through to their accomplishment.

Putting Your Lesson into Perspective

So now in retrospect, let me review the important points I have presented during this leg of our journey into the realm of true warriorship. Hopefully you have come to understand and appreciate the importance of "higher" warrior motivation to longevity and fulfillment in your financial risk-taking endeavors. I have tried to help you see above the basics of simple incentives to an appreciation of how history's most accomplished risk-taker, the *samurai*, was able to keep on pushing himself forward even in the face of insurmountable odds or possible defeat.

I have tried to make you wary of the three primary "motivation-eaters" of *stress*, *anger*, and *fear*, with anger and fear being the way the primordial fight-or-flight reflex is experienced by modern man, and stress being the collective effect of trying to resist or ignore the other two.

And if you have been attentive so far, you can also probably see why I describe warrior motivation as being a tabletop upon which all of your other warrior-trader efforts will depend, and how the legs of this table, represented by the four pillars of warrior motivation (mortality awareness, life purpose, soul passion, and higher goals and objectives) each equally serves to provide the tabletop with stability as they stand upon the grounded foundation of the true Way of the warrior.

If all of this has made reasonable sense to you and you have made a commitment to assimilate this wisdom into your own situation, then we have accomplished our mission so far. It also means that it is time to take yet another step along the true Way of the warrior-trader, as we begin to study how the *samurai* viewed himself and his relationship to everything around him!

True Tales of the Warrior-Trader

By the time I first spoke by phone with C.M., of Dallas, Texas, he was a physical and emotional wreck. He had previously heard me speak at a trading conference. The fact that he then went to the trouble of calling me to inquire about my consultation services and training programs was a good indication that he had finally recognized that he needed some help—serious help! But the interesting thing about his call was the kind of help he seemed to be asking for.

C.M. began by telling me that he was a 48-year-old venture capitalist and futures trader who invested heavily in offshore oil-drilling operations throughout the world as well as petroleum futures. He went on to say that he was twice divorced, was overweight, suffered from chronic headaches, and had had a triple-bypass operation on his heart earlier that year after a "mild" heart attack. Hearing this, I immediately knew that, considering these substantial problems, he and I (if I were retained to help) had our work cut out for us. But what shocked me was his going on to say, "The reason I've called is to see if you can help me with my investing motivation. Somehow it's just not fun anymore!" This statement almost blew me away. How could anyone, I wondered, hope to stay motivated (or even stay alive!) while carrying around the kind of harmful and inefficient "luggage" he was hauling?

I promptly informed C.M. that the real secret to the samurai's indomitable spirit and motivation was their holistic approach to training and living. I further stated that I wouldn't even consider taking him as a "motivational" client unless he agreed to an out-and-out holistic "personal overhaul"—which he finally agreed to after about a month of deliberation.

In the subsequent months, C.M. effectively used Zen meditation and the universal truths of the samurai's Kyokushin (both of which I will cover later) to first control his formerly out-of-check emotions, which had vacillated between anger and fear. Then he also came to grips with the reality of his mortality, which in turn helped him to develop a soul passion for fitness and survival. A proper diet and fitness plan were the result. Finally he re-evaluated his reasons for engaging in the risky business of venture capitalism and trading, which resulted in his looking more closely at the potential good the projects he funded might do for the world, rather than just the potential profit margin they offered him.

It is interesting to note that approximately two years later when we happened to see each other again at another conference, I was delighted to see that C.M. looked happy and vibrant, and was energetically carrying himself like the 10 million bucks he was worth. Undoubtedly, he was a totally transformed man! But what made me smile, both inside and out, was his parting comment as we later went our separate ways. Turning and looking at me over his shoulder, and with a knowing "warrior's-twinkle" in his eye, he mockingly asked, "Hey, when are we ever gonna work on that motivational stuff anyway?"

CHAPTER 3

The Way of Warrior Self-Perception

TRUE TALES OF THE BUDO

The head priest of the Henshoji Temple placed the flaming torch beneath the 10-foot tower of interlaced cedar logs, signaling the official commencement of the Festival of Harmony. As the logs began to burn, so too did the hundreds of flat cedar planks upon which the attendees had earlier scripted their person prayers, hopes, and dedications. As the planks were consumed by the ever-increasing heat of the blaze, their prayers were symbolically transformed into energy rising up toward the heaven. There they would hopefully be received and acknowledged by the various deities and saints whose respective supernatural protection and assistance were being petitioned.

Known as the Yamabushi, *these mountain warrior-priests of central Japan had gathered together for this annual test of their minds, bodies, and spirits, and to reaffirm their sense of harmony within themselves and unity with the five basic universal elements of fire, wood, water, earth, and air. Before the festival's end, they would subject themselves to a series of three physically and emotionally formidable tests from which they prayed to emerge unscathed and spiritually renewed. They were about to undertake the rigors of* shugendo, *"the Way of enlightenment through torturous self-discipline"!*

As the darkness of night falls, and the burning tower has been reduced to a huge mass of glowing embers, the temple attendants begin the task of carrying shovels full of the fiery coals to the 20-foot-long pit prepared earlier in the day. After the coals have been evenly distributed along the length of the shallow pit, they form what looks like a three-inch-thick, 20-foot-long seething, iridescent carpet ready to be traversed by the warrior-priests . . . barefoot! Starting with the head priest, the attendees proceed to walk smoothly and steadily down the length of the fire trail, each emerging harmlessly at the other end, having unquestionably reaffirmed the harmonious relationship of mind, body, and spirit, and the protective capacities of the latter.

A few minutes later the spiritually charged warriors proceed to a nearby cavern containing a shallow pool fed by the melting snow in the mountains above. Stepping into the ice-cold water, now clothed only in loin-cloths, they sit submerged up to their necks in the dangerously cold water with only the power of their focused Ki, or life force, to generate the warmth necessary for survival until the light of dawn comes.

As morning light breaks, the warriors emerge from their frigid baptismal experience with a sense of renewal and rebirth, and proceed to climb to the crest of a rocky overhang not far from the opening of the cave. Here their third and final shugendo experience will take place when their feet will be securely tied to a long length of natural vine, after which they will be lowered over the edge of the overhang. There they will precariously dangle, upside-down over a 300-foot ravine, during which time they will come to accept their destiny and their unquestionable death, which would take less than five seconds to occur should their fate dictate that the vine should break! After the prescribed time has passed, each is lifted up and released from his bondage, their ordeals victoriously completed, and their warrior self-perspective and inner strength renewed and fortified once again.

The Synergistic Warrior

As I take a step back and look at the big picture of my overall presentation to you, I feel that the ideas presented in this chapter might very well be the most insightful and transformational in this entire book. The information in the first two chapters was essentially preparatory in nature. My objective was to set down an adequate foundation for further learning and deeper understanding of the true Way of the warrior, specifically the Way of the warrior-trader. I encourage you now, however, to be particularly attentive and open-minded to the ideas and perspectives I am about to reveal and to give them your most serious consideration.

The one thing that was truly special and unique about the life-long training of a *samurai* was that it was totally holistic in nature. *Holistic* literally means "to bring together or to address *all* parts." The *samurai*'s equivalent to this word was *kokoro* (literally meaning "to unify into a single action"). Additionally, it could easily be said that the abilities and performance of this legendary warrior might have represented history's first record of the principle of synergy, a word that was coined and gained popularity in corporate America in the 1980s. *Synergy* literally means "an overall effect greater than a sum of the individual parts." While the corporate world was referring to the cooperation between their various divisions and management teams for the sake of enhanced productivity and profits, they came short of recognizing the possibility of synergizing the "internal team" of the individual! The team I am referring to is that of body, mind, and spirit.

The Difference between East and West

In the Western world the body, the mind, and the spirit have always been looked upon as distinctly separate components. The tendency has also been to assign responsibility for the welfare (and hopefully development) of these individual components to separate and unrelated institutions. What I mean by this is that typically the welfare of the body is viewed as the responsibility of the health care and fitness institutions. The improvement of the mind is relegated to our many educational institutions. And the strengthening and/or salvation of the spirit is generally entrusted to the so-called religious institutions. Despite the obvious fact that body, mind, and spirit exist in us interactively and interdependently, no institution or practice has evolved within the confines of our seemingly advanced, high-tech society that specifically specializes in the holistic and synergistic enhancement of individuals and their performance.

. . . typically the welfare of the body is viewed as the responsibility of the health care and fitness institutions.

Fortunately, natural evolution of thought and the higher consciousness within each of us have a way of taking care of things. This is evidenced by the growing feeling and recognition in a great many people that there's something missing in the way they do things or the way they live and view their respective lives. People from all walks of life are being led by some inner need to discover the holistic benefits of numerous body–mind–spirit resources like yoga, meditation, breathwork, the martial disciplines, and, of course, books like this one. And thankfully for our purpose, the *samurai* dutifully recorded their philosophy and means to this end for us to now benefit from.

"Universal Physics" and the Warrior

Before we look closer at the *samurai's* Way of *kokoro tai-shin-ki* (literally meaning "to bring mind, body, and spirit together in one action"), it is of great importance that I also convey yet another point of view held by this insightful warrior. In all things and events occurring within physical nature, the *samurai* viewed all such manifestations as occurring at three distinct yet interdependent levels of physics: (*1*) *the simple-physics level*, (*2*) *the superphysics level, and* (*3*) *the metaphysics level.*

As in all things, they saw each level of physics manifested within themselves as well. Their body (*tai*) resulted from and depended on *simple physics* to exist and function. Their mind and will (*shin*) resulted from and depended on *superphysics* to experience and assess the environment, and to direct the functioning and actions of the body. And most importantly, their spirit (*Ki*) resulted from and depended on *metaphysics* to ultimately provide the power or life force to execute the orders given to the body by the mind.

The "Centering Triangle"

To help you construct a mental picture that can be useful to you for future reference, let me suggest you take a pencil and draw the following series of shapes. First, draw an equilateral triangle with each side being about four inches in length (see Figure 3.1). The triangle (and many other three-pointed symbols) is commonly used in Japan to represent the *kokoro tai-shin-ki* (body, mind, spirit) trinity and their unification. Now, around each of the three points of the triangle, draw a circle about two inches in diameter (see Figure 3.2).

Each of these three separate circles represents the completeness of each component of the trinity, and you should label each circle as such. The first circle represents the *simple-physical* body (*tai*), the second circle represents the *superphysical* mind (*shin*), and the third represents the *metaphysical* spirit (*Ki*).

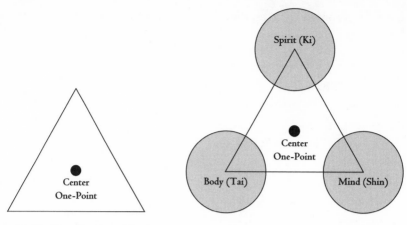

Figure 3.1 The "Centering Triangle" – Part I   Figure 3.2 The "Centering Triangle" – Part 2

Orient your drawing so that *tai* and *shin* form the two ends of the base of your triangle. Now place a large, bold dot in the center of the triangle and label it "center/one-point."

The drawing you have created is a graphic representation of the way the *samurai* viewed the structure and interaction of everything in the physical universe, including himself and his actions, since he recognized himself to be an exact microcosmic representation of that universe. The next alteration I would like you to do to your drawing will depict how and why the *samurai* trained themselves the way they did.

Convergence into "the Zone"

With your pencil now draw a short one-inch arrow from each inside corner of the triangle straight toward the center/one-point of the diagram. These arrows depict the intended direction of movement toward the middle of each of the respective circles resulting from physical training and/or meditation. Imagine that the circles do in fact begin to move toward the center/one-point, and as they do they begin to overlap like three of the Olympic circles. For clarity's sake you could lightly draw this inward motion or transition.

Continuing their inward migration, the circles will eventually overlap within the confines of the triangle, forming a single darker or heavier circle surrounding the center/one-point (see Figure 3.3). What you are now

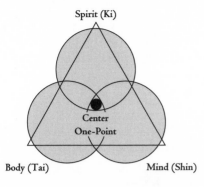

Figure 3.3 The "Centering Triangle"
Approaching the Centered State

Figure 3.4 The "Centered" State

looking at represents the physical, mental and spiritual objective underlying everything the *samurai* warrior did, whether it be preparatory or tactical. This all-important convergence of body, mind, and spirit into an overlapping state is referred to as "centering" (see Figure 3.4), a state most athletes would refer to as being in "the zone"! This is a critically powerful subject that I will address specifically in Chapter Eight, "The Way of Warrior Centering." At that time I will also have you make some further additions to your "centering-triangle" diagram, so keep it handy until then.

Breaking Down the Way of Centering

But for now, let's see if we can bring these potentially "lofty" body–mind–spirit ideas down to a level that's easier to understand by looking closer at a couple of contemporary examples you might more readily grasp (and perhaps even try for yourself sometime). In doing so, we'll compare the differences between how a warrior and a nonwarrior might handle the same situation. So first, we'll look at a semirisky activity that practically every "karate guy" has attempted at one time or another—breaking a board with his hand. Then we'll look at a much higher-risk activity—one that *you've* probably done—taking a trade in the markets. You may be surprised to see that the body–mind–spirit connection as well as the roles of *simple physics, superphysics,* and *metaphysics* are virtually the same in both examples, *as they are in everything!*

Someone is holding a 12×12-inch pine board up in front of you and, likewise, someone is holding one for your nonwarrior buddy. The mission for each of you is to execute a single punch and break your respective board cleanly in half. Both you and the nonwarrior take your hands and proceed to fold your fingers into tight fists. While the nonwarrior may simply look at his hand and see just a clenched fist, you should see and understand much more. As a true warrior, you should recognize that *simple physics* (the body) are responsible for allowing the fist to form and exist. You would see that *superphysics* (the mind) directed or willed the hand to transform into the efficient weapon it now represents, and will soon further direct this weapon as to the precise manner of executing the required blow. And then you should also see and appreciate that the weapon is comprised of and surrounded by *metaphysics* (the spirit), possibly feeling and looking like a glowing iridescence, and that this life force will reinforce and protect the weapon as it passes through the target.

The Moment of Truth (or Pain?) Arrives

As the time to execute arrives, the nonwarrior's psychology is to just give the board a good whap and hope his hand doesn't break in the process. You, however, have checked the alignment of your wrist and the tightness of your fingers. (The "body" or *Ki* circle moves in toward the "center" of the triangle.) You have imagined the execution clearly in your mind and know precisely how the hand will be directed to strike. (The "mind" or *shin* circle also moves in toward the "center" of the triangle.) And most importantly, you know that it is your decided destiny to break the board and that there will be a "higher" life force reinforcing your action as you strike it. (The "spirit" or *Ki* circle now moves in toward completion of the convergence.)

As the moment of truth arrives, the nonwarrior (in a primitive attempt to get his adrenaline pumping, his physical brawn at least a little organized, and his mind past the fear of the pain he is inadvertently anticipating) forms a meanacing grimace on his face and releases a deep growl that escalates into a scream. He then lashes out wildly and violently at the board, which results in one of two probable outcomes. Either he breaks the board, much to his surprise, but in doing so may sloppily break a couple of other things as well, or he doesn't break the board, just like he feared and antici-pated, and is now experiencing the stinging pain he feared he would. As he shakes his hand in disgust and discomfort he thinks to himself, Damn, I don't believe I want to do this again!

But on the other side of our story, for you there is no such moment of truth. Instead, it is just another simple moment in time that demands imme-diate unified action, a moment not unlike many other moments in your existence during which the forces of body, mind, and spirit—*simple physics, superphysics, and metaphysics*—suddenly synergize (or *"center"!*) creating a "unified force greater than the sum of all your individual parts." As destiny and opportunity would demand, and as we would expect from following the true Way of the warrior, you find yourself in the triangular "zone" ready to strike—*now!* (see Figure 3.4.) You release a unified bolt of concentrated action directed at the epicenter of the target and, like you had expected, it breaks cleanly and suddenly in half with a loud crack. Your fist snaps back to its original poised position unharmed, totally ready for the next board . . . and the next . . . and the next . . . and the next one too, if need be!

So, as in all things in nature, the same body–mind–spirit trinity exists for both you and your nonwarrior partner. However, your awareness and *uti-lization* of it resulted in completely different perceptions, states of mind, expectations, execution, results, and—maybe most importantly—resultant emotional aftermaths! And I'll venture to guess—if I've judged your warrior potential correctly—that you've already begun to draw some insightful parallels between this board-breaking exercise and financial risk-taking. Am I right? If not, let me help you with another example.

Now a Shot at "Breaking" the Market

To set this situation up we'll assume from the start that both you and your nonwarrior friend are, by definition, commodity traders. We'll further assume that, as luck would have it, you live in the same town, utilize the same real-time data-feed, and have invested in the same trading system. To elimi-nate other imaginary variables, let's say your system has a proven track record of profitability in one specific market (like the S&P 500) when executed with accurate consistency. One hour after the market opens, there is a strong flurry of oscillatory activity, followed by a suddenly appearing upward trend. In response to these emerging conditions (which are both risky and opportunistic) your system is about to give you a signal to buy. Now the scene is set!

The nonwarrior sits watching the screen, taking this all in, aware of little more than the lines, numbers, and graphs appearing before him, the growing sense of tension and anxiety mounting in his gut, and the fact that a moment of truth seems to be imminent. He looks at the phone and then looks at his hand, wondering if he's ready. Suddenly he gets the "Buy!" signal, but instead of taking action immediately, he continues to nervously watch the screen, remembering the hit he took a couple of days ago when the market had suddenly nose-dived right after he had taken a position. What if that happens again? Should he wait a little longer to be sure the price will continue its upward climb?

His hands begin to sweat and his heart begins to beat faster as he watches what should have been a substantial window of profit for him continue to widen. Anger and frustration suddenly set in as adrenaline pumps feverishly through his body. His face grimacing, he releases a deep growl that escalates into a frustrated, "Damn, I've gotta do it *now!*" He clumsily grabs the phone, hits the autodial, and places his order. Just as he hangs up, he watches in dismay as the price begins to rapidly reverse just as he had feared and anticipated it would. Before his stops take effect and his position gets closed out, he has lost money. Finally, shaking his head of the sting of this turn of events, he thinks to himself, *This business really sucks sometimes! I don't know why I even do it!*

The Warrior-Trader's Experience

On the other side of town, things evolve differently for you, the warrior-trader. As you watch the flurry of oscillatory activity in the S&P prices, you recognize that at any moment *suki* (literally meaning "a short-lived opportunity to strike at an opponent's defensive opening") may occur.

You sit balanced and centered in your chair, recognizing and appreciating the *simple physics* of your body and computer technology that puts you in touch with the markets. Breathing smoothly and deeply into your *hara* (the center/one-point of your physical body, located just below the naval), you also relax your hand in anticipation of its pending trip to the phone. (The "body" or *tai* circle moves toward the center of the triangle.) Your *superphysical* mind, which is free of any emotional leftovers from the loss you incurred yesterday, calmly evaluates *today's* market conditions, including the upward price trend that has suddenly taken shape.

Your superphysical mind, which is free of any emotional leftovers from the loss you incurred yesterday, calmly evaluates today's market conditions, including the upward price trend that has suddenly taken shape.

Knowing that a "Buy!" signal is inevitably coming, and trusting your system's statistical track record and the Universal Law of Averages (one of the *Kyokushin*), you are fully prepared to command immediate interaction between your hand, your phone, your voice, and your broker. (The "mind" or *shin* circle also moves in toward the center of the triangle.) At the deepest soul level, you believe in what you are about to do, and that the *metaphysics* of a "higher" life force will reinforce your action. (The "spirit" or *Ki* circle moves in toward completion of the convergence.) You are in the "triangular zone"!

The signal to buy comes as expected, and you become a bolt of efficient action as you execute your will . . . and your order. Being the true warrior-investor that you are, you have assumed your stance (or, in this case, your position) for better or for worse. As your destiny would have it, today it is for the better, as you watch the prices continue to tick upward. Still calmly vigilant 30 minutes later, you "capture" your profits by closing out your position as prices take a decisive downward swing. You sit back with a warrior's appreciation of a well-executed battle plan, and you think to yourself, Life is what I make of it. Trading is my Way of making it better every day!

Putting These Lessons into Perspective

So as a matter of review, it has been my mission in this chapter to provide you with some degree of insight as to how the *samurai* warrior viewed the makeup of himself and the natural universe he lived in. I hope that you will begin to see for yourself the truth and importance of the body–mind–spirit trinity within you and the obvious benefits of centering them into a unified force greater than the sum of the individual parts. I would also like to see you begin to look for and recognize the three distinct levels of physics that account for and exist within every situation and thing around you.

As your experience with these ideas grows, I am certain that you will determine the same thing that I have: that regardless of whether you are walking on burning coals, sitting in freezing water, hanging precariously from a cliff, breaking a board with your hand, or, of course, engaging in financial risk-taking, it is of the utmost importance to be aware of and then utilize these truths to your advantage.

In subsequent chapters in Part Two, "The Samurai's Psychology of Engagement," I will be providing you with precise methodology for getting "centered" and putting yourself into the "triangular zone" at will, as well as specific ways to apply the numerous other truths I have related so far. But before we get involved with such tactics, we need to explore the Way and benefits of warrior mindfulness, which happens to be the next step of our journey!

True Tales of the Warrior-Trader

At one time or another we've all had the experience of needing to get psyched up for some very important event or presentation. What I find interesting about this are the many ways high-risk "performers," particularly in the field of investment banking and market trading, go about this. Many such performers, such as S.O. of New York City, come from a background in high-level collegiate or professional sports where quirky "ritual" and "superstition" are almost the norm when it comes to "get'n in the zone," as he put it.

S.O. is an investment banker and institutional trader with a major New York financial firm. I first met him at one of my training retreats. Admittedly, I found him to be quite animated and charismatic and a hell of a lot of fun to be around. Somehow he quickly came to view the two of us as being peers since we both had a background in national-level championship competition—he in basketball and me in sport-karate. He seemed to particularly enjoy comparing stories of psychological self-preparation back in "the good old days." But the more stories we compared, the farther apart we seemed to be in our fundamental beliefs and methods for preparing for high-risk performance situations.

To the average listener it might seem that we were indeed similar in that we both used self-psyching methods today that originated in our more youthful years of athletic competition. But that was where the similarities ended. S.O.'s approach(es) back then seemed to revolve around external (and somewhat impractical) idiosyncratic rituals and good-luck charms such as wearing the the same underwear repeatedly, walking into the gymnasium backward, or wearing one red sock under his regular uniform socks. He had also come to believe that these things either attracted good luck or repelled bad luck, depending on the circumstances.

While all of this may have been fine and good at the time—and for the purpose of winning an important athletic competition—I explained to S.O. that such approaches seriously lacked "conceptual integrity" and practical ongoing applicability in a business setting. What he needed was an internal (and functional) mental picture of what being "in the zone" was like plus a method of preparation that addressed not only the three components of his being, but the three levels of physics that ultimately determined the outcome of every event of our lives. In short, he needed some way to genuinely "synergize" himself—rather than fool himself—into preparation for "battle."

Throughout our weekend together, I proceeded in numerous ways to show S.O. that the same meditations, visualizations, and philosophies I used 25 years ago to prepare to step into a ring with an opponent were no different than those I employ today (and the same methods you will learn in this book) to prepare for some high-risk venture or presentation. And the reasons they still work, I pointed out to him, are because they are conceptually valid, they are easy to replicate, and they address and harmonize all of the empowerment resources at my disposal.

Months later, when I spoke with S.O. again during a post-training follow-up interview, he admitted that preparing himself for the critical, multimillion-dollar proposals to prospective clients—around which his career and success revolved—had indeed become much easier and more dependable than ever before! Upon asking him to summarize as best he could the internal changes that had contributed to this improvement, he explained, "Well, rather than trying to pretend to be a psyched-up ball player trying to pitch an investment plan, I've now come to see myself as a genuinely centered, confident warrior. But not just any warrior—a financial samurai warrior—since samurai means 'one who serves and protects'! Instead of trying to psych myself up to defeat my investment prospect's resistance, I now totally prepare myself to serve my prospect's needs and to protect his money—and my reputation—at any cost. Somehow they're able to pick up on this mind-set, and things just seem to fall in place better than ever!"

*Looking beyond the scope of his words, and with a teacher's pride and satisfaction, I realized that S.O. had come to learn and apply, in his own special way, a very important but simple samurai precept—that the Way of self-perception is often the critical difference between life or death, success or failure, or just winning or losing—*especially for the warrior-trader!

CHAPTER 4

The Way of Warrior Mindfulness

TRUE TALES OF THE BUDO

Yoshinaga Kenshi, his sword poised at his side, stood blindfolded and motionless in the center of the large room. Approximately 20 of his sempai *sat along two sides of the room, anxiously awaiting the master's famous demonstration of his seemingly supernatural powers of "mind vision" and swordsmanship. Standing, unclothed from the waist up, in various self-assigned positions at random distances from him were four of Yoshinaga's top* shihan *(senior instructors), who had bravely volunteered to participate in this incredibly dangerous exhibition for the* sempai.

Each of the respective volunteers had a different fruit in his possession, each soon to be the target of the Kenshi's razor-sharp katana. *The first was holding an unpeeled banana in his mouth, his arms securely held behind his back. The second held an apple in the flattened palm of his right hand, while his left hand was secured behind his back. The third, reaching over the top of his own head with his right arm, held a cucumber against the jugular vein on the left side of his neck, his left arm and hand held tightly against the front of his body. The fourth held a watermelon directly against his stomach, holding it vertically with his right hand on its top and the left hand on its bottom.*

The details as to how the bearer of each respective fruit would pose both the fruit and his body had been carefully instructed in advance of the demonstration. It was also agreed that the assistants would select their respective fruits after the blindfold was put in place over his eyes in order that Yoshinaga would not know who held what fruit. The master further explained to everyone that his breathtaking objective was to assess the locations and directional orientation of all four assistants, to determine who they were and what fruit they held, and then to cut each fruit in half in a succession of four different cuts. Of course, his concurrent mission was to also leave his trusting assistants unharmed as well!

With the room in total quiet and stillness, Yoshinaga began by taking a slow, deep breath and then releasing it, followed by a kind of curious cocking of his head this way and that. He then moved forward with a violent stomp, then stopped, turned, and repeatedly did the same advancing stomp in several directions. After this he held his right hand high above his head and began to snap his fingers several times as he rotated himself 360 degrees. Following this there was a long pause with no detectable motion other than the master's breathing and an occasional repeat of the curious cocking of his head.

Finally, after a series of faster breaths, Yoshinaga Kenshi suddenly drew his sword. He advanced confidently toward the left side of the shihan *holding the banana in his mouth, and proceeded to loudly shout the bearer's name while cutting the fruit in half with a lightning-fast swing.*

Moving quickly in the other direction, he drew his blade high over his head as he advanced on the shihan *with the apple, then cutting as he shouted the second bearer's name. The apple suddenly fell into two parts, with the blade sitting motionless against the* shihan's *palm. Lifting the blade one inch, Yoshinaga retreated one foot and then advanced at a 45-degree angle from his current position toward the third target.*

Swinging the blade in a large circle, he executed a clean diagonal cut while simultaneously calling the name of the bearer, as he had with the previous two. The bottom half of the cucumber fell with a splat to the floor. Suddenly returning to center of the formation of assistants with a swift, catlike motion, the master twirled the katana *between his fingers, reversing his grip, and then seemed to take a blind bearing on the fourth* shihan *and his melon.*

With a loud yell that seemed more like a battle cry than the name of the last fruit-bearer, Yoshinaga rushed forward, his sword's blade trailing behind him. At the last second he suddenly veered sharply left, causing the trailing blade to cut and pass completely through the melon. Moving instantly back to the center of the formation once again, Yoshinaga twirled and wiped his blade in the traditional act of chiburi *(cleansing of blood) before returning it to its resting place at his side.*

After removing the blindfold and verifying the well-being of his assistants, Yoshinaga Kenshi turned to address the sempai, *who now sat in stunned silence, jaws gaping open in disbelief. He said to them, "What you have just witnessed was not a demonstration of magic or some supernatural skill! What you have seen was simply an example of* shinjutsu, *the* samurai's *'skills of the mind,' and the power of mindfulness at work. As you continue to train in the true Way of the warrior, you will come to understand and duplicate everything I have done here!"*

The Three Minds of the Warrior

The *samurai's shinjutsu* (literally meaning "skills of the mind") provided the framework upon which his incredible mentality was built. The three basic components of this framework were *is-shin, mu-shin, and zan-shin*. Although you will come to understand each of these mind-states and their unique functions in the course of this and subsequent chapters, I feel it will be helpful for you to have a brief preview of them now.

Is-shin (literally meaning "one mind") is a state of mind of which the warrior exists completely and totally in the present moment. As he experiences this "nowness" he usually isolates his perceptual awareness and thoughts to one thought, experience, or action. It is generally most useful to him the instant of executing an attack, inasmuch as it tends to eliminate fear and hesitation (which I will cover in Chapter 11, "The Way of Warrior Fear-Management"). When *is-shin* is expanded to include all sensory perception at once, it is referred to as *mindfulness,* the primary subject of this chapter.

Mu-shin (literally meaning "empty mind") is a state of mind that is completely void of all thoughts, emotions, or perceptual awareness. It has been my experience that this mindlessness is the most difficult concept for Westerners to intellectually grasp and practice, since it involves letting go of any and all intellectualizing for brief periods. You will discover in Chapter 5, "The Way of Warrior Mindlessness," that the warrior finds this state invaluable in cleansing the mind of unwanted clutter and nonproductive emotions, and for getting in touch with his inner spirit.

Zan-shin (literally meaning "ready or receptive mind") is a state of mind in which the warrior is completely tuned in and sensitized to what is going on around him as well as to any situations that may be evolving before him. Yet, his mind is unattached to and unbiased by any particular thought or anticipation. *Zan-shin* is considered the ultimate and most potent state of mind for the warrior (especially the warrior-investor), inasmuch as it allows him a kind of supervigilance and a readiness to respond with lightning-fast effectiveness to whatever may occur.

I should point out here that *zan-shin,* as important as it is, cannot specifically be learned or practiced. It is simply the natural result of routinely practicing mindfulness and mindlessness in the course of everyday activities, along with the regular practice of *Budo-Zen* mediation (which I will cover in Chapter 8, "The Way of Warrior Centering"). That is why I have dedicated this and the next chapter to these two critically important mental skills, starting here now with the Way of warrior mindfulness!

A World of Perceptual Information Awaits

Incredibly, there is an entire world of perceptual information out there that most people will never have the pleasure or benefit of knowing. Helping you to break out of your possible numbness or insensitivity to that dimension of perception is my primary objective in this look at warrior mindfulness.

So what comes to your mind when you consider the word *mindfulness?* Most people would think it to mean "attentive," which wouldn't be too far off the track. Some might see it to mean "having the mind full," which would also be right, especially for most Westerners who tend to spend every waking moment with their heads filled with useless thoughts and static. In fact, having the mind so full of such useless thoughts and static contributes to most people's never being able "to fulfill the mind's perceptual capabilities," which happens to be the definition of mindfulness I would want you adopt.

It is a simple fact of life that the average human being possesses five senses through which we can, and do, perceive the world around us. In case you've forgotten, they are the senses of sight, hearing, taste, touch, and smell. The reason I thought you might have forgotten them is because that is what happens in a very literal way for most people! Because of the senses' ready availability to your brain, you tend to forget them or, more specifically, take them for granted. And that's when you really begin to lose out.

Sometimes "Better" Is Worse

The more and more we advance technologically at the individual and societal levels, the less and less we pay attention to the most advanced technology known to exist—human physiology! As smart and advanced as we think we are, we are still probably centuries away from truly understanding the intricacies and seemingly miraculous potential of the human mechanism. And it should be remembered that it is through the five senses that this incredible and probably unduplicable mechanism stays abreast of the outside world it coexists with.

Fortunately for the "less advanced" animal kingdom, there is no mechanical or scientific technology to have dampened their acute senses and awareness. Optical technology allows us to vividly see objects great distances from us, but a hawk or cougar can see movement in the grass a mile away with its own eyes. Audio technology can create a device to eavesdrop on a conversation a mile away, but a deer or rabbit can do it with its ears. We can create a sophisticated device that can "feel" tremors in advance of an earthquake, but a horse or a cat can detect them without assistance. There are devices that can detect and track a trail of gases, but any good hunting dog or lion can do the same. Expensive, complicated DNA testing can determine if a blood sample comes from one of your relatives, but a bird or a wolf can do that with a simple lick or sniff.

At this point you may be inclined to argue that these skills I've mentioned are unique to the animal kingdom, and the humans just don't possess such capabilities. But that just doesn't hold water when you take into consideration the natural abilities displayed by members of numerous scientifically undeveloped (often warrior/hunter) cultures like Native-American, Australian aborigines, isolated African tribes, and the Eskimos of the Arctic regions, to name a few. The fact is, such supersensory abilities appear to be an automatic feature of the human mechanism unless some dampening or eroding influence (like lack of use and/or scientific "sophistication") enters the picture. And the word *supersensory* brings me to my next point and observation.

The Physics of Mindfulness

In the last chapter you learned that the *samurai* viewed all things and events as existing at one of the three levels of physics: *simple physics* (the "body" of the universe that gives it form and functionality), *superphysics* (the "mind" of the universe that perceives and directs it), and *metaphysics* (the "spirit" of the universe that energizes it and is its life force). Therefore *supersensory* implies that it is a function of mental superphysics, and, as a warrior knows, anything mental can be improved or enhanced through conscious effort. So how and why do you go about elevating your existing "simple sensory" perceptions into the higher "supersensory" capabilities? Well, it's really not that hard to do, as you will soon discover for yourself.

The way I see it, the mind's capacity to function and serve you at different levels of efficiency is no different than a muscle's. How would you go about improving the efficiency of a muscle? You would exercise it, of course. And why would you want to do that? Because the muscle's purpose of existence is to serve, and it can only do its best when it is in nominal condition. So if you want your mind to serve you and to perceive the world and events around you at the highest possible level, you will logically seek to exercise it accordingly. That is the Way of warrior mindfulness, and it may surprise you to find that you are practicing it to some degree already!

EVERYDAY SELECTIVE MINDFULNESS

What I have discovered over the years is that most people experience what I call "selective mindfulness" to some degree. By this I mean that they have, for one reason or another, heightened their perception of a particular sense through some kind of specialized activity, hobby, interest, or sometimes even a handicap. Let me give you some simple examples that I've observed in various people I know.

In the office building where my clinical practice was formerly located, there was a concession stand downstairs run by a blind man named Larry. Sometimes late in the day I would go down to take a break, since Larry always had a good joke or two to share with whoever came in. On one particular day I noticed that he was preoccupied as he carefully sorted through what appeared to be several dollars' worth of change.

At first I assumed that he was simply separating the various denominations into separate piles in order to count down his receipts for the day. But then I noticed he had already done that and was now "looking" at select

What I have discovered over the years is that most people experience what I call "selective mindfulness" to some degree. By this I mean that they have, for one reason or another, heightened their perception of a particular sense through some kind of specialized activity, . . .

coins from each pile, every so often taking one and putting it in his shirt pocket. Being the innately curious guy I am, I couldn't help but ask him what he was doing, to which he responded that he collected rare coins as a hobby. What he had been doing was feeling with his fingers the minting date and location of each coin and searching for any printing abnormalities that might increase its value. Not only could he feel things with his fingers that most people couldn't see with their eyes, but he could also identify everyone who came in the room by their "signature" footsteps and/or smell!

My brother Steve, who owns a restaurant and is a self-styled gourmet cook, can take the smallest taste of any soup or sauce and tell you its exact ingredients. Interestingly, he can even tell you the material of the pan it was prepared in and whether it was heated on a gas or electric stove.

My sister Karen, a true audiophile, is supersensitive about the music and sound system she listens to. She can describe the exact instruments being played in even the most complex piece of music, even though she has never played an instrument herself. She can also tell you (within a few hertz) the exact setting of someone's graphic equalizer and whether it's the "right" setting for the music being played.

My mom, who has seen and cared for more than her share of colds and flus in her lifetime, can take one look at your color and tell you if you have a fever, and exactly what your temperature is. And to top that, she knows a Hispanic midwife who can detect if a woman is pregnant the same way, with nearly 100 percent accuracy.

And on the humorous side, Sophie, a petite Thai friend of ours who, by her own admission, is a little spoiled and still lives with her parents, knows exactly when to ask her father for money. It seems he "walks just a little different" when he has "extra cash" in his wallet, which I guess goes to show that practicing mindfulness can be more profitable for some than for others, if you get my meaning!

You've Got to Push Yourself and Your Senses

The point of these examples is to illustrate that a lot of people, and probably you too, already experience some form of higher mindfulness in their lives. But I would hope you would agree with me that simply enhancing one of five senses is a waste, and that it is certainly not enough to elevate your mental functioning to the level we seek. Rather, you must make it one of your first warrior missions to encourage all five senses to be the best that they can be!

The good news here is that by simply reading this chapter you have already progressed through the first two phases of learning. You are now in the conscious competence phase, which means that converting your "simple senses" into "supersenses" is simply a matter of choosing to do so and then waking up to what there is to sense. The simplest and best way to do this is to just routinely direct your awareness to one of your senses at a time, preferably in a rotating order that stays the same every day. Taking a "mindfulness break" requires only 15 to 30 seconds to determine what one particular sense is currently receiving, and then "extending out" for a moment to see what else it might detect.

> *The good news here is that by simply reading this chapter you have already progressed through the first two phases of learning. You are now in the conscious competence phase, . . .*

Like the Zen maxim says, "Wherever you are, *be there!*" It's that simple. And with repeated conditioning all five senses will soon begin to simultaneously feed your mind enhanced data with increasing unconscious competence. The result will be such an elevated level of awareness of and sensitivity to everything in your existence, including investment opportunities, that you will be astounded!

Unveiling the "Magic" of Mastery

As a closing note to this chapter, you might be interested to learn how Yoshinaga Kenshi accomplished his demonstration in the *True Tale of the Budo* that opened this chapter.

The violent stomp he made in several directions created vibrations that were dampened by the feet of his assistants, which provided him with an initial bearing as to their locations. The snapping of his fingers while turning 360 degrees produced a combination of echoes and "dead spaces" that enhanced his bearings. By cocking his head in different ways he could ascertain who the assistants were and the directions they were facing by their respective scents and the unique sounds of their breathing. He knew by the fragrance of each fruit, who held what and, accordingly, the exact pose and position they would be maintaining.

As Yoshinaga advanced to make each cut with a loud yell, the rapid dampening of the yell further assured him of his orientation. During the milliseconds the blade was passing through the various targets, Yoshinaga's tactile sensitivity told him exactly when he had completed the cut. The slow, deep breath and release at the start of the demonstration was him clearing his mind of all static and interfering thought. This warrior mindlessness cleared the way for accurate reception of the critical sensory information he and his trusting assistants were depending on, especially the guy holding the cucumber on his neck . . . who coincidentally was *me!*

So now would be a good time for us to proceed to our study of the Way of Warrior Mindlessness before I start shaking and sweating all over again.

True Tales of the Warrior-Trader

You never know when or how the warrior-mind or mindfulness might come in handy or prove profitable! Take, for example, an interesting twist of events that happened for G.L. of Colorado Springs, Colorado.

G.L.'s first soul passion is developing and writing computer software for the financial industry, something he does on a relatively full-time basis. But that's not to say that he's not interested in the markets, especially stocks. So, to augment his programming income he maintains a fairly diverse stock portfolio that he trades himself, and he prides himself in using his personal instincts about investing in up-and-coming new companies. At the time he trained with me, G.L. admitted that he was "rather unorthodox" in the ways he sometimes selects his stock investments. But it was the method that developed several months after he began regularly practicing Zen—which includes mindfulness—that got my attention.

As he tells it, G.L. began getting profitable stock market tips from a stock analyst in his dreams. Interestingly, the analyst looked just like himself. Knowing that I had done a considerable amount of research in dream dynamics, he called to ask me whether I thought his dream stock advisories were somehow psychic in nature (and I suspect to also reassure himself that he wasn't going off the deep end by practicing this "Zen stuff," as he often called it). While I was admittedly fascinated by his story, I was initially inclined to believe that there was probably a more "earthly" explanation to his experiences. Being considerably familiar with the rather incredible potential of a warrior's Zen-mind—and following an educated hunch of my own—I decided to do a little investigative research into what the Hardy Boys would probably have called The Case of the Dreamland Stock Analyst.

After asking G.L. how he kept up with the daily performance of his stocks (by reading The Wall Street Journal, it turned out), I requested the NYSE stock signals for his 10 most regularly checked holdings. Then I asked him for the listing signals for the five new stocks he had invested in at the advice of the "dreamland stock analyst." Gathering up as many recent back issues of The Wall Street Journal as I could—especially those just prior to the dates of G.L.'s dreams—I went to work. And what I soon discovered left me both amazed and truly impressed with the abilities of G.L.'s Zen-mind.

After marking G.L.'s top 10 stocks in the paper with a fluorescent yellow highlighter pen, and then marking the "dream stocks" in blue, an interesting pattern began to emerge on the page. It turned out that, by holding The Wall Street Journal's stock market pages out at arm's length, I could see that each of the 'dream stocks' signals were all printed within three inches of one of G.L.'s regularly checked stocks. This immediately indicated to me that somehow G.L.'s mind had been unconsciously following the dream stocks peripherally, an ability often associated—but usually in less dramatic ways—with the regular practice of mindfulness! It would seem that once G.L.'s unconscious mind had peripherally (but mindfully) determined enough of an advancing change in these stocks' prices, it managed to communicate this to his conscious mind in the form of a tip from his inner dream-analyst!

"Impossible!" you say? Well, it would appear not, especially to one mindful warrior-trader in Colorado Springs, whose total "dream stock" value has increased more than $10,000 as of this writing! I think I feel a nap coming on, don't you?!

CHAPTER 5

The Way of Warrior Mindlessness

TRUE TALES OF THE BUDO

During the waning days of the feudal period of Japan, there were many ronin, or masterless samurai, who roamed the villages in search of employment and duels. On one particular day in a small village in southern Honshu, a poor but distinguished practitioner of chado, the Way of the tea ceremony, accidently brushed by one such ronin, inadvertently insulting him. Outraged, the ronin boisterously challenged the humble teaman to a "fight to the death."

"But kind sir, I am not a warrior but a humble man of tea," the chadoshi fearfully said, "and I am quite sorry if I have accidently offended you! Please accept my apology, as I know nothing of swordsmanship." But the ronin would not hear of this, refusing to back down.

"We will meet at the edge of town as the sun rises," he said as he handed the teaman his spare sword, "and I suggest you start practicing now!" With this he turned and walked away in a huff.

Not knowing what else to do, the chadoshi ran to the home of a well-known sword master named Tomichi who resided in the village, and proceeded to relate to him the story of his deadly dilemma. Upon assessing the teaman's situation, the sword master said, "This really is a bad situation, since you will undoubtedly die under the ronin's blade! The only help I might possibly be able to render would be to help you understand isagi-yoku, the art of dying with dignity."

Not knowing what else to do, the chadoshi proceeded to ceremoniously prepare and then pour tea for them both. There was something particularly special about the way he did this, and it caught the attention of the sword master, giving him an idea. He exclaimed, "You need not die! I will teach you the proper way to hold and poise the sword. Then simply put yourself in the state of mind I just witnessed as you prepared the tea and you can win this duel!"

The teaman couldn't believe his ears. He had never as much as held a sword before, much less possess any ability to cut someone down with it. What "state of mind" could the sword master be referring to? Answering this unspoken question, the sword master replied, "What were you thinking as you prepared and poured this tea? Were you thinking, I am just a lowly teaman?"

"Quite the contrary," the teaman responded. "In fact, I wasn't thinking of anything at all."

"And that is how you will win!" the sword master laughed. "Tomorrow when you face the ronin, draw your sword and poise it high over your head, the way I will show you! Then, after you've fully committed in your mind to strike him down at his first move, don't think of yourself as a teaman or a swordsman. In fact, don't think of anything at all. Be perfectly mindless as you were in preparing this wonderful tea!"

The next morning as the first rays of the sun peaked over the nearby hills, the ronin arrived at the designated spot as did the chadoshi. After the usual formalities that accompany such duels, both men drew their swords in preparation to fight. The ronin held his blade out in front of him in the chudan no-kamai position, and began to ominously circle around his opponent. The teaman slowly lifted his blade high over his head in the classical hasso no-kamai position that the sword master had shown him. As he had been instructed, he then cleared his mind of all thoughts as he looked directly into the ronin's eyes.

A quiet, incredibly long pause then occurred as the ronin stared at the teaman's poised sword, and the perfect clarity in his eyes. Finally, unnerved by what he saw and sensed, the ronin surrendered saying, "I was wrong! I do not have the ability to defeat you! Please accept my apology!" With that he resheathed his sword, bowed to the chadoshi, and left the village, fearful for his life.

The Samurai's View of "Nothing" and "Everything"

Before we delve into the Way of *mu-shin* (the empty mind), I feel it is of equal importance to first present some kind of overview of the *samurai's* feelings about the universal principle of "empty." If you ever do much reading of Asian philosophy or literature, particularly Chinese and Japanese, you will quickly discover a great emphasis on the importance of the "great void." In fact, Miyamoto Musashi, in his classic dissertation on warriorship, *The Book of Five Rings*, dedicated the final summary chapter of his work to this subject. And there is a profound reason why he did. But to help you understand this reason, I must step ever so carefully into the sensitive arena of conventional religious and spiritual thought.

Most Westerners, particularly those of the Judeo-Christian persuasion, don't give a whole lot of analytical thought to where and what "God" is. With all due respect, it has been my experience that they tend to fall back on such pat answers and preprogrammed rhetoric as "God is everywhere," "God is in Heaven," "God is love," or "God is the creator of all things." Interestingly, nearly all Eastern religious or spiritual thought agrees with this. The only difference between them is that people of the latter persuasion take these definitions a step further—to a living, breathing, practical level. At this further level, "God"—also referred to by many other names such as the "One," the "Universe," and, of course, the "Void"—can be seen in every thought, action, object, and situation in existence, without exception. But to get to my particular point, let's get a little more scientific with this idea.

Looking Closer at "Reality"

Consider a simple rock. It has tangible weight, depth, width, height, color, and shape. Not many people would argue that it doesn't exist. Yet the closer we look, the more it becomes apparent that its so-called existence is, indeed, something of an illusion. Someone once said, "God made everything out of nothing, but sometimes the 'nothing' shows through!" How true this may be!

To a quantum physicist the rock represents much more than "just a rock." This guy will proceed to tell you that the rock is a coordinated arrangement of molecules, with mostly space in between them. Then he'll say that these molecules consist of a coordinated arrangement of atoms, with mostly space in between them. He'll then have to proceed to say that these atoms consist of a coordinated relationship between various subatomic particles (that aren't really particles at all) with differing electrical charges moving at light speed around each other, with mostly space in between them. And then finally he'll say, as far as science knows, these subatomic particles are really made up of illusive little pieces of "nonstuff" like quarks and nutrinos that are made up of nothing but the eternal void of so-called time-space.

So somewhere along the line our rock seemingly ceased to exist, or at least to have definable reality as we normally interpret and perceive it. For the pragmatic thinker, this truth can present either a genuine conceptual dilemma or a new way to view the universe and his relationship to every thought, action, object, and situation in existence, including the markets and trading—which is why I have cautiously ventured into this sensitive discussion to begin with. In fact, I feel I would have been seriously negligent in proceeding with this lesson on the purpose and value of mindlessness without such a preface. This is because I ultimately want you to understand that whether you're looking at the rock, the markets, or anything else for that matter, at the core of that "something" is that omnipotent "nothing" the *samurai* called the void. And as far as I can tell, the practice of mindlessness is the most natural way to commune with it, which I guess is why the Bible says, "Be ye still, and know that I am God!"

The Nature of Mindlessness

So moving on with the lesson, it can be said that warrior mindlessness is an intentionally evoked state of mind in which you are literally free of any thoughts, emotions, or sensations for brief periods of time, usually ranging from a couple of minutes to a couple of hours. In some extremely advanced practitioners it can even be as long as a couple of days. There are essentially two fundamental purposes for practicing intentional mindlessness; these purposes have been of equal importance to the *samurai*. These two objectives are to simply *clear* and to *harmonize*, each producing uniquely profound benefits that are both important and useful.

. . . warrior mindlessness is an intentionally evoked state of mind in which you are literally free of any thoughts, emotions, or sensations for brief periods of time . . .

A World of Mental Clutter

It is an easily observable fact that our minds tend to be filled with an endless barrage of seemingly innocuous internal dialog, emotional leftovers, and a sundry assortment of mental "static." To verify this, just sit with your eyes closed for a moment and "have a listen." I'm quite sure you'll find some, and I'm equally sure that it's not all harmless. The fact is that it can seriously impede your ability to perform complex tasks, to make important critical decisions, to be in touch with your higher intuition, and to keep body, mind, and spirit centered in the "triangular zone" we discussed earlier. And don't forget what I pointed out in Chapter 2—that it is common medical knowledge that it is harmful to your physical well-being to remain attached to negative emotions such as fear and anger for any prolonged period of time.

So it should almost go without saying that the most logical antidote to the detrimental effects of this mental and emotional clutter and static is to regularly practice mindlessness, during which you literally "clear it out" for a short while. Each mindless "clearing" session you engage in also tends to weaken the harmful potential of each separate piece of clutter after the fact as well, and can eventually cause the clutter to disappear altogether. Mindfulness, like its counterpart mind*less*ness, also contributes to your ability to live comfortably and confidently in the present moment, which of course is the only moment you have any real control of in your life.

Regarding harmonizing, here too the resulting benefits should be more than obvious in light of what I previously discussed in my preface. What could be more beneficial to any objective, be it a life-or-death duel or taking a position in the markets, than "getting in touch" with the very source of everything? As far as I'm concerned, there *is* a higher unified source out there (and *in* here), possessing a unified mind, creating a unified effect. Getting in touch and in harmony with "it" can only serve to improve your intuition (which we'll cover in Chapter 9, "The Way of Warrior Trust and Intuition") and your odds for success and fulfillment.

Getting Started on the Way of Mindlessness

If I have accomplished my mission so far, then I have brought you to a point where you are beginning to appreciate the potential value of practicing warrior mindlessness on a daily basis as well as its important place in the framework of *samurai shinjutsu*. If that is true, then you will also be wanting to give it a try as soon as possible. I encourage you to limit your experimentation, at first, to two simple exercises I will detail shortly. This is to allow your experience and patience to grow in uncomplicated, gradual steps that we can build on later. In Chapter 8, "The Way of Warrior Centering," I will provide you with detailed instruction in the hows and whys of *Budo-Zen* meditation. At that time you will begin to integrate everything I have covered in these first five chapters into one simple process.

But for now, simply remember that you want to exercise your mind like you would exercise a muscle. And to efficiently exercise a muscle, you must *push* and *pull* to get proper tone, and so too is it with your mind. For the best long-term results, you want to limit your daily practice to the mindfulness exercises (*pushing*) presented in the last chapter, and these two simple exercises in mindlessness (*pulling*).

> *. . . for now, simply remember that you want to exercise your mind like you would exercise a muscle.*

Eyes-Open Exercise

While sitting comfortably straight in a chair, look at a watch or clock with a sweeping hand. Try to position the timepiece in such a way that you are able to look slightly downward at it during the exercise. The objective is to simply look blankly at the clock for increasing periods of time without experiencing any thoughts including any thought or awareness of the clock, the sweeping hand, or the passing of time itself. Your objective is to reach increasing mindless durations of 15 seconds, then 30 seconds, then 45 seconds, and so on.

Eyes-Closed Exercise

This exercise is exactly the same as the first, including the presence of the timepiece, with the only difference being that your eyes are closed for the duration. With this exercise it can be helpful to start by being totally aware of your breath (mindfulness) for 10 or so respirations. This is to isolate your awareness to the internal level and to minimize internal distractions. Your duration objectives are the same here as they were in the eyes-open exercise.

Your Patience *Will* Pay Off

As I mentioned in the last chapter as I previewed *samurai shinjutsu* for you, it has been my experience that mindlessness is the most challenging warrior discipline for Westerners to grasp or practice. As you will determine for yourself, your primary obstacles to success here (and in every other undertaking in life) are impatience, boredom, distracting mind-static, and a lack of a sense of inner-motivation to continue trying, all of which are typically nonwarrior maladies. But I assure you that with practice it *can* be accomplished, and I will further assure that the results will be well worth your time and persistence.

> *. . . mindlessness is the most challenging warrior discipline for Westerners to grasp or practice.*

Throughout this section I have attempted to assist you, my *sempai*, in laying a foundation of understanding of how and why the legendary *samurai* warrior existed as well as his philosophy and methods for attaining the indomitable mentality he historically displayed. The true Way of the *samurai* was not an easy path to follow, as is true of anything of real value in life. But if you truly believe trading and financial risk-taking to be your destiny, then I encourage you to push on to be the best you can be at it.

I am convinced that understanding the *samurai's* Way of existence, what motivated him to keep going when the chips were down, how he viewed himself and his relationship to the universe around him, how he trained his mind to perceive that universe to the highest possible degree, and how he cleared his mind of superfluous distractions and clutter will unquestionably enable you to achieve that goal in the most efficient way—the Way of the warrior-trader!

True Tales of the Warrior-Trader

Sometimes the simple advantages of the Way of warrior-mindlessness can really impact the life of a warrior-trader, as M.M. of St. Louis, Missouri, discovered.

M.M. works as an institutional trader for a medium-size bank as well as trading his own account on a part-time basis. It was easy to tell by talking with him that M.M. was not only intelligent but a fairly good trader as well. But intelligent or not, he had a problem that had always given him considerable difficulty! Taking tests tended to freak him out—especially professional certification tests like the SEC's series-7 and CTA exams!

After reassuring him that "clutching" during test-taking is a common problem, even among very intelligent people, I proceeded to explain some things to M.M. about the basic memory/recall process itself. I pointed out that the ability to remember anything (especially testing materials) hinged upon three simple (and natural) steps or processes: impression followed by natural retention and, finally, recall. I further explained that most people who try to cram for a test tend to think they can force the retention process by studying harder when they do. Then, likewise, when taking the actual test, they tend to try to force the required memory from their mind similarly to the way they had put it in. This philosophy and approach can only lead to tension and anxiety—and test-taking catastrophe—as M.M. had personally experienced.

After making the previous points clear, I explained that the solution to this was indeed very Zen—a balanced blend of warrior-mindfulness and mindlessness. I went on to tell him that the true warrior's Way to study is to first be fully mindful of a small amount of material or information. After such mindfulness, it is imperative to then clear the mind as completely as possible for a very short time. Then simply move on to the next important paragraph, page, fact, or whatever with what could be called an empty mind. It is important to never "try" to remember per se—just let natural retention do its job, because it will!

When test-taking time comes around, I explained, the test should be handled just as the samurai would have handled a battle against multiple opponents—one strike and one opponent at a time! All that matters is what is in front of you now—not before and not later—but only now! I told M.M. that this is made possible by clearing the mind as he approached each question, just as he had cleared after studying each bit of information when preparing for the exam. This way the answers were more likely to simply "flow" from his unconscious memory just as the samurai's offensive and defensive techniques flowed from his in the heat of battle!

M.M. took this lesson to heart and then applied it with an open mind. I am pleased to say that he passed his certification exams. But going beyond the scope of the exams, he has since acquired a new respect for and confidence in his ability to absorb information of all types and, perhaps more importantly, to readily recall or access the information when the situation presents itself. Without a doubt, the Way of warrior mindlessness (and mindfulness) has had a positive impact on his life!

PART TWO

The Samurai's Psychology
of Engagement

CHAPTER 6

The Way of Warrior A.C.T.I.O.N.

TRUE TALES OF THE BUDO

In all of Japanese history, one of the most extraordinary examples of the samurai's execution of a battle plan can be found in the famous story of "The 47 Samurai." In 1701, Naganori Asano, who was the daimyo *(head of a province) of Ako, was insulted by Lord Yoshinaka Kira, an even more powerful* daimyo *of the court of the* shogun *at Edo. In the confrontation that followed, Asano drew his* katana *and attempted to cut down Kira, but instead only minimally wounded him. Asano was well aware that to draw one's sword inside the castle of the* shogun *was an infraction of samurai etiquette punishable by death, an outcome he was ready to accept as a result of his actions. Out of respect for him and his honorable reputation, Lord Kira gave Asano permission to commit* seppuku, *the traditional ritualistic act of suicide by self-disembowelment, which he did.*

Upon hearing of this tragedy, 47 of Asano's most loyal samurai *vowed among themselves to avenge their master's fate even though they knew this would ultimately result in their own deaths as well. This was because the Code of 100 Articles, which consisted of strictly detailed guidelines for* samurai *behavior, prohibited the taking of revenge by* samurai *without first informing the appropriate authorities and obtaining their official seal of approval for such action. The 47* samurai *faced a difficult ethical dilemma inasmuch as they would obviously not receive official permission for revenge against such a powerful lord as Kira, yet the* samurai's *code of honor, their* bushido, *clearly dictated that they "could not coexist under the same heaven with the enemy of their master"! It was quickly agreed upon by all 47 that, first and foremost, they had to serve the highest law of their* Bushido Code, *which was, of course, loyalty.*

The samurai *were well aware that Kira and the other authorities were expectant of an attempt at revenge by the* samurai *of Asano. But in order to mislead them into thinking otherwise, the* samurai *agreed to temporarily disband and seemingly lead the lives of masterless* ronin. *They would leave their families and live like drunks and other dishonorable men long enough for the authorities at Edo, including Kira, to forget about the possibility of a vendetta. They further agreed to reunite one year later, at a precise time and place, to then take their revenge on Kira after he was lulled into a sense of security and least expected it.*

On the snowy, inclimate night of December 14, 1702, each of Asano's 47 samurai arrived at the designated spot and reaffirmed their unified vow to avenge their master's death. Assisted by the weather and the element of surprise, they proceeded to attack Kira's residence, cutting down all of his samurai. Upon capturing Kira, they offered him, as he had Asano, the opportunity to commit seppuku. When he declined their offer, they decapitated him with the very blade Asano had used to take his own life. With Kira's head in hand the samurai marched openly through town and proceeded to the grave of their master. When they arrived they placed Kira's head and Asano's sword on his grave, along with a written proclamation that read, "We have come to pay homage, Lord Asano. We could not have dared to come unless we had completed the revenge that you began. Every day we waited seemed like three autumns to us. We have delivered Lord Kira to you and returned the sword you entrusted to us. This is the respectful statement of your 47 samurai."

Of course, all of the samurai surrendered to the authorities and were subsequently sentenced to death, as expected. Almost poetically, the samurai met their death simultaneously by committing seppuku together within the walls of the prison. In their last moments each was strengthened by the satisfaction of having lived up to his personal code, by having accomplished his mission, and ultimately knowing that he was dying for what he believed and stood for.

The Essentials of Engagement and Action

We now begin the most powerful (and my personal favorite) section of our study—the *samurai's* psychology of engagement. In this chapter I specifically address his Ways and means for preparing and executing a particular plan of action.

It has been my experience, in both my martial arts training and my "real-world" endeavors, that there are essentially three "action catalysts" that support effective action and ultimately lead to a successful mission. They are (1) a firm, well-grounded stance or position, (2) a workable "harmonize, then enter" tactical philosophy, and (3) a dependable "psychology of action" suitable for unwaivering application in any situation. And just as a matter of additional food for thought, I have also observed that, inversely, there are essentially three "action blocks" that contribute to ineffective action (or none at all) and typically the failure of a mission. They are (1) overanalysis (experienced as "analysis paralysis"), which leads to (2) self-doubt (experienced as fear), which leads to (3) hesitation (experienced as missed opportunity and then anger).

It might be interesting for you to note that the similarities between the martial discipline terms and the market trading terms of position, pacing, entry, and analysis paralysis (as well as many others) are purely coincidental, inasmuch as they existed in the martial disciplines centuries before the markets or trading came into being. Yet these similarities point out once again the validity of viewing market engagement as a war game and viewing trading as warriorship. No one could disagree with the observable fact that the opportunity for making money cannot exist until some action is taken in that war game somewhere. And since your actions (which are dependent upon your "warriorship") will either make you or break you, it would be well worth our time to look closely at the catalysts that enable them to happen.

ACTION CATALYST 1: A WELL-GROUNDED STANCE

The first action catalyst I mentioned had to do with having a well-grounded stance or position. By this I am referring to your physical and attitudinal postures, which incidentally are interrelated. At the physical level, just watch someone who is powerful and accomplished enter a room full of people and you can tell that they have those traits just by the way they hold themselves. You almost immediately recognized them as someone to be respected, depended on, learned from, and/or cautious of. During my youthful years of martial art competition, I always knew who meant trouble just by the way they walked into the ring and the way they assumed their initial fighting stance. Their body language clearly conveyed to me that they intended to be in the fight to the bitter end, win or lose, and that it was my misfortune to have drawn them as my opponent.

What I have always found interesting about such physical posturing is the effect it has on the mind of the bearer. Countless warrior maxims allude to "immovable stances lending to an unbendable mind." Although I will be covering the physical implications of this in Chapter 8, "The Way of Warrior Centering," right now it is psychological stancing and positioning that we want to look closer at.

It is important in all matters to know where you stand on things—in other words, to take a position. It has often been said that, "If you don't stand for *something*, you'll fall for *anything!*" In this chapter's opening story of "The 47 Samurai," it was their unwaivering position on loyalty that first empowered them to put their plan for revenge into effect. And so it is with you, too, in trading and in life. You simply *must* come to know what you believe in and come to live or die by it. In fact, that's how you'll know if you're right to begin with. If your beliefs or positions are such that you are willing to risk all or even die for them, then you can count on them as being valid. I will be covering the issue of trusting your beliefs in greater detail in Chapter 9, "The Way of Warrior Trust and Intuition."

Your Stance Should Truly Be Your Own   But how do you come to acquire such a psychological stance or position to begin with? There is only *one* true way and it's really quite simple: analytical research combined with personal observation. You've got to do your homework and decide for *yourself* where you ultimately stand on an issue—no one can do it for you! I have noticed a very real tendency among traders to depend too heavily on the advice and opinion of other "experts" in formulating their own trading philosophies and beliefs. While it is possible to borrow from someone else's research and analysis, it is up to you to test those ideas and validate their appropriateness for your situation. In fact, nothing is possibly more dangerous to you or your success than assuming a stance or position based purely on someone else's recommendation. I have seen countless students try to emulate my presumed "technically correct" way of holding my *shinai* and moving my body in *kendo* (full-contact fencing with a bamboo sword) only to find themselves repeatedly defeated in competition because my "example" wasn't appropriate for their particular physique or quickness level!

In fact, nothing is possibly more dangerous to you or your success than assuming a stance or position based purely on someone else's recommendation.

To be able to take effective action on any battle plan, whether it be real combat or market trading, your stances or positions must be yours and yours alone, and based exclusively on your own analysis and observations. Otherwise you will never be able to truly live or die by them. But regarding analysis and observation, remember also that the first action block is overanalysis! The correct time for analysis and observation is *well before* the time for action arrives—not *during*.

For example, every trader working with a new trading system tests and analyzes its performance in "paper-trading" before putting real money on the line. This is the phase during which the psychological stance is developed, or at least should be. When the time *does* come to put that money on the line, it is no longer time for analysis. By that point you either believe or do *not* believe that the signals your system gives you will be valid. In the martial disciplines, trying to initiate effective action from an "I'm not sure" stance is called "tentative entry" into battle. In such a case, you are sure to get maimed or killed, or in trading jargon it would mean "a paralyzed trigger finger" or possibly "broke." Therefore, a firm attitudinal stance or position is something you absolutely believe in—not something you *might* believe in. It's that simple.

ACTION CATALYST 2: HARMONIZE, THEN ENTER

The second action catalyst I listed was a workable "harmonize, then enter" philosophy. While this might sound complicated or confusing at first sight, in reality it is a principle that is easy to understand and apply, and one that you inevitably practice in many situations already. But it would probably be helpful if I first explained how the *samurai* viewed and applied it in his situation.

You learned in an earlier chapter that the Japanese word for *life force* is *ki* (pronounced "key"). It is additionally important to remember that *ki* is responsible for and at the heart of every thing and situation that exists. If you add the prefix *ai* (pronounced "eye") to *ki*, it becomes *aiki*, which literally means "to blend with oncoming energy." Inversely, if *ki* is followed by *ai* as a suffix, it becomes *kiai*, which literally means "to send or focus energy," usually into one place or action. So what we end up with is a pair of philosophically complementary antonyms: *aiki* and *kiai*, representing the *yin* and *yang* or *in* and *yo* of the Asian martial arts.

At my *dojo* we use a little rhyme that helps students to keep this functional dichotomy in mind:

To bring conflict to its peaceful ending,
be sure to practice blending, then sending!

This gets to the very essence of the *aiki/kiai* tactical philosophy, which simply points out that the only efficient way to accomplish what we want in this world of conflict and competitiveness is to first get in step in the great dance of life before you try to lead! My own life and martial arts experience have taught me that, undoubtedly, to first patiently harmonize with a situation as it evolves will certainly render you far more opportunities for productive and profitable entry than if you simply "butt heads" with it. You can see many examples of this truth at work in the world around you every day!

The 47 samurai used *aiki* (blending) when they decided to spend one year acting and living like drunkards in order to avoid the notice of Kira and the authorities. Then on the designated night, they used *kiai* (sending) to launch a swift, deadly surprise attack on Kira's stronghold. Perhaps you've known someone who has patiently waited, sometimes for years like these *samurai*, to execute a vendetta or other plan of action when the timing was finally just right. I've known them!

Some Everyday Examples of "Blending, Then Sending" Think about the freeway on-ramp. When you accelerate down the ramp to make your entry into the freeway traffic, do you just take a bead on some point in front of you and put the pedal to the metal hoping that the other cars look out for you? Or do you first accelerate, then look to your left to spot your potential entry point, and finally adjust your speed up or down in order to blend with the opening you plan to enter? I would like to believe that your tactical common sense leads you to employ the latter *aiki/kiai* technique rather than the first, although I've certainly seen a hell of a lot of people use *kiai only* . . . and to everyone's peril.

What about conversation? We've all known people who just blurt out what they're thinking even though the listener doesn't have a clue as to where the talker is coming from with his comment. And then there is the conversation dominator who loves to hear himself talk and doesn't give a hoot about what

I would like to believe that your tactical common sense leads you to employ the latter aiki/kiai technique rather than the first, although I've certainly seen a hell of a lot of people use kiai only . . . *and to everyone's peril.*

you've got to say. Neurolinguists will tell you that the only way to effectively communicate an idea to a listener is to first get in sync (*aiki*) with the listener's frame of reference. You are better off using language structure that listeners can and will identify with, in order to gradually solicit rapport with them before you begin to more powerfully lead (*kiai*) them and their opinion in the direction you want them to go. This is the true art of diplomacy and effective debate.

And since this *aiki/kiai* principle applies to all things and situations, it naturally applies to trading the markets as well. Any trader worth his salt knows that it is imperative to first get in sync (*aiki*) with the market flow and direction, and to know precisely when and where (the stance) he intends to enter (*kiai*). Once *in* a position, the same principles start all over again as preparations for getting *out* begin. Highly successful traders I have come to know seem to have inadvertently developed an intuitive *aiki/kiai* sense about the markets, which serves them very profitably indeed. But the other interesting thing I notice about these special traders is the way they employ *aiki/kiai* in literally everything they do—from opening a door, to conversations with me, to driving on the freeway. Everything about their actions and behavior reflects a relatively high level of mastery and application of these principles, which in turn should give you a clue as to their importance in successful action-taking!

Some Simple Aiki/Kiai *Exercises*   Once I convince students of the importance of "blending, then sending" on their overall action-taking psyches, a common complaint I hear is that they want the opportunity to practice *aiki/kiai* regularly but that they are stuck in a chair-sitting situation all day with no way to do so. After I point out the rather narrow scope of their perspective on "practice opportunities," I usually recommend the following drill that they can do wherever they are and that will in fact help to condition their *aiki/kiai* senses.

Take a white golfball and hold it between your fingertips like a gem would be mounted in a ring, only hold it upside down facing the floor. Sit at the front edge of your chair and hold the ball out in front of you with your arm straight, above eye level, in a position as if you were going to drop the ball to the ground. The idea here is to release the ball from the fingertips and, as it begins to fall, smoothly move the hand downward faster than the ball is falling in order to get ahead of it.

As you drop your hand downward, simultaneously exhale with an audible "ooosssh" sound. Your hand should be in a lead position by the time the ball passes your spread knees, so you can "scoop" under it and catch it somewhere below the seat level. There are two things you are nominally seeking to accomplish: (1) your hand should "merge" (*aiki*) with the ball with little or *no sensation* of impact and (2) there should be *no noise* (like "plop") as your hand and the ball intercept (*kiai*)!

Now after trying this a few times, with boredom beginning to set in, you might say of this drill, "This is nothing more than a simple coordination exercise!" And damn if you wouldn't be right. But the truly operative words in your comment would be *simple, coordination,* and *exercise! Aiki/kiai* really is *simple*—so simple, in fact, that you may take it for granted and not see the bigger implications it offers. *Coordination* could be described as the Western definition of *aiki/kiai,* since it means "a harmonious working relationship between two or more objects or events." And finally, the only way to produce a *conditioned* response in any area of behavior is through repeated practice or exercise! So that's why you're sitting there playing with your balls. And if you find that boring, then try using a raw egg in the exercise just to make things a little more interesting and a little more risk-oriented as well!

ACTION CATALYST 3: A DEPENDABLE PSYCHOLOGY

Now let's move on to the third and possibly most powerful action catalyst, a dependable "psychology of action" suitable for unwaivering application in any situation. For the *samurai,* their *Bushido* Code served to provide the blueprint for their decisions and actions.

All of us would do well if we lived our lives within the seven tenets of this moralistic code: *loyalty, rectitude, courage, benevolence, courtesy, veracity,* and *honor.* However, I have found the *Bushido* Code and all of the wonderful wisdom contained therein to be a little too abstract for the Western mind, leaving too much "gray area" for interpretation that can ultimately render many of its tenets useless. Plus just reading and understanding it does not necessarily shed any light on how the *samurai* found themselves empowered to action as a result of living by it.

Although I do teach the specifics and moralistic importance of the *Bushido* Code to my regular martial arts students, I have found a much more understandable way to communicate *how* the *samurai* prepared his psyche for necessary action.

The *Samurai* A.C.T.I.O.N. Plan

Over many years of practicing the Way of the Japanese martial disciplines myself, I have done a considerable amount of self-observation and self-analysis. By thinking back in detailed retrospect after I successfully executed a high-risk plan of action, I have been able to determine that the mind of the risk-taker (whether it be me, a *samurai*, or the most successful trader in the world) goes through a six-step process or flow chart just before and upon initiating decisive action, especially that of a high-risk nature. For ease of understanding and easy remembering, I have organized these six steps into what I call the *Samurai A.C.T.I.O.N. Plan.*

The acronym A.C.T.I.O.N. consists of the first letter of the first key word of six warrior maxims that are essential in preparing the risk-taker for action. Although I have arranged the maxims in the order of occurrence in the mind, they are all of *equal* importance to the overall action-oriented psyche. The *Samurai* A.C.T.I.O.N. Plan is as follows:

Accept . . .	*all possible losses before entering the battle!*
Center . . .	*yourself in body, mind, and spirit!*
Trust . . .	*your warrior skills and intuition!*
Imagine . . .	*success clearly with the mind's eye!*
Only . . .	*exist in the present moment to control fear!*
Never . . .	*stop or look back once action has begun!*

Believe me when I say that it will be very much worth your while to commit this plan to your deepest memory. It will serve you many ways for the rest of your life if you will let it. For all intents and purposes you will find, like I have, that this arrangement of ideas can provide you with a reasonably infallible blueprint for psychologically preparing you for the action you need to initiate in your life, especially in the area of financial risk-taking. It can also serve as a "self-diagnostic" tool when things are not going well for you. Just be honest with yourself concerning how you handled or felt about a particular situation, then look at the *Samurai* A.C.T.I.O.N. Plan. If you are indeed being honest, you will be able to quickly spot the area of psychological or attitudinal deficiency that contributed to the less-than-desired results you experienced.

Looking Deeply into the "Plan" Can Change Lives

Interestingly, I have seen both martial artists and traders completely overhaul the way they approach their respective disciplines after simply reading and interpreting the *Samurai* A.C.T.I.O.N. Plan at its face value. But what if we looked beneath the surface of these all-important maxims? Wouldn't that yield even greater understanding and an even higher potential for action-oriented success? I have found that it does, so in the next six chapters I will discuss the inner meaning of each of the individual maxims and many of the insights I have observed and experienced with them over the years.

> *I feel that traders and other financial risk-takers have the potential to apply and benefit from the psychological Ways of the* samurai *more than any other type of* professional . . .

As I said in my introduction to this book, I feel that traders and other financial risk-takers have the potential to apply and benefit from the psychological Ways of the *samurai* more than any other type of professional that I have had the pleasure of teaching them to. I am also confident in my belief that the *Samurai* A.C.T.I.O.N. Plan, in combination with a strong attitudinal stance and your *aiki/kiai* tactical philosophy, can transform your trading and financial risk-taking endeavors into the true Way of the warrior-trader! So let's move on and see what you can learn as we take a closer look at the benefits and importance of *acceptance.*

True Tales of the Warrior-Trader

As silly as it may sound, I don't believe I'll ever get over feeling excited when I receive a package from a foreign country, especially one that bears a return name and address of someone I've never met or heard of before. Maybe it's a remnant of my youthful years when I believed in Santa Claus and the tooth fairy. But whatever it may be, I still remember the excitement I felt in July 1992, when I received an interesting package from Australia that bore the notice, "Please do not fold—photos enclosed!"

When I opened the envelope I was intrigued to find an 8×10 photo of a youth soccer team posing in front of a banner that read, *A.C.T.I.O.N. PACKERS, 1991 DISTRICT CHAMPIONS.* My curiosity pricked, I hurried to read the personal letter that accompanied the photo, which was from G.S. of Sidney. In the letter, G.S. related that a trader friend of his had heard me speak at a Los Angeles conference on futures trading. It seems that his friend had picked up a copy of a miniposter of the Samurai *A.C.T.I.O.N. Plan* I had distributed at my program and brought it back to to G.S. along with other conference materials.

According to G.S., the simple, yet powerful message of the *A.C.T.I.O.N.* formula immediately impressed him, so much so that he framed the poster and put it in a prominent position over his trading station at home. This way, whenever things were not going well, he could just look up at the plan and figure out what he was doing wrong that day. He indicated that the presence (and guidelines) of the plan made an immediate impact on his personal attitude as well as his market trading performance! But then one day several weeks later, he continued in his letter, something else about the *A.C.T.I.O.N. Plan* suddenly became obvious to him—that the plan could be applied to any type of adversarial situation, especially competitive team sports!

G.S. proceeded to take down the poster and make 15 copies of it, one for each member of a relatively unsuccessful youth soccer team he coached three evenings per week. He then proceeded to make his players memorize the maxims and recite them before each practice session; at the end of each practice he would have different players give their personal impression of the inner meaning of a particular maxim. Once they had memorized and gotten a grasp of its meaning, G.S. went a step further and renamed their team the *A.C.T.I.O.N. Packers*, which he said reflected the kind of game they were committed to bring to their opponents each and every time they played!

By the end of the season, according to G.S., the results were nothing less than remarkable. His team went from finishing second-to-last in the previous season to finishing first in their district the current year! And at the end of the season the team was so excited about their win that they had asked him if they could send a copy of their team's victory picture to "the samurai guy whose picture was on the *A.C.T.I.O.N.* poster," which G.S. proceeded to do!

"What an incredible endorsement of the accomplishment potential of the true warrior-spirit, whether it be that of a young soccer player or an indomitable samurai!" G.S. concluded in his letter to me. And he went on to say, "It seems to me that it doesn't matter whether you are trading the international markets or taking on the defending champion Sidney Kangaroos, if you have a sound plan of action (or, in this case, a good *A.C.T.I.O.N. Plan*) and the willingness and ability to execute it, you will inevitably be victorious!"

I couldn't agree more!

CHAPTER 7

The Way of Warrior Acceptance

TRUE TALES OF THE BUDO

During the time of the Tokagawa shogunate, it is told that Tokagawa Ieyasu decided to seek special tutoring in the Ways of the sword for a number of his lesser-skilled samurai. *To accomplish this Ieyasu solicited the services of a highly reputed* kenshi *(sword master) whom he knew to reside in the area.*

On the designated day Ieyasu's samurai *gathered in the courtyard to be interviewed and inspected by the* kenshi *before their training began. As he walked among the ranks of the allegedly unskilled warriors, something about one particular man caught and riveted his attention. The* kenshi *said to the soldier, "Sir, it is obvious to me that you are no novice at the Way of the sword. Your advanced mastery and spirit are unquestionably apparent. Is someone attempting to perpetrate a hoax upon me here?"*

"I assure you, master," replied the soldier, "that I am without any advanced skill or knowledge of the sword! I am here to benefit from your tutelage in order that perhaps I might someday better serve Lord Ieyasu, and I am in no way attempting to deceive you!"

"If that be the case, how is it then that I sense such a powerful, indomitable presence within you?" asked the kenshi.

"I could not know!" the samurai *responded. "In fact, ever since I was young, my sorely lacking skills with the blade were something of an embarrassment to my family. I was told that with skills like mine, it would be best if I prepared to die, since surely I would be killed in the course of my first battle. Not knowing what else to do, I proceeded to do just that. Every day I thought about my death in vivid detail . . . what it would be like . . . how it would feel . . . the many possible ways it could happen . . . the honor of dying for our shogun's cause. With the passing of time I eventually came to totally and completely accept the inevitability of my death, and along with this acceptance seemed to come a complete lack of fear of its eventual arrival. This is all that I can imagine you sensed in me, master!"*

Hearing this, the kenshi *proceeded to show the* samurai *his two favorite sword-fighting techniques, after which he awarded the fearless* samurai *the highest certificate of proficiency he could bestow! He then sent the warrior back to the service of Tokagawa Ieyasu that very same morning.*

Accept All Possible Losses before Entering the Battle!

This is the first of six maxims that make up the *Samurai* A.C.T.I.O.N. Plan. And even though all six are of equal importance to the warrior and financial risk-taker, this first maxim actually sets the stage for everything else to happen. The famous Zen master and noted philosopher D. T. Suzuki was once quoted as saying, "Acceptance is that fine line between misery and ecstasy," and I couldn't agree more.

How many people do you know that literally make their lives miserable, along with those of the people around them, by failing to simply accept and then learn from the repercussions of their actions? Instead of accepting and learning from their defeats, they tend to internalize and then personalize the loss, thereby compounding it into a loss of self-respect and confidence as well! But for you and I, this *must* not and *will not* be the case, since there is no place for such an emotional travesty and miscarriage of justice in the mind of a true warrior!

Risk Is the Real Issue

My somewhat philosophical lesson to you here is not so much about accepting "all possible losses" as it is about accepting *risk.* I think it goes without saying that a person who has faced and accepted the intrinsic risk in a given situation has also accepted all possible losses he might incur. Thus it is an appreciation of risk that we should discuss above all else. Risk is what always has and always will make the world go round, and it is important for you to appreciate how essential it is in the grand scheme of things. Every major accomplishment of man has been the result of some individual or group of individuals pushing on with their dream or vision in the face of what were probably overwhelming odds against them. To be successful in trading or any other type of financial risk-taking, it is inevitable that you must adopt such a philosophy for yourself as well.

A great many years ago one of my Japanese *sensei* give me a lecture on acceptance of risk and losses, and it has stuck in my mind and heart ever since.

Sensei had noticed my tendency to be preoccupied with my defense during *kumite* (empty-hand sparring) and not concentrate enough on my attacking opportunities. Taking me aside and going over to a blackboard, he said, "There are two kinds of people in this world. First, there are those who follow life's lead and spend their time and energies defending against whatever life might throw at them, then living off the leftovers of the battle. Then there are those who courageously attack life by taking advantage of every opening and opportunity that may present itself, thereby setting the pace of life and living off the spoils of victory."

Then *sensei* proceeded to draw a Japanese character on the blackboard. He explained, "This is the ideograph for 'risk.' It is not a word like you use in English, but rather a picture of an idea. What you see depicted here is 'opportunity riding a dangerous wind.' If you see the word *risk* written in English, you can't help but think about moving slowly and cautiously. But when you see *risk* written in Japanese, you can't help but think about moving ahead swiftly, like the wind! As a budding young warrior you *must* begin to move like the wind in combat, taking advantage of every strategic opening, while accepting that at any moment you may be struck down by your opponent."

As I said, this lesson has stuck with me for many years and has been valuable in countless high-risk situations I've faced in my life. And from this lesson have emerged two glaring, indisputable truths that I want to pass along for your consideration and assimilation.

OPPORTUNITY IS PROPORTIONAL TO RISK

The first obvious truth is that the degree of opportunity that exists in any situation is usually directly proportional to the degree of risk, almost without exception. In the *samurai's kyokushin* (universal truths and laws) this is called the *law of risk versus reward*, which I will cover again in Chapter 14, "The Way of Universal Law and Truth." In other words, it is an inescapable fact (or law) that there just can't be opportunity without some kind of risk! You don't have to like this arrangement, but you do have to learn to accept and live with it!

ACCEPTANCE: THERE IS REALLY NO BETTER WAY

And that brings me to the second truth I've come to recognize, especially in working with traders. I have come to find, surprisingly, that not everyone believes in or accepts the law of risk versus reward. I have met people out there (and I bet you have too) who delude themselves into thinking they can skirt around the danger of risk and just go directly to the reward. They usually think they can accomplish this with a wide assortment of defensive risk-evading measures (that usually come up short of their expectations in the final analysis) instead of concentrating on taking advantage of the opportunities with a good rational offense or plan of action. In other words, they spend their precious time and money looking for that holy grail that will protect them, only to discover that the risks simply have changed, not disappeared.

> *. . . not everyone believes in or accepts the law of risk versus reward.*

The same people that tend to disregard the law of risk versus reward also tend to argue with me about the possibility of "accepting all possible losses" being helpful to them. Their contention is that it seems to them that to accept all possible losses is defeatism of the worst magnitude. "You're supposed to be in the battle to *win!* It would be self-defeating to accept defeat before the battle even begins," is their usual argument. And you and I would have to agree with them *if* our thinking was limited to conventional "think-positive" pop psychology. Fortunately it's not, and this is *not* about positive thinking to begin with. It's about empowerment to *action*, and the only way to be truly empowered is to be free of fear and inhibition. Only by optimistically accepting our *potential* losses can we face the risk and move on to effective action.

The Three Types of Acceptance

That brings me to another interesting perspective about acceptance that may be valuable for you to consider and may account for the confusion expressed by some people over this issue. Believe it or not, there are three different kinds of acceptance, each of which produces a different outcome—some positive and some negative.

. . . there are three different kinds of acceptance, each of which produces a different outcome—some positive and some negative.

The three types are optimistic acceptance, pessimistic acceptance, and indifferent acceptance. Each deserves scrutiny. For the sake of clarity I will also give you a simple example of each that I have observed in one of my favorite environments—casino black-jack tables! We'll compare the different outcomes of three different players who simultaneously sit down at the same table to play, each bringing with him a different situation and type of acceptance.

THE NATURE OF OPTIMISTIC ACCEPTANCE

Optimistic acceptance is the type wherein you truly accept the risks and potential losses that stand between you and a desired reward, but your emotional focus and vision are clearly placed on the successful accomplishment of your mission. This is the type of acceptance practiced by most successful risk-takers before and during execution of the necessary action.

Our first metaphorical casino player arrives at the blackjack table with a thousand-dollar bankroll in his pocket. He buys in for $500, but he has established a stop-loss of $300. Now he knows upon sitting down at the table that there is a chance he will lose as much as $300, and he accepts that risk and potential loss for the right to play the game and possibly win. In fact, that's exactly what he wants to do—win! Because he has accepted his possible losses in advance, he is free to play his blackjack system confidently and can rely on his intuition more assertively. He *wants* and *expects* to win (because he has a *samurai*-blackjack mentality), but he still knows that his $300 might not survive. But as "luck" would have it, today things go profitably for him and he ends up several hundred dollars ahead.

THE NATURE OF PESSIMISTIC ACCEPTANCE

Pessimistic acceptance is the type wherein risks and potential losses are accepted, but with a sense of defeated resignation. This type of acceptance is usually accompanied by comments such as, "Oh, what the hell. I may as well get this over with!" It pretty much goes without saying that such an attitude would inevitably lead to failure. In fact, everything about this type of acceptance leads toward expecting or even manifesting negative results through the incredible power of *sakki*, a mind-over-matter power we all possess and control whether we know it or not, and which I will cover in Chapter 10, "The Way of Warrior Imagery."

Our second metaphorical casino player also arrives at the table with a thousand-dollar bankroll in his pocket. The problem is that this is his last thousand dollars and he must make $500 to pay his past-due $1,500 mortgage. Like player 1, he knows that he might lose his money and he accepts that as a possibility. But he really ignores the truth of the situation—that he can't *afford* to lose—and that will be his downfall.

He buys in for $1,000 to give himself plenty of betting power and begins to play. The first few hands go his way, which brings about a wave of optimism. But the next hands draw him down, causing him fear and desperation as he watches his money disappear. He panics and follows his losses with some bigger bets, but his sense of pessimistic acceptance causes him to look for and expect "killer cards" to emerge from the shoe. And wouldn't you know it—he *gets* them. He tries changing seats at the table, but his "luck" seems to follow him there too. In no time he finds himself $900 down, at which time he dejectedly gets up to leave mumbling, "Damn, I *knew* this would happen!"

Now, indifferent acceptance is a very powerful but rare animal of a totally different color. This type of acceptance usually accompanies situations where there is no perceived risk involved in the action taken, the operative word here being *perceived.* By this I mean that the magnitude of risk versus reward is a very individual perception, differing with each person, depending on his situation and depth of backup resources.

For example, a person who is broke might be willing to risk his life in a venture for $10,000, whereas a person with $200,000 wouldn't dream of doing such a thing for such a "small" reward. Or look at it another way. A person with $20,000 wouldn't be worried about risking $100 to make $100, whereas a person with only $200 to his name wouldn't dream of risking half of his net worth for the possibility of increasing it by 50 percent.

So as you can see, it's all relative! But let's consider some of the interesting ramifications of indifferent acceptance as we watch our third metaphorical casino player.

Player 3 is a successful businessman. In fact, he is a multimillionaire. Today he took the day off and he has come to the casino to just kick back, enjoy the view, and either win or lose some money. He too has a thousand-dollar bankroll, and he proceeds to buy in for $1,000 as he makes light chitchat with our other two players and the dealer. His play begins relaxedly and indifferently progresses on an even keel, as he splits his attention between the game and an attractive drink waitress.

It seems to the other two guys as if player 3 gets blackjack about every third hand, so often in fact that the dealer has to steal his attention away from the waitress long enough for him to pull his winnings back. It's like magic, as if winning hands were somehow attracted to him. Before he knows it (literally), he finds himself $1,500 up. And since he and his new waitress friend have discovered they both share an affinity for prime rib, he picks up his pile of money and they head for the casino steakhouse.

So as you can see from these metaphorical examples, all three players accepted their possible losses in their own unique way. However, it is optimistic acceptance that should be the goal of the warrior and, of course, the warrior-trader. Each of the three types of acceptance exhibited in the examples seemed to yield different results depending on the mind-set of the individual. But optimistic acceptance is the most *dependable* and *replicable*, and offers the greatest amount of manifestory possibilities of the three (which I will cover in greater detail in Chapter 10).

How *You* Perceive Things Is *Everything*

Another important point drawn from these examples that I would encourage you to always remember is that your ability to accept risks and losses is very dependent upon *your* personal perception and appraisal of risk versus reward, and no one else's. This is particularly true in matters of financial risk-taking, as I've pointed out in several examples already.

> *. . . your ability to accept risks and losses is very dependent upon your personal perception and appraisal of risk versus reward, and no one else's.*

It has been my personal experience, with both casino gaming and trading, that I am most capable of optimistic acceptance if 30 percent or *less* of my financial "war chest" is at risk at any given time. This gives me the reassurance that even in the aftermath of loss, I still have the potential to attempt several comebacks whenever I'm so inclined. You, of course, will have to judge your own comfort zone in such matters, and I am confident you will do so wisely and realistically.

My objective in all of this is to give you food for thought and to make you look closer at yourself, your situation, and your current tendencies in facing risk and accepting losses. As I said at the beginning of this chapter, it is the genuine acceptance of risk and potential losses that enables the other five maxims of the *Samurai* A.C.T.I.O.N. Plan to work. Always keep in mind that it is risk that has always made this world go round, and that without it there could be very little opportunity for you to even take advantage of to begin with. So welcome risk, embrace it, and genuinely accept its purpose and importance in your business and your life. In doing so, you will inevitably come to understand and be empowered by the Way of warrior acceptance, and you will hopefully find yourself able to face life and financial risk-taking in the true Way of the warrior-trader!

A Final Thought and "A Warrior's Prayer"

As we prepare to move on to our study of warrior "centering," I would like to conclude by sharing something with you that a preacher/trader alumni of my program once sent me engraved on a beautiful plaque. His adaptation of the famous *serenity prayer* seems to put his religious faith and warrior mentality into cooperative perspective. As a gesture of appreciation to this insightful man, I am pleased to present *"A Warrior's Prayer"* for your consideration and possible use:

> *Lord, grant me the physical strength to face this risk with poise and confidence, the wisdom to accept the losses I might incur, and the spiritual faith to see that whatever happens is for the higher good!*

True Tales of the Warrior-Trader

J.W. of West Caldwell, New Jersey, originally came to my training program to overcome what he described as "an irrational fear of pulling the trigger." He really couldn't understand this lack of confidence, since as a chiropractic physician he had for many years relied heavily on his confidence as a competent healer to assist patients who were often in great pain or discomfort.

Throughout our retreat together, J.W. appeared to truly grasp the essence of warrior psychology. He seemed genuinely excited about the prospect of going back home and applying what he had learned to his relatively new career in trading the S&P 500! In fact, I know for a fact that he did quite well for several months through the post-training follow-up period after we had worked together. However, some months after we had again last communicated with each other, I learned from another alumnus who also knew J.W. that he had once again begun to seriously struggle with his old fear of pulling the trigger. So I gave him a call to find out what was going on.

J.W. seemed glad to hear from me, but at the same time also seemed penitent for not calling in and telling me of the return of his old problem. So after reassuring him not to worry about it, I asked him to give as me as detailed a description of the problem as possible so I might give him a clue as to the solution.

He at first said that he couldn't understand what had happened to him, since he had been doing so well with his trading in the months following his training. In fact, he said, he had been doing so well that his father and one of his best friends from medical school had asked him to trade their money along with his. It was then that he said that it wasn't so bad for him that his fear and hesitancy had returned, but that he really hated letting his father and friend down in the process. And that was the clue I needed.

In reality, things had changed for J.W. and his trading situation, but he was just too close to it to recognize what had happened! When he had left my training program, he had come to understand the importance of accepting all possible losses before entering the battle, and he had initially done well in trading his money due to this change in his perspective! What he didn't recognize was that he had not come to accept the possibility of losing his father's or friend's money the way he had accepted the risk of losing his own! Therefore, the trades he was formerly taking for himself with confidence and warrior-like acceptance, he could not take in someone else's behalf!

When I verbally fed this observation back to J.W., you could almost hear the light going on in his mind and a weight being lifted from his chest simultaneously. He immediately acknowledged that my assessment was right on target, and hesitantly admitted that the only way he was ever going to be able to trade again at his fullest potential was to return his father's and friend's funds to them—at least for the time being.

I am pleased to say that as of my last conversation with J.W., he was again trading confidently and profitably, as he and I both knew he could. Maybe someday he will be in a position to trade other people's money again. Who can say? But I can say that when and if that day comes, J.W. will undoubtedly recognize the importance of accepting all possible losses—both his and his client's—before he can hope to be victorious in that emotionally demanding war game we call trading!

CHAPTER 8

The Way of Warrior Centering

TRUE TALES OF THE BUDO

As the sempai *(special student) sat on the large flat boulder, there was a cool wetness to the* Japanese *air as it touched his face. The sun was just beginning to make its slow ascent above the horizon, and the first streamers of golden light mystically pierced through the remaining morning fog. It was a peaceful and inspiring scene, yet what was even more striking was the way the orange-red glow illuminated the calm, focused face of the* bugeisha-kenshi *(master of the* samurai *sword) who knelt on the ground several feet away.*

Yoshinaga sensei *(revered teacher) was fully attired in the traditional garb of his warrior ancestors, the legendary* samurai *of feudal Japan. To the* sempai, *there was a sense of surreal timelessness about this scene, perhaps the way one would feel if he found himself looking at an ancient ghost or specter. It was as if he had been thrust back 700 years into Japan's past. Somehow the* sempai *instinctively knew that he was witnessing something far more important and far more powerful than his inexperienced mind could yet appreciate or comprehend.*

From the vantage point on the rock, he could detect the sensei's *smooth, deliberate "belly breaths" as he sat on his knees in the traditional* seiza *posture of the* samurai. *Poised in his left hand was a razor-sharp 300-year-old* katana, *still nestled in its long polished* saya *(scabbard). His back straight and his head erect, there was an incredible intensity and clearness in his eyes, without the slightest hint of distraction.*

Following his stare, the sempai *began to realize what the master had been so intently concentrating upon since the beginning of daybreak. As the sun began to shine through the foliage, it produced a silvery halo around each leaf where the dew and fog had begun to condense. It was obvious that his* sensei *had been focusing on one leaf in particular about four feet in front of him and two feet above eye level. A delicate orb of moisture had been slowly forming, preparing to drop from the tip of the leaf, and as it grew larger there was the unmistakable feeling of energy rising within the master. In fact it felt as if lightning were about to strike!*

Suddenly it happened! As the dew drop released its clinging hold on the leaf and began to fall toward the ground, the quiet and serenely centered kenshi became an explosive blur of movement and energy. As he launched forward with his right leg, there was a sudden sound of splitting air as the blade sped toward the falling target at what seemed like the speed of light. As if it were its destiny, the glistening edge of the katana sliced dramatically through the drop of water, instantly converting it back into the mist from which it had come!

As the blade completed its cutting arc, the master effortlessly twirled the blade between his fingers, reversing its direction of travel, and in one smooth movement, returned it to its saya as swiftly and efficiently as it had been drawn. Within a shorter time than it takes most people to swallow once, the entire event had transpired and the bugeisha-kenshi was back in seiza again—physically, mentally, and spiritually recentered again—as if nothing had happened!

His morning training session now over, yoshinaga sensei stood and stepped over to the sempai's rocky perch. As he began to voice his only comment of the morning, it seemed to the sempai as if he were hearing 30 generations of powerful, insightful master-warriors speaking to him in unison! He said, "The Way of the warrior is more than being able to defeat an opponent. True warriorship is, above all else, the Way of self-discipline and self-control. In order to prevail over the opponent or situation that comes leaping at you, you must first be centered in body, mind, and spirit! Remaining centered in the face of hardship, risk, or fear is the ultimate objective and outcome of martial training! Kokoro-shinjutsu—unification of body, mind, and spirit—is the warrior's one true Way and means of accomplishing it!"

Center Yourself in Body, Mind, and Spirit!

This is the second of the six maxims in the *Samurai* A.C.T.I.O.N. Plan. As you can probably assess from my previous references to this chapter, it is the most *physically* important part of the plan and the true Way of the warrior. That is why you will find this chapter to be the longest and most extensive chapter in the book. Due to its length and to help you grasp the overall scope of this important subject, I will make it a point several times throughout to put my main points back into overall perspective for you.

A New Look at the Centering Triangle

As I detailed in Chapter 3, the most important skill a physical warrior *or* warrior-trader can possess is an ability to "center" himself into the "triangular zone" anywhere and anytime. To help you remember this important idea, it would now be helpful to pull out the "centering-triangle" diagram I had you draw in Chapter 3.

As you look at the diagram, you will see the triangle has a bold dot or "one-point" in the center, while its three corners are encircled by three separate circles or "balloons." The bottom-left circle represents the body, the bottom-right circle represents the mind, and the top circle represents the spirit. You should also see how I had you depict the circles moving inward, toward the one-point, into an overlapping condition.

Finally, your diagram should depict a *single bold circle* sitting within the confines of the triangle, representing the centering of all three circles around the one-point. Hopefully you will recall that this is a state wherein body, mind, and spirit become synergized into one unified force resulting in an overall effect greater than the sum of the individual parts! And since the process of accomplishing this is *physical* in nature, we now begin a pivotal and transformational phase in your learning experience.

It's Time Now to Get Physical

Up until now, everything I have discussed and conveyed to you has been about developing a warrior's psychology, philosophy, and attitude. In other words, it has essentially been of a cerebral nature. But there comes a point in the development of warrior centering where there are things to do rather than think in order to get the results you seek. I call this a pivotal and transformational point in the program because it is the physical practice of centering that tends to separate the casual from the serious student

But there comes a point in the development of warrior centering where there are things to do rather than think in order to get the results you seek.

of the Way of warrior-trading. So let me challenge you to move out of your comfort zone after reading this chapter and actually try the various *physical mechanics* of centering I detail herein, methods that have been tried and proven over many centuries of warrior experience.

Important Additions to Your Centering Triangle

Look at your triangle diagram again. I would now like you to make some very important additions to it. If the three corners of the triangle (and their respective circles) represent the body, mind, and spirit, then its three sides or *facets* can represent the *three physical processes* through which the warrior causes centering to take place.

The three techniques for warrior centering are

1. *Haragei* (body posturing around and movement from the one-point).
2. *Kokyu-kihara* (breathing into the energy-center).
3. *Budo-zazen* (warrior Zen meditation).

On your diagram, label the bottom line linking the body and mind circles as *kokyu-kihara*, the right diagonal line linking the mind and spirit circles as *Budo-zazen*, and the left diagonal line linking the body and spirit circles as *haragei*. Although I will detail the specifics of each facet of the triangle separately, continue to keep in mind that all three are necessary for true centering to exist. Leave out or neglect any of the three, and the result will be an overall imbalance in your psyche.

Haragei: The Way of Posturing and Movement

One of the most important principles in all martial disciplines, *haragei* is central to the correct execution of any physical technique or action, whether it be of a combative or business-related nature! Many of my warrior-trader students have found it to be of great value in the execution of their trades, particularly during very risky or volatile market phases. *Haragei* refers to the way you hold or carry your body at all times, but especially during the execution of tactical action. It also involves the recognition of a center or one-point from which the energy for all action originates.

The practice of *haragei* can be condensed into three basic rules:

1. Keep your body aligned.
2. Maintain and move from your one-point.
3. Keep your weight underside.

Each of these rules is easy to follow and will quickly become habit with even a minimum amount of practice. However, they do require some explanation in order for your practice to be correct and beneficial.

HARAGEI RULE 1: KEEP YOUR BODY ALIGNED

Imagine that at the crown of your skull you attach a string that is long enough to hang down to your knees. Further imagine that you attach a weight to the end of the string, and that this string and weight arrangement can somehow hang and swing freely from the top of your head, down through the center of your body to an area between your knees. This "plumb bob" will now serve to tell you when your body is aligned or misaligned, and is an imaginary tool that works well for my martial arts students as they learn the proper stances and body positions used for combat. It will work just as well for correcting noncombative posturing.

The idea here is simple but also easy to overlook if you have never been made aware of its importance. No matter where you are or what you are doing, the plumb bob should be hanging between your knees. This means your head should be squarely on top of your shoulders . . . your shoulders should be squarely on top of your midsection and torso . . . your torso should be squarely on top of your waist and hips . . . and your legs (whether they are spread or together) should strongly support everything else on top of them. If any of these body components are off-center, they will be misaligned with the imaginary string.

The most common posturing mistake made by most people usually involves the relative position of the head, shoulders, and back. If the head and shoulders droop forward, the plumb bob will incorrectly hang in front of the legs. If the back is too arched, it will cause the head and shoulders to lean back, and the plumb bob to hang behind the legs. So as you can tell, the point here is that any time the plumb bob hangs to the left, right, in front, or in back of the midpoint between the knees, you are *not centered.* The only exception to this is when you are sitting or kneeling. In this case the hips and waist take on the role of the legs, and the center point for your plumb bob (which you can now imagine to be shorter) becomes the base of the spine or the rectum.

While the physical correctness and advantages of posturing yourself in this way may be obvious, the mental and spiritual benefits may escape your notice if I do not point them out.

The Physics of Proper **Haragei**   In Chapter 3, I explained that the *samurai* was aware of the *simple physics* (body), *superphysics* (mind), and *metaphysics* (spirit) in everything. The simple physics of correct alignment naturally allows the body's various components to work in harmony together. But it may surprise you to discover that when you stand, walk, sit, or kneel with correct posture, the superphysics of correct alignment also causes you to feel more confident, emotionally balanced, and attitudinally centered. I made mention of this interrelationship between *physical* posturing and *psychological* posturing back in Chapter 3 as well. This is the reason that centered posturing is the first physical principle I teach students in my *dojo.* I can see a literal transformation take place in an individual lacking in confidence or self-esteem just by having them practice keeping their body aligned.

While the first two benefits of correct alignment are important, it is the *metaphysical* benefits I would really like to highlight for you. I have already tried to help you understand that at the core of all things and events—at the core of the very universe—is *ki* (life force). In the Japanese language the word *haragei* also means "intuition" or "gut feelings." Therefore aligning the body also aligns the spiritual energies of the body/mind with the rest of the spiritual universe and all that it contains, including the markets. When a critical situation arises, like a menacing figure emerging from a dark alley, the warrior's *haragei* enables his intuition to be at its peak sensitivity. Likewise, when a market suddenly begins to become volatile, the warrior-trader's *haragei* enables him to intuitively "read" and respond to what is happening with quick, efficient action orginating from his one-point! And that brings us to Rule 2.

Haragei Rule 2: Maintain and Move from Your One-Point

Aikido master Koichi Tohei once said, "If this great sphere that is the universe were condensed, it becomes the *itten* or one-point in the lower abdomen." All Asian cultures see the soul or spirit as centering itself in the small round area three inches below the navel. This area is called the *itten* (literally meaning "the one-point") or *hara* (literally meaning "belly" or "center of life force"). The idea and importance of such a one-point really aren't too hard to grasp if you give it a little bit of philosophical thought.

As I mentioned in an earlier chapter, one of the primary differences between Eastern and Western religious/spiritual thought is that from the Western perspective, God, Heaven, or the universe is somehow "out there" and that you exist separately on the periphery of it all. On the other hand, Eastern spiritualism holds that God, Heaven, or the universe exists "in here" and that you coexist at the center of it! If you draw a line on a piece of paper, mathematicians and physicists will tell you that the line extends infinitely in *both* directions. So where is the middle or center of the line? The answer is, "Wherever *you* are." And so it is within you too that there has to be a perceptual center of it all, and that center is your one-point.

To maintain your one-point simply means to be aware of it—to recognize it as being the source and beginning of every action you initiate. When I am helping martial artists or other athletes to improve their performance, I cannot overemphasize the importance of having their technique originate from and revolve around their one-point. After grasping and applying this idea, the improvement in their technique and execution is usually remarkable.

After grasping and applying this idea, the improvement in their technique and execution is usually remarkable.

Some Examples of Haragei One-Pointedness   My brother-in-law John had been playing tennis seriously for many years before I met him. John aspired to someday play professionally and eventually become a teaching pro. Even though he's quite tall and lanky, I could tell immediately that he had tremendous potential to accomplish his dream. I became convinced that if he would just center his serves and defensive play around his one-point more, he could make it happen.

After about a year of practicing *haragei* and letting its one-pointedness naturally overflow into his tennis, his performance suddenly began to blossom into its full potential. I am proud to say that John has since become an accomplished tennis competitor and highly respected United States Professional Tennis Registry instructor for a large tennis program, where he now passes along the principles of *haragei* and one-point to his students.

Now Practice **Haragei** ***Yourself*** You can begin to practice *haragei* one-pointedness for yourself very easily, and you can do it in the process of any motion you make. Simply set the idea into your mind that all motion originates from your *hara* (lower belly). Then whenever you walk from one side of the room to the other, get up out of your chair, or do anything else for that matter, just let that initial "pulse" of energy that sets you in motion begin from that point . . . that is, the one-point.

You will find it even more interesting to apply one-pointedness in such static efforts as opening a stuck jar, wrenching loose a supertight hex nut, or pushing or lifting something very heavy for a short distance. It is in these situations that you can genuinely feel the power and effectiveness of one-pointedness, especially when it is correctly combined with correct body alignment and keeping your weight underside (which I will cover next). And although you may not immediately see the connection between such actions and financial risk-taking, I absolutely assure you that it's there and that it will come to you in time!

HARAGEI RULE 3: KEEP YOUR WEIGHT UNDERSIDE

At first glance, it may seem hard to understand how it could be possible to "put" your body weight one place or another. And it may initially be even harder to appreciate why anyone would want to do such a thing anyway, even if he could. Admittedly, most people who tend to be routinely concerned about getting weight *off* their underside would initially flinch at a rule that implied that they needed to *keep it* there. But that would only be because they are missing the true meaning and intent of the rule.

Keeping your weight underside is actually a psychophysical principle wherein you literally "think" your weight to your lower body for increased stability and improved posturing. The great founder and master of *aikido* Morihei Ueshiba was known for his incredible public exhibitions of *haragei* in which he demonstrated what he called the "immovable stance."

Ueshiba *sensei* was a very small man in stature, but in his remarkable demonstrations he would assume a spread-leg stance and challenge anyone to be able to push or lift him out of it. Over the years countless numbers of men tried in vain to move the master, sometimes three or four trying simultaneously. Ueshiba never claimed this feat to be anything other than the power of *haragei* at work, by aligning his body, lowering his one-point by bending his knees, and mentally "putting the weight of the universe" into his legs.

Experience the Power of Weight Underside for Yourself   While all of this may sound like so much Japanese folklore, you can experience the phenomenon for yourself by trying a very simple and fun exercise that all of my retreat attendees do with each other. I call the exercise "Guess my weight!" Most participants find it very interesting and quite convincing. All you need to try it yourself is the assistance of a partner who is bigger and/or stronger than you.

Once you have found an agreeable partner, have him put his arms around you from the back, going *under* your arms, and clasping his hands in front of you at about the sternum. Hold yourself straight up and relaxed, and imagine that your body is as light as a feather. Now stop breathing for a moment and indicate to your partner to *slowly* (to avoid injuring your ribs!) lift you into the air about four inches and then put you down. Ask him to guess your weight out loud.

But then it will be your turn to surprise him. Have him put his arms around you again the way he did before. But this time flex yours just a little and imagine that your lower body weighs a ton. Take a slow, *deep* breath below the level of his arms into your stomach, and, as you do, also imagine that your one-point is immovably attached to the earth.

As you indicate for your partner to *slowly* attempt to lift you again, stiffen your belly while you release the breath with your mouth open and from the back of your throat. As he struggles with your "increased" weight, keep the breath coming out and continue to "extend" your weight down into the ground. In many cases, he will not be able to lift you at all.

But if he does, ask him to guess your weight a second time. More often than not, he will guess a number 50 percent or more higher than his first guess. And you will have proved to yourself that *haragei* and keeping your weight underside somehow *do* transform you into a more unified, undisturbable force.

I will be the first to admit that there's not much of a market out there for an "instant weight-gain" program. But on the other hand, if following the three rules of *haragei* can enable you to feel (and be) more stable, confident, and centered before, during, and after all of your actions, then I feel it could prove invaluable to your trading and financial risk-taking psyche and performance. Assuming that you agree, we'll now move on to our study of the second facet of your centering triangle, *kokyu-kihara* (breathing into the energy center), which, by the way, you already employed in the second part of the "guess my weight" exercise.

Kokyu-Kihara: The Way of Breathing

Sadly, breathing is an automatic process that most people in Western culture take for granted. After all, they've been doing it without paying much attention ever since they were born. But if you are receptive to all possibilities, you will soon learn that breathing serves purposes that go far beyond simply keeping you alive. The Eastern cultures have recognized the critical importance of breathing "correctly" for thousands of centuries, which is why references to it permeate the writings of literally every warrior-philosopher in history. This is particularly true of the great Chinese and Japanese warrior-scholars, such as Sun Tzu and Miyamoto Musashi, who continually referenced the vital importance of *kokyu-kihara* (literally meaning "to breathe into the energy center") to the warrior's strength, courage, and indomitable spirit.

Interestingly, remnants of this ancient understanding can even be found with our own lingual interpretation of breathing. In the English language the medical term for breathing is *respiration.* This word can be traced back to its Latin origins to mean "the process (*tion*) of taking in or renewing (*re*) the spirit (*spira*)." Even then, the medical authorities of the time recognized that breathing not only keeps you alive, but also keeps you vibrant through the restoration of the spirit or life force.

In a similar way the *samurai* also recognized and applied this perception to a very high level. He saw that the simple physics of breathing kept the body alive and functioning as it should. He knew that the superphysics of breathing stimulated and afforded access to the higher functions of the mind, especially those in charge of intuition and highly refined tactical skills. And he unquestionably recognized that the *metaphysics* of breathing brought in new *ki* (life force), which would protect and energize his entire being.

Ancient Knowledge Confirmed by Modern Technology

Modern neuropsychological research and knowledge validate many of these ancient points of view about breathing. Thanks to advanced brainwave monitoring technology, scientists are well aware that the human brain functions via electrical impulses or waves that vary in frequency from a high of 32 cycles per second (CPS) to a low of 2 CPS. The various frequencies of brain functioning have been classified into four ranges or "bands" of activity (*beta, alpha, theta,* and *delta*), each of which is characterized by its unique role or function in the human mechanism. And more specific to our purpose here, they are also each associated with unique breathing characteristics.

THE BETA BRAINWAVE CHARACTERISTICS

The fastest of these bands is the *beta band,* the higher end of which tends to be associated with a lack of coordination and an inability to execute tasks requiring critical or rational judgment. It is also associated with nervousness, anger, fear, anxiety, panic, and irrational thinking. It is nearly always characterized by fast, panting thoracic (upper-chest) breathing. On the other end of the band, low-beta waves are associated with the ability to execute complex tasks requiring coordinated motor skills and normal concentration. Low-beta rhythms are usually coincidental with fairly even breathing of an average nature.

THE ALPHA BRAINWAVE CHARACTERISTICS

The *alpha band* is a narrower band of brainwaves that are generally associated with calmness, serenity, creativity, and intuitive thinking. Alpha waves, which are generally produced during a fully awake state, are usually coincidental with much slower, deeper abdominal breathing. The production of alpha rhythms (and theta rhythms) is the typical objective of most self-hypnotic and meditative processes.

THE THETA BRAINWAVE CHARACTERISTICS

The *theta band* is one that is most commonly referred to as the "twilight state" since it tends to occur with the eyes closed and just before and just after unconscious sleeping begins. Most experienced meditators think of this phase of brain activity as being very transcendental inasmuch as it puts the meditator in touch with his higher consciousness, his psychic abilities, and often creative or visionary dreams. Many artists and inventors effectively use this "preconscious/subconscious" state to obtain new inspiration, ideas, and solutions to work with. The type of breathing associated with theta rhythms is deeply abdominal, as it is with alpha rhythms, but can be of a somewhat faster pace—particularly after REM (rapid eye movement) sleep begins.

THE DELTA BRAINWAVE CHARACTERISTICS

. . . by intentionally breathing deeper you are also able to generate those same rhythms in your brain at will—a skill you will soon find invaluable in everything you do!

The bottom end of the brainwave spectrum is made up of the *delta band*, which is associated with very deep, almost comatose sleep. The human body needs and uses the delta state for healing and regeneration. Breathing during this period is automatically and by necessity very slow and regular, and deeply abdominal in nature.

Even though it is helpful to you in understanding yourself to know these facts about the various brainwave rhythms and the breathing patterns that are naturally associated with them, there is another very important validated scientific observation I want you to be quite aware of! And that is that the relationship between brainwaves and breathing patterns is reciprocal in nature. I mean by this, for example, that not only do you get deeper breathing patterns when your brain is generating alpha and theta rhythms, but, inversely, by intentionally breathing deeper you are also able to *generate* those same rhythms in your brain at will—a skill you will soon find invaluable in everything you do!

The Important Common Denominator in All of This

In presenting all of this technical information about brainwaves and breathing patterns, it is my objective and hope to help you see two valuable common denominators in it all. In fact, they are common denominators that can also be found in most of my true warrior tales that open each of these chapters.

The first denominator I want you to see is the *value* and *importance* of *kokyu-kihara* to the warrior's centeredness and effectiveness! But second and more specifically, I want you to notice that whenever mention is made of higher consciousness, intuition, highly accurate performance, emotional stability, mental focus, or any other worthwhile "inner benefits," it is deep belly-breathing that facilitates *access to it!* Believe it or not, it is the simple act of breathing—something you've been doing all along without knowing of its potential—that serves as the warrior's primary tool to instantaneously put himself into the triangular zone of centeredness!

The great founder and master of *karate-do*, Gichen Funakoshi, often said, *"If you know the art of breathing with the belly, you will have the strength and courage of 10 tigers!"* And since this was true for the warriors of old, it is equally true for you today—and *today* is as good a day as any for you to begin!

The Practice of *Kokyu-Kihara*

The best way for you to get started on the right foot with *kokyu-kihara* is to first become aware of what muscles do what when you breathe. You will find this easy enough to do by simply placing one hand on your chest and the other hand on your abdomen while you are either standing straight up or lying down flat.

In one of these two positions, take what you currently feel is a slow, deep breath. As you do this, if your chest rises or if your shoulders come up with your breath, then you are probably taking a thoracic breathe. Keep in mind that when you breathe, your diaphragm is supposed to move *down*—not up—in order to expand and inflate the lung sacks fully. When the diaphragm moves up, as indicated by the rise of the chest or neck, the capacity of the lungs is reducing, and the brain will produce the less desirable high-beta waves. Alternately, when the diaphragm moves down, the brain tends to generate more alpha and theta waves, which is what you want for the purpose of self-control and centering.

In order to get the hang of *kokyu-kihara* inhalation, first start by pushing *outward* with the muscles of the abdomen to familiarize yourself with how they work. Most people are only familiar with these muscles' ability to pull *inward*, and that's why they tend to breathe in their chests. Once you get a feel for the outward functioning of these muscles, it will be additionally helpful to practice pushing with a heavy book or some other object resting on your abdomen.

Eventually, you want to begin to practice slowly inhaling through your nose while imagining that the air is traveling to the back of your head, down the back of your neck, down your back, and finally into the abdomen. It should be easy to further imagine that your abdomen and chest are a series of two balloons, the abdominal balloon filling first, followed by the chest balloon, until you are completely inflated.

Kokyu-kihara exhalation is done in just the opposite way. While you hold the one-point outwardly flexed, start exhaling by allowing the chest to deflate first with the air moving up the front of your chest and out your open mouth (not through pursed lips). Once the chest area seems to be deflated, allow the overall deflation to continue down into the abdomen and one-point. Concentrate on releasing and then even *pushing* all of the air from your body to complete the full respiratory cycle.

With practice you can learn to extend your exhalation phase for as long as 60 seconds, particularly if you tighten the throat as you exhale, causing you to release the air with a sound something like a whispered "Aaaahhhhh." Such extended exhalations will later facilitate proper *Budo-zazen* meditation, which I will be detailing for you shortly.

ROUTINE PRACTICE OF *KOKYU-KIHARA*

In reference to the *kokyu-kihara* process I have just described, you may be wondering if it is necessary to breathe this way all of the time. The answer is that breathing abdominally is the *correct* way to breathe, whether you are a warrior or not. Watch a baby breathe and you will see what nature intended respiration to look like—abdominal!! However, the exercise I have detailed here is exaggerated for the sake of proper learning and conditioning. With practice you will eventually notice a tendency to breathe "into your belt" from the one-point all the times, without giving it a second thought. But when the time for critical *action* arrives, you will do it with intent and exaggeration—putting yourself into the "triangular zone"!

VALIDATING YOUR *KOKYU-KIHARA*

After you've practiced *kokyu-kihara* for a while, should you want to validate for yourself that what you are doing can and *is* having a positive effect on you and your body, let me make this suggestion. Since you probably don't have access to biofeedback equipment like my retreat attendees when they train with me in person, I would suggest that you let your heart be your guide to the truth.

All you have to do are a few push-ups or some other exercise that will quickly elevate your heart rate. Once you've got the heart beating faster, sit straight up on the forward edge of a chair and fairly quickly execute the inhalation process. Then begin to properly (but again fairly quickly) release the air. Notice the immediate reduction in your heart rate as the air goes out! Repeat the procedure several times until you feel you have the heart at its resting rate. This should readily serve to convince you of your growing inner control and the long-term value of your warrior-trader *kokyu-kihara!* If it does, then it's time to move on to our study of the third warrior centering technique and final facet of your centering triangle!

Budo-Zazen: The Way of *Samurai* Zen Meditation

The practice of Zen spans a period of over 2,500 years. Although it has been practiced by many different cultures, it could be said that it reached a pinnacle of practical application as a result of the legendary *samurai.*

Despite what many people initially think, Zen is not a religion. It offers no Heaven, no Hell, no guilt, no miracles, and no particular salvation other than a dramatic improvement in the quality and depth of your performance and existence.

Despite what many people initially think, Zen is not a religion. It offers no Heaven, no Hell, no guilt, no miracles, and no particular salvation other than a dramatic improvement in the quality and depth of your performance and existence. Zen is not dogmatic or holier than thou. And although within the ranks of its practitioners there are masters and students, beyond the mechanics of its practice that I will cover here, there is nothing specific that can be taught or learned, per se. It is a personal and private path that you must travel alone, not unlike trading, with many potential lessons along the Way.

You may find it particularly difficult to reap the potential benefits from the practice of *Budo-Zazen* meditation if you constantly try to relate your meditation experiences back to trading and financial risk-taking. I assure you that these connections *will* come, given that you open your mind to the possibilities, practice persistently, and let things "just happen" as they should. Remember that Western culture, like many a trader, is always on the lookout for a quick fix—something with instantaneous results. Nothing could be farther from the principle of Zen and the true Way of the warrior, as suggested in the brief story that follows.

A young samurai *sought out instruction in meditation from a famous Zen master for he wanted more discipline and intuitive response in his swordsmanship. Upon being granted an interview the* samurai *asked the master, "How long will it take me to master* Zazen *and experience enlightenment?" The master replied, "It could be 10 minutes or 10 years." To this the young warrior responded, "That could be much too long! What if I study extra hard and meditate twice as much as your other students?" The insightful master answered without hesitation, "In that case. . . 100 years!"*

Obviously the Zen master understood that haste and impatience will inevitably lead to lack of progress, frustration, and a loss of motivation to continue. So take your time and simply enjoy the experience of the meditation procedure I will teach you, and don't worry about how it connects to your trading.

This way you may surprisingly find yourself striking the center one-point of your triangle (as in Zen archery) without even having to aim. How about that!

Over 25 years of teaching Zen meditation to countless students, I have developed a format that I think is easy to remember and easy to learn. The meditation format I teach consists of five steps, and each step consists of principles that I have already detailed in this and previous chapters. Therefore there is nothing new to learn except the sequence involved, which should make it easier for you to begin right away with your practice. And even though we are now in the process of working through the acronym in the *Samurai* A.C.T.I.O.N. Plan, please indulge me further as I introduce yet another acronym and "plan" to help you remember the method of meditation I am about to detail.

The *Samurai* S.T.I.L.L. Meditation Plan

Because *Budo-Zazen* meditation is the warrior's process of making his body, mind, and spirit quiet and still for a brief period, I refer to it as the *Samurai S.T.I.L.L. Meditation Plan.* The acronym contained therein is again made up of the first letters of the first key words of five simple instructions:

> *Sit straight* . . . with your body balanced and centered. Then . . .
>
> *Take breaths* . . . slowly and deeply into the one-point. Then . . .
>
> *Introspect* . . . on your purpose for meditating. Then . . .
>
> *Let IN* . . . all sensations available to your mind. Then . . .
>
> *Let GO* . . . of all thoughts and awareness indefinitely.

Although these instructions are essentially self-explanatory, I would like to give you a few pointers on each that have been helpful to my students in the past.

SIT STRAIGHT WITH YOUR BODY CENTERED AND BALANCED

You learned of this earlier in this chapter as I discussed the three rules of *haragei.* This instruction requires you to apply all three as you (1) align your body, (2) maintain your one-point, and (3) keep your weight underside. The word *zazen,* which literally means "seated meditation," can be a little misleading inasmuch as many Zen practitioners actually kneel in the traditional Japanese *seiza* posture when they meditate. You might try both sitting and kneeling to see which is more comfortable for you personally.

If you choose to kneel, the recommended method is to sit back on your feet with a soft cushion between your feet and buttocks. If you choose to sit, the best method is to sit on a firm cushion (called a *zafu*) that will elevate your buttocks four to six inches above the ground. Your legs should be crossed with your feet criss-crossing in front of you. More advanced practitioners place the right foot on top of the left thigh, or vice versa (called a half-lotus posture), or the right foot on top of the left thigh and the left foot on top of the right thigh (called a full-lotus posture). Whichever leg position you opt for, remember that the knees should *always* be lower than the hips! This allows for proper body alignment and blood and *ki* circulation during meditation.

Take Breaths Slowly and Deeply into the One-Point

You learned of this when I detailed *kokyu-kihara*, the third fact of the centering triangle. I find it most comfortable to take a series of three breaths— long extended breaths—one for the sake of the body, one for the sake of the mind, and one for the sake of the spirit. This is often referred to as the "three breaths of Zen" or *san-chin.*

After taking these three "major" breaths, I usually allow my breathing to return to a smooth, even pattern and let my attention be exclusively aware of the feeling of the air moving in and out of my body, before I begin any introspection. In Zen jargon this is called "following your breath."

Introspect on Your Purpose for Meditating

There must be a purpose for meditating, even if that purpose is to simply do nothing for a while. At this phase of your meditation process, your mind is in a very programmable state, which provides you with the nominal opportunity to input such things as a positive affirmation, a goal you want to achieve, a feeling you wish to engender, or even a question you need answered. It makes no difference what it is, as long as it's benevolent and for your higher good. And you need not spend much time in this step. One to two minutes is more than enough time to be effective!

LET *IN* ALL SENSATIONS AVAILABLE TO YOUR MIND

You learned of this in Chapter 4, "The Way of Warrior Mindfulness." The objective here is to quickly and effortlessly take in *everything* that reaches your five senses. Some people prefer to meditate with their eyes open and comfortably staring at an object like a candle or blank wall. This is to minimize the possibility of sleep during the meditation.

If you choose to leave your eyes closed, then heighten your awareness of the remaining four senses, particularly your awareness of your body functions. Body temperature variations, blood circulation, and salivation (or lack of it) are all good areas for meditative mindfulness. And don't forget to include sounds (both close and distant), various smells, and all tastes available for your detection. In short, take in everything you possibly can before the next and most important step.

LET *GO* OF ALL THOUGHTS AND AWARENESS INDEFINITELY

You learned of this in Chapter 5, "The Way of Warrior Mindlessness." As I mentioned back then, I recognize that this is the hardest aspect of warrior mentality and meditation for Westerners to catch on to at first. But just remember that mindlessness really is a natural thing to experience, and that through mindlessness you get in touch with the ultimate "nothingness" that is everything.

It is perfectly natural for thoughts and images to creep across your mind during meditation. Don't worry about it, and don't fight it. Just think of your mind as a revolving door that allows the transient thoughts or images to flow right back out into the nothingness where they came from. It's as simple as that, and I assure you that you *can* do it with patience and regular practice.

So that pretty much sums up my tips and thoughts for now on the mechanics of *Budo-Zazen* meditation, except to say that the typical meditation period ranges from 15 minutes to an hour and is preferably done two times per day—morning and late afternoon. This also brings us to the end of our study on warrior centering. As I said I would at the beginning of the chapter, let me encapsulate what we have covered herein to put it all into summary perspective for you.

Putting the Chapter and Lessons into Perspective

Referencing your drawing of the centering triangle once again, remember that centering is that state in which the body, mind, and spirit circles come to perfectly overlap within the sides of the triangle, evenly encircling the one-point in the center. This is to create a unified effect greater than the sum of the individual parts.

The physical processes or means of facilitating such centering are represented by the three sides of the triangle, which are labeled *haragei, kokyu-kihara,* and *Budo-Zazen.* Remember that the practice of all three (and their respective rules I detailed for you) is essential to proper centering, with failure to do so resulting in serious imbalance in your overall warrior-trader mentality and psyche.

And perhaps most important of all, I want to remind and encourage you once again to physically *try* the various drills and exercises I have described, and to do so with an open and receptive mind. My promise to you is that the results of your efforts will both surprise and please you, and that those efforts will surely center and secure your understanding and application of the true Way of the warrior-trader!

True Tales of the Warrior-Trader

Since centering is a somewhat lengthy and diverse subject containing several issues of consideration, there are numerous anecdotes I might relay concerning their many applications to trading. But there is one simple short story I think you will enjoy, since it is one that brings a smile to my face and a nod of approval from my head when I think about it.

M.C. of Little Rock, Arkansas, explained to me that, before he began to practice the samurai Way of trading—particularly the principles of haragei—*he, like so many other traders, had sometimes experienced long periods in which he just couldn't bring himself to "pull the trigger" on desirable trades. Thus, drawing upon his new understanding of warriorship, he figured that if the one-point was the center of the universe (including the trading universe), then maybe it would be wiser for him to somehow turn over the responsibility of actually intitiating a trade to this "seat of his consciousness."*

This rather insightful idea eventually evolved into a process in which M.C.'s eyes and brain were responsible for watching the real-time data coming in, but when a signal to trade is indicated by his system, this job of placing the trade order was the exclusive responsibility of his one-point. The way M.C. describes it, when the time comes for action, he experiences a sudden swelling of energy in his one-point that then causes his hand to quickly move to the phone and hit the autodial button for his broker. When someone answers on the other end, his brain comfortably takes over again and he begins to speak, just as it would if he were answering the phone instead of calling out!

Now as odd as all of this may sound to you, there are two important points I would like to make. The first and perhaps most important point is that it worked for M.C. He used a combination of psychological creativity and an understanding of warrior principles to effectively solve his problem! And by anyone's standards, that should be what counts. But my second point should serve to further endorse the use of this technique—and possibly exonerate M.C. from any accusations of lunacy on his part!

In the course of M.C.'s training program, I had mentioned to his group that the great samurai Miyamoto Musashi sometimes used a detachment technique not unlike M.C.'s when he faced an ominous opponent. It seems that he would similarly turn over responsibility of tactical response to an adversary's attacks to what could be described as a "second inner-personna" that "lived" in his one-point. Therefore, thanks to haragei and one-pointedness, both Musashi and M.C. overcame potentially dangerous hesitation by turning the jobs of offensive counter-attacking and order placement, respectively, to whom they both called Bujin-san (which means "Mr. Inner Warrior-Spirit")!

An interesting idea to say the least, don't you think?

CHAPTER 9

The Way of Warrior Trust and Intuition

TRUE TALES OF THE BUDO

The six prospective candidates for the rank of godan *(fifth-degree black belt) kneel quietly and expectantly along the side wall of the* Bujinkan *dojo in Noda City, Chiba Prefecture, Japan. This is the* hombu, *or "home-dojo," of Dr. Masaaki Hatsumi Soke, the thirty-fourth grandmaster of the* Togakure-Ryu, *a direct lineage of warriors spanning eight centuries of Japanese history. These* yondan-sha *(fourth-degree black belts) have come from various points of the globe to spend time under the watchful and intuitive eye of the* soke, *in the hopes that they might possibly pass the demanding series of tests deemed necessary by the* ryu *for advancement to the title of* shihan *(master-instructor).*

Four days have already passed. And even though this is the fifth and most frightening day of their testing regimen, it seems to each godan *candidate as if he has already gone through Hell!*

The first day had been dedicated to psychological and spiritual cleansing to prepare their bodies, minds, and spirits for the ordeal to follow. All of the yodan-sha *had experienced the intensive demands of* misogi and shugendo, *consisting of extended meditation under an icy waterfall followed by the traditional* goma *fire ceremony and a 20-foot firewalk over the resulting coals. This was followed by three days of personal interviews with the* soke *and nonstop demonstrations in front of his critical stare of countless requisite techniques of the* Togakure-Ryu's *martial Way. But in the* soke's *opinion, all of these other requirements pale in importance compared to the final test that is about to take place. It is the test of* Budo-kanzuru—*the Way of warrior trust and intuition!*

Grandmaster Hatsumi, pointing to one of the stoic candidates, indicates who will have the dubious honor of attempting the test first. The selected yondan-sha *comes out to the middle of the* tatami *surface and kneels down in the* seiza *position facing away from the* soke, *holding his back straight and head erect. In his grip, the* soke *holds a razor-sharp* katana *as he stands directly behind the warrior kneeling before him. Once things have settled into a quietness wherein only the sounds of breathing remain, the grandmaster slowly lifts the long blade high above his head in preparation to strike!*

The candidate is painfully aware of what is expected of him. At any given moment, the soke *will bring his blade down at a blinding speed to the point in space now occupied by the candidate's head. Before the blade can reach its destination the* yondan-sha *must roll instantly to the left, hopefully avoiding the cutting edge that will soon descend upon him. He also knows, however, that to simply avoid the blade is not enough to pass the test, since his evasive maneuver must not begin before the* soke *begins his cut. To do so or to be cut by the blade would mean automatic and irrevocable failure—period!*

As the godan *candidate sits in* seiza, *his first natural instinct is to rely on his supersensory capabilities to possibly hear the first rustling sounds of grandmaster Hatsumi's* hakama *pants or to feel the vibration of his body as he moves to cut. But he then quickly realizes that to depend on such clues would not allow enough precious time for the necessary evasion. There is just no other way to come out of this challenge unscathed, or much less to pass the test—he simply must rely on his* Budo-kanzuru! *To begin evading at the very instant the* soke's *cut begins means he has to clear his mind of all thoughts and guesses, and trust his ability to intuit the vibrations of the grandmaster's* sakki—*his inner resolve to cut now!*

After what seems like an eternity to those observing, there is a sudden simultaneous explosion of breath, steel, and body motion! Within the fastest blink of an eye, it is all over. Now poised motionless in space, where only a fraction of a second before had been the head of the candidate, is the glistening katana *of Massaki Hatsumi Soke! Kneeling unharmed three feet to the left of the blade, and now facing him, is the* soke's *newest* godan-sha—*and the next* shihan *of the 800-year-old Togakure-Ryu!*

Trust Your Warrior Skills and Intuition!

This is the third maxim of the *Samurai* A.C.T.I.O.N. Plan, and within its simple message you can find three very precious jewels of warrior wisdom. The first is that every warrior *must* possess fighting skills and methods that have been firmly committed to the realm of his unconscious mind to afford immediate accessibility. The second is that the warrior, after mastering his fighting system and getting in tune with the nature of warfare, will naturally come to possess gut-level intuition within his realm of specialization. And the third jewel of wisdom is that, in order for his fighting skills and intuition to be effectively useful, the warrior must *also* possess unconditional trust, or faith, in their viability! So for the sake of discussion, let me start with a few observations about the sometimes overlooked power of believing.

The Power of Believing

If you take a moment to think about the principle of believing, you may come to realize, as I have, that it tends to happen in two progressive levels. Through intellectualization and experience, you first come to trust in something. This could be best described as a *process* based on a series of trials and errors. After a period of time, as well as a series of reinforcing positive experiences, trust can evolve to the next level, gut-level belief. Gut-level belief in something can best be described as a *condition* called faith, which I hope you come to recognize as being far more powerful and desirable than simply trusting! The word *condition* indicates that the belief has *completely evolved* through the *process* of trusting and has become unshakably fixed at the gut level or one-point.

It is interesting to note that the one thing that *all* religions have in common is their point of view concerning faith. Without exception, it is the teaching of every major (and minor) religious and/or spiritual system that access to the ultimate manifestory power of the universe is afforded by faith. In the famous New Testament story of Jesus and the centurion, the centurion petitions Jesus to heal his devoted house servant who has fallen deathly ill. He tells Jesus that he absolutely knows, "If you only say the word, Lord, my servant shall be healed!" Rather than taking credit for himself, Jesus tells him in no uncertain terms, "Go home to your servant now, for *your faith* has made him well!"

Importance of Faith—
A Trans-Spiritual Consensus

Countless stories, metaphors, and parables attesting to the unlimited manifestory power of faith can be found in the writings, scriptures, scrolls, and oral teachings of virtually every spiritual and religious tradition known to man. And what's my point here? Simply to point out that the collective wisdom of all humanity endorses the idea of accessing a higher power through the *process* of trusting and the *condition* of faith. I additionally want to highlight that, based upon this collective transspiritual consensus, an element of belief (either trust or faith) is absolutely essential to effective action and consistent success, whether it be in warriorship, financial risk-taking, or life in general!

. . . the collective wisdom of all humanity endorses the idea of accessing a higher power through the process *of trusting and the* condition *of faith.*

Most importantly, I want to encourage you to not only develop intellectual trust in your skills or system, but also let your trust ultimately *evolve* to the higher gut-level *condition* of *faith!* And the word *evolve* brings me to a final important point and a *warning* I would have you consider concerning this subject!

Two Types of Faith—One Good,
One Dangerous

Inasmuch as I am lauding the importance and benefits of faith to the warrior-psyche, I would be remiss if I didn't additionally point out that there are really *two* kinds of faith—one good and the other one potentially dangerous! I label them *evolved faith* and *presumed faith*.

Evolved faith is the type of faith I've already been discussing. I refer to it as such due to the manner in which it came into being—through trial, error, and eventually proving itself to be valid at the gut level. Evolved faith will never

> *Evolved faith will never desert you and will always back up your actions . . .*

desert you and will always back up your actions, no matter how intensive or threatening a situation might be. On the other hand, *presumed faith* is the type of faith adopted by someone simply because someone told them something was so.

The potential danger in this should be obvious. Faith that has not passed through the tempering fires of the trusting *process* and gut-level validation will easily bend or break under pressure, like a poorly constructed sword. The harm that can result from the standard belief being proved wrong is that it can leave a person faithless or spiritually impotent in the warrior sense.

Presumed Faith and the Trader

Unfortunately, I have seen and heard of many traders who have fallen prey to presumed faith. They bought into their trading system after being convinced by some smooth developer or salesperson that the system would produce profits in one way or another. Perhaps they wanted to believe—maybe even *needed* to believe—that this was true, only to discover too late that he was misled or misinformed. In many such cases this resulted in the novice trader giving up on the markets altogether due to either a lack of funds or a loss of faith or maybe even both. And even sadder is that they may often walk away with two *new* prejudices (which are really misguided beliefs): "Everyone selling a trading system is a liar and crook!" and/or "I can't make money in the markets!"

The bottom line here is that you simply *must* formulate your trust and faith for *yourself* by learning and testing your skills or 'system' before believing in them at all. And that brings me to the second jewel of wisdom to be found in our "A.C.T.I.O.N." maxim—that of "warrior Skills"!

The Power of Warrior Skills

My comments on this subject will be relatively brief, but of paramount importance. Common sense would reasonably tell you that before you could trust your warrior skills in a situation involving risk, those skills would have to be firmly committed to the subconscious mind. The *samurai* would never have considered going into battle to test some new technique or system of fighting before thoroughly practicing it in controlled scenarios.

I would like to believe that this would be true of all traders as well, but unfortunately I have met many of them who prematurely "engaged" the markets before properly completing the appropriate preparatory steps! Never forget that that's the purpose "paper-trading" serves—the theoretical practice of a "system of fighting" in a controlled scenario. The argument I hear against extensive paper-trading is "You can't get the *real* feel of a system's performance capability until you've got money on the line." I don't necessarily disagree with this statement, but it is still a foolish philosophy at the very least. And it is certainly outside of the true Way of a warrior-trader! I think what proponents of such a naive approach are *really* saying is that they really won't know how *they* will feel about the new system or how well they will execute it until the risk of financial (and emotional) loss is at stake.

The true warrior knows that he *must* practice his methods and techniques to a point of near-perfection *before* ever trying to trust them to serve him in battle. He knows that there is simply *no* other way besides dedicated practice to acquire enough mastery of a particular technique to honestly be able to call it an *unconsciously competent* "skill." As you may remenber from my introduction to this book, every student *must* pass through four requisite phases of learning before his knowledge can be dependable "under fire."

Don't Forget the Four Phases of Learning

As matter of review, I would suggest that you take a brief glimpse back at that introduction and my description of the importance of (1) *unconcious incompetence*, (2) *conscious incompetence*, (3) *conscious competence*, and (4) the ultimate objective of learning, *unconscious competence!*

If you don't take the time to pass through *each* of these very necessary phases, there will exist great gaps and weaknesses in the foundation of your knowledge. Additionally (and maybe more importantly), without dedicating yourself to the appropriate practice and emulation of battle conditions, it would be almost impossible to develop a warrior's sensitivity and inner vision that naturally accompany such mastery. And that brings me to the third (and my favorite) jewel of warrior-wisdom found within the "A.C.T.I.O.N." maxim we are studying—*warrior-intuition!*

The Magic and Marvel of Intuition

Intuition is probably the greatest gift of human consciousness that exists. It is a perfectly natural phenomenon that everyone possesses, without exception. And frankly, I don't believe I've ever met anyone who couldn't tell me of one kind of intuitive experience or another that they've had. I've talked to wives who "knew" their husbands were cheating on them, parents who "knew" their children were in danger, detectives who "knew" that a suspect was lying, and even martial artists who "knew" the instant when a sword began to descend on their heads. The list could go on and on. I suspect that you too could make a list of such intuitive examples, probably drawing from your own experiences!

Intuition is probably the greatest gift of human consciousness that exists. It is a perfectly natural phenomenon that everyone possesses, without exception.

Intuition has been of keen interest to me ever since I was a small child. Some of my earliest "semitraumatic" childhood memories are intuitive in nature. I remember "knowing" such things as my sixth grade teacher, Mr. Baugh, dying of a heart attack at home in bed. I somehow "knew" when Friskie, my pet collie, got taken away to the dog pound while I was at school. I particularly remember "feeling" heartsick at the very moment another guy kissed my first girlfriend, Kathy, at a seventh-grade birthday party I wasn't invited to. And I'll never forget being afraid to come home one afternoon that same school year because I "knew" my mom (who would naturally tell my dad) had found the girlie mag that one of the neighborhood delinquents had bequeathed to me when he moved away.

I feel fortunate that these intuitive experiences tended to stay with me and naturally overflowed over time into my martial arts training and discipline. This has afforded me a kind of "inside straight" to experiencing and understanding warrior-intuition in a way that few contemporary Western martial artists ever will. I say this not as a matter of pride or ego, but more so as a prequalification of my comments and observations on this subject.

Nothing could be worse or less effective than studying under someone who has only "book learning" to back up or qualify his teaching. Intuition, particularly warrior-intuition for the past 30 years, has been an integral part of my life experience. And in the last 15 years, trusting that same warrior-intuition (and the rest of the *Samurai* A.C.T.I.O.N. Plan) has had a powerful, positive impact on my financial risk-taking endeavors including several entrepreneurial ventures, casino gaming, stocks and commodities trading, and, most recently, dedicating a major percentage of my time to teaching the Way of the *samurai* warrior to other financial risk-takers like you!

So please remember that my comments and observations come to you from *experience*, not theory! And if you are open-minded to the possibilities these ideas engender, as my warrior-intuition now tells me you are, you and your trading will benefit immensely.

The Way of Open-Mindedness

The first observation I would like to make about intuition has to do with open-mindedness, something I just referred to in my last sentence. It has been my experience that you must first come to believe that there *is* such a thing as intuition. Based on what you've probably experienced for yourself, that shouldn't be too hard for you to do. Then simply expand that belief into a recognition that intuition is relevant to literally every thing and every situation in the universe, including the markets. In fact, the word *universe* literally means "one song" or "one vibration." Thus intuition is nothing more than *allowing* the mind's ear to open up to that universal song that is always there and dependably available to anyone and everyone that would hear it—including *you!*

It seems to me that a very important obstacle to experiencing and using intuition for your advantage is scientific and technological

It seems to me that a very important obstacle to experiencing and using intuition for your advantage is scientific and technological prejudices.

prejudices. By this I mean that the established scientific viewpoint of something as intangible as intuition is that it is only so much metaphysical hogwash. Modern science has unfortunately limited the acceptable definition of *reality* to the three quantifiable dimensions of width, height, and depth and measurable energies such as heat, light, and electromagnetism. This means that there just isn't room in the "tangibly" biased belief systems of most scientists—and many traders—for something as abstract as intuition. Yet in spite of their tendency to disclaim the existence (much less the usefulness) of intuition, this same group of scientists and traders can tell you of countless intuitive experiences they've had in their lives. Go figure!

Some Helpful Observations about Intuition

So to put intuition, particularly warrior-intuition, into a more scientific light, please consider some of the thought-provoking observations I have noted. Many of the warrior-trader *sempai* I have trained have found them helpful in putting intuition into a clearer, more believable perspective as well as helpful in developing some degree of trust or faith in it!

Neuropsychologists and parapsychologists (whose respective specialties exist on opposite ends of the acceptability spectrum) both agree that the experience of intuition is a function of the right cerebral cortex or "right brain." Additionally, these same respected neuropsychologists have determined, through accepted scientific method, that the right brain is also responsible for such conditions as sadness, grief, creativity, impulsiveness, love, and fear. As far as I can tell, these conditions should be right up there with intuition on the list of nonquantifiable, immeasurable, and otherwise intangible (and therefore nonexistent?) conditions of human consciousness. Yet the reason they're not is because of the very visible and commonly accepted *side effects* these conditions produce.

Let's consider some everyday examples. You can't quantify love, but you *can* tell when someone is in love. You can't quantify anxiety, but you *can* measure its effects on the body. You can't quantify creativity, but you *can* buy the results of it to hang on your living room wall. Therefore, by carrying this same standard forward, I propose that even though science can't quantify intuition, you *can* see evidence of its existence in the prompt tactical actions and situational adjustments taken and made by those who have experienced it—like the *godan* black-belt candidate in the opening story of this chapter!

Some Reflection about My Own Intuition

The fact that I have always been so intuitive can probably be attributed to several things. I always have enjoyed a strong sense of curiosity, had a vivid imagination, been open to nontraditional experiences, and read lots of books on science fiction and paranormal phenomena. And let's not forget the many years of physical, mental, and spiritual training in the Japanese martial disciplines.

I suspect this rather eclectic array of interests and activities inevitably caused me to be more open-minded and receptive to the less tangible aspects of consciousness than were my peers. But this in no way means that you have to do or be interested in such things in order to develop functional intuition. In fact, other than simply being open-minded to it, I have determined that such intuition is *actually* facilitated or engendered by either one or both of two very common human conditions that are experienced by most of us at one time or another: *passion* and (surprise, surprise!) *skill!* So let's take a brief look at each.

Passion's Contribution to Intuition

Back in Chapter 2, I spoke of the importance of *soul passion* to the Way of warrior motivation. Now you will be able to see yet another major benefit resulting from this powerful force. Passion is a deeply emotional (and therefore right-brain) experience that engenders many psychic-level outcomes, not the least of which is intuition. Whenever a person is passionate about a person, object, or activity of some sort, he will nearly always experience some kind of intuitive "connection" with it. My father-in-law Don and his rather unusual pastime provide a perfect example.

Don is retired from a long, successful career in sales and marketing. His definition of being retired is finally having the time and flexibility to indulge in his two favorite activities: playing tennis and searching for and collecting what he calls "junktiques" and "discarded treasures." To accommodate his first love, Don spends part of his day working as an assistant manager at a local tennis center where he finds plenty of playing partners and as much free court time as his arms and racquet can stand. But when he's through with his fitness and competitive "fix" for the day, it's time for him to indulge in his second (and I suspect even more powerful) passion.

Off he goes on his daily mission to save one or more poor discarded items from "seeing their untimely and unappreciated end at the city dump," as he puts it! But what's really fascinating about his passionate quest is that he can "feel" these items calling out to him to be saved, sometimes from all the way across town. He has often amazed other family members by describing the item or items in detail—as well as what the area around these "treasures" would look like—before they got to them.

Modern science would say that this is simply coincidence or luck, and the skeptic would accuse Don of planting these items in order to impress us later with his "intuitive" finds. But I know differently. Don becomes connected to these things because he has a genuine *passion* for "saving" them from a wasteful demise and then finding them a new home where they will be appreciated. In other words, he is on a warrior's passionate mission of justice, and his warrior-intuition helps him to fulfill it! And by the way, Don also makes a nice income from placing these "orphans" in their new homes, which I think is only fair. Don't you?

The Roles of Skill in Intuition

But what about *skills* and intuition? The stories that immediately come to mind are those of Nelson and Robert, my senior *hanshi-dai*. The title of *hanshi-dai* is a sometimes dubious honor bestowed by a *shihan* upon one or more *sempai* who have dedicated many years to their training and have proven their dedication to the operational philosophies and objectives of a *dojo*. Unfortunately for them, it also means that they are the heirs apparent to the obligation of paying the monthly rent and utilities. But my intuition about them tells me that they would assume this responsibility without hesitation if anything were to happen to me.

I have watched these two gentlemen gradually evolve into highly skilled and dedicated warriors over a period of many years now. I can still remember when Nelson first entered the *dojo*, a tall, lanky guy who had *never* participated in any kind of sports or athletics in his life. Needless to say, his athletic skills and coordination were essentially zilch in the beginning, but what he *did* have that ultimately got him to the level he is today was the burning desire to be the *best he could be!*

As his physical coordination gradually improved and as his *unconscious competence* with the many combat techniques became more obvious, something else emerged as well. Nelson began to display an uncanny ability to "read" what was on students' minds, like when they wanted but were afraid to ask a question. Today, Nelson not only "knows" that they want to voice a question, but more often than not, he also "knows" what the question is before they verbalize it. In my opinion, it was Nelson's efforts toward elevating his martial skills to their highest possible level that caused his gift of intuitive mind-reading to become obvious and useful to him and the students he serves.

Robert's evolution was similar, but the intuitive results have turned out to be more tactical in nature. Over the years as Robert's warrior skills became more *unconsciously competent*, he developed an interesting ability to sense when someone intending to enter the *dojo* was approaching the front door. He could also tell you if they were male or female and if they were going to be a "good" visitor or a "bad" visitor. By this I refer to the fact they we have a fair number of crackpots who visit the *dojo*, usually in search of a place where they can learn to improve their odds in their weekly barroom brawls and skirmishes. Naturally we want to have nothing to do with these sorts of people, and Robert's intuitive insight has helped us more than once to see through their up-front story about "wanting to get in shape" so we could appreciate the real truth and danger of having them train with us.

Putting the Chapter and Lessons into Perspective

The summary message in these stories, as well as the rest of this chapter, is once again simple but profound. To be able to "trust your warrior skills and intuition" you must first come to understand the nature of trusting and,

To be able to "trust your warrior skills and intuition" you must first come to understand the nature of trusting and, through that understanding, allow your trusting beliefs to naturally evolve into gut-level faith.

through that understanding, allow your trusting beliefs to naturally evolve into gut-level faith. To have beliefs formulate within your psyche that you can trust or have faith in, you must also patiently practice your fighting (or trading) system until it is firmly committed to your subconscious mind, where it will be transformed into *unconscious competency*—the only kind that is *truly* trustworthy!

Then, remember that intuition is natural and experienced by everyone, and that useful warrior-intuition almost always accompanies *passion* and *skills*. So passionately dedicate yourself to being the best you can be at your specialty. By also opening your mind to all possibilities, I can assure you that the trust, warrior skills, and intuition *will* come. And when they do, you will also be ready to put the incredible powers of warrior imagination and universal synchronicity to work in your trading—which is our next intriguing topic of discussion and study!

True Tales of the Warrior-Trader

Mark Twain once cynically remarked, "There are three kinds of lies: lies, damn lies, and statistics." Many people would agree with Mr. Twain's rather contemptuous opinion of "contrived numbers," but sometimes statistics can mean the difference between faith and fear, as L.S. of Fort Lauderdale, Florida, discovered not too many years ago!

When L.S. originally contacted me concerning a short-term intensive consultation concerning what he described as a "confidence problem," I wasn't at all sure if I had any clinical or warrior-based philosophies that could help him. And the reason for this was simple—L.S. seemed to be doing all the right things already. He had been consistently paper-trading his system for over a year, and he seemed to thoroughly understand both his and his system's strengths and weaknesses. In short, it seemed to me that L.S. had dotted all his I's and crossed all his T's, and with the audited track record he had compiled during paper-trading, he had no reason to distrust either his or his system's performance potentials under live trading conditions.

When I confessed to L.S. that I felt it could very well be a waste of his time and money to come to my dojo *for such a consultation, he emphatically disagreed. In most cases this would have been the end of it, since I had no desire to take a fee for no value rendered. But something L.S. said in defense of the idea struck home with me and caused me to change my mind. He said that he had a gut-level intuition that something worthwhile would come from our getting together. And since I am a firm believer in such instincts, I reluctantly agreed to the meeting—and in the end, it turned out* he was right!

On the day L.S. arrived for our meeting, it was considerably stormy. In fact, he was over two hours late arriving due to his flight being rerouted twice to get around the considerably bumpy weather. When he did arrive, I met a man who was white-faced and weary looking. On our short drive to my dojo, *L.S. explained that he had a genuine dislike for flying, even though he had to travel by air quite often. When I asked him how he managed this, considering the rather obvious anxiety he had experienced during his flight to come see me, his somewhat curious response was, "Well, basically, statistics save my ass." Naturally intrigued, I asked him to elaborate for me!*

"You see, I'm a person who just has to be in control of things," he said. "When I fly on a commercial airliner, I know I am turning my faith—and I guess my destiny—over to a man and a machine I don't know anything about. So back when I began having to travel by air more frequently—and experiencing anxiety in the process—I decided to learn everything I could about air-travel safety statistics. And what I learned was that, statistically, I am far safer on a commercial airliner than I am even taking a stroll around my own neighborhood. At this point, yes, I am still anxious when I fly. But that doesn't keep me going. I just make it a point to continually recite flight safety statistics whenever a plane is taking off and somehow it gets me through it," he concluded.

It was then that I knew the possible solution to his trading problem. As far as I was concerned, the whole while L.S. was describing his anxiety about flying and how he had come to overcome it, he could have just as well been describing his fears about the capabilities of his trading system. I believed that in the same way he had used statistical "facts" to validate flying even in the face of potentially uncomfortable anxiety, it was possible he might be able to use the accumulative success statistics he had gathered during paper-trading to validate live trading, even in the face of some doubt or anxiety about doing so.

After several hours of working on the fundamentals of warrior-psychology and warrior-trading (with a particular emphasis on drills relating to trusting and intuition), I presented my idea about using "statistical confidence" to L.S. I was pleased when he latched onto the idea right away, and even more pleased when, without me having said anything about it to him, he mentioned the similarity between my idea and his experience in doing the same thing for flying.

Several weeks after returning home, L.S. called to tell me that, lo and behold, the approach had worked excellently and that he was live trading successfully at last. And at the conclusion of our follow-up conversation, he took the opportunity to preach to me a little, giving me back a small dose of my own medicine. He said, "You see, my instincts were right about making the trip to come and see you. If I hadn't come, I wouldn't have had the rough-weather flight, you wouldn't have learned about my fear of flying and my use of statistics to help it, and we wouldn't have come up with the idea of using my faith in statistics to help me get started live trading. So you see, sometimes you have to have a little faith—because things just have a way of working out!"

I guess he and the ancient samurai were right about trust and intuition after all! Lesson learned!

CHAPTER 10

The Way of Warrior Imagery

TRUE TALES OF THE BUDO

The small group of six ninjutsu-ka had been steadily hiking for approximately 15 hours, only stopping ever so briefly for water and nourishment. The majority of their predominantly nocturnal pilgrimage had been guided by only lantern light and the occasional illumination of a nearly full moon peeking in and out from behind the clouds. Thankfully, the purple hue of early dawn enabled the highly motivated pilgrims to increase their pace up the sometimes treacherous ascending mountain path they had been following for so many hours. They were intent on reaching their destination by midmorning in order that they might spend as many precious daylight hours as possible with their mysterious and reclusive host.

Only the day before had the cryptic invitation been hand-delivered to Masaaki Hatsumi Soke, who then had passed it along to the six newest shihan *of the Togakure-Ryu. Inasmuch as the invitation was written in the ancient form of Japanese* kanji, sosho, *the shihan immediately knew it had come from someone deeply grounded in the tradition of the warrior Ways. The message had simply read, "Please come tomorrow." Below the vertical line of script was the* hanko *(personal seal) of Matsuyama Saito, an elderly and mysteriously reclusive practitioner of* okuden-sakki *(the secret teachings of the power of intent).*

Within the lore of Japanese warrior history, there exist countless legends and tales of warrior-mystics and warrior-wizards often living in remote mountainous areas, and possessing incredible powers of mind-over-matter. These esthetics were generally said to have been retired warriors who had at some point reached such a high state of psychological evolution and spiritual enlightenment they chose to live out the rest of their lives in secluded meditation and prayer. But those destined to be fortunate enough to cross paths with these warrior-recluses were often rewarded with mind-boggling demonstrations of the powers of mind and intent over objects, nature, and events.

Matsuyama Saito was one such modern-day warrior-mystic, living out his life in the seclusion of a simple mountain retreat in northern Chiba Prefecture. Because of his reputed abilities in the Ways of okuden-sakki *and the rarity of his being willing to accept visitors, not to mention six* gaijin *(foreign outsiders), the* shihan *had been immediately aware that a highly unusual honor and opportunity had been bestowed upon them. But to take advantage of this opportunity it had been necessary to depart almost immediately and travel through the night to reach master Saito's home by "tomorrow" as the invitation had dictated, since it was many miles away and only accessible by foot.*

A few hours after the break of dawn, the group of weary travelers spotted the simple dwelling as they broke through a stand of trees. As they did, the shihan *could see master Saito working peacefully in his vegetable garden. Looking up, the master motioned for them to come closer and take rest next to him and his obviously healthy plants. After introductions were made and conversation had begun, it seemed at first like the master was making pleasant small-talk about their arduous hike, as he spoke of being pleased with their "undertaking the long journey" and "reaching an important destination." But soon it became evident that what he was referring to was their long years of training in the martial Ways, and having passed the* godan *testing of Masaaki Hatsumi. It further became clear that, from this mountain top so many miles from the event, he had "sensed" their success of two days earlier, prompting him to send the invitation by way of a courier. Since passing the "test of the blade" indicated that each of them possessed the warrior's inner vision to some degree, he felt it would be appropriate to share with them a glimpse of the next level of warrior power!*

For an hour or so Matsuyama Saito talked to the shihan *of the powers of the mind, the interconnectedness of all things, nature, and events, and the Ways of* okuden-sakki. *And even though his visitors found his stories, comments, and explanations interesting and compelling, the master knew his words must at some point be backed up by physical demonstration in order for the truth they contained to permanently imprint on their minds—and the time had come for just that.*

Master Saito pointed to a dog sleeping about a hundred yards down the hillside. He proceeded to explain that through the power of his imagination, he would enter into the dog's dream in the form of another dog attacking from the rear. Closing his eyes, a calm look coming across his face, the master directed the group's attention away from him and back to the sleeping dog. Suddenly, without warning or any visible reason why, the dog yelped and jumped up and around, seemingly in a panic. After looking cautiously and disbelievingly in all directions, he moved over to a tree nearby and lay down once again.

Even though the demonstration had been fascinating, the comical way the dog had reacted had left a smile on everyone's face, rather than having created the impact master Saito intended.

Taking this into account, he then directed the group's attention to a small, fluffy cloud floating proudly alone in the northern sky. He then said that, once again using the power of his imagination, he would "enter the cloud as a ball of heat, causing it to break into pieces and quickly evaporate into nothingness." The shihan turned their eyes, now squinted from both brightness and involuntary skepticism, back towards the distant cloud. Within a matter of seconds, a large hole formed in the center of the cloud that then spread outward, causing it to break into four separate sections. Within one minute each of the individual new cloud sections had, as predicted, dissolved into nothingness. This provoked genuine exclamations of awe and surprise from the mouths of the six spectators, each unconsciously doing so in his own native language. Having this time evoked the response he wanted, Matsuyama Saito knew it was time to take his visitors one more major step toward appreciating the power and potential of warrior-imagination.

After being invited into master Saito's one-room home, the shihan's eyes were greated by a beautiful array of approximately 40 handmade butterflies. Each had been marvelously crafted from natural materials, most predominantly beautiful feathers representing every conceivable color and hue. It was obvious to all six visitors that the master held a great love and respect for one of nature's most elegant and lighthearted creatures. The most unusual thing about this collection, however, was the way in which they were displayed. With the exception of six butterflies lying loose on a small table near the side of the room, all of them were suspended at various heights in the air by very thin strands of colorless thread.

After each of the visitors was handed a loose butterfly from the table, everybody settled into a large circular arrangement on the floor, with their backs to the middle, sitting cross-legged as master Saito suggested. Soon the air in the room settled down, as did the suspended butterflies, and it was time for the final demonstration to begin. Master Saito once again began to speak, saying, "All things and events are interconnected. The guiding and creating force behind all those things and events is thought—yours, mine, and that of the universe! The butterflies you now hold in the palms of your hands, as well as those suspended around this room, may at first seem 'inanimate' to you. But in reality they contain the same life force as you and I. With the proper thoughts directing their destiny, they too can become as 'animated' as you and I. Watch now as this truth comes to life before your eyes!"

Master Saito again closed his eyes, the look of serenity descending onto his face as before, while the six shihan sat motionless with their eyes open, quite curious, and not knowing what to expect. Each also sat with his artificial butterfly in the palms of his flattened hands as they had been instructed.

For a while there seemed to be nothing but a great expectant calm permeating the room. But soon, from the midst of that calm, something else seemed to be coming into existence—a "feeling" of energy or life force that defied description! Though they remained perfectly motionless as *they had been instructed, the visitors' eyes began to move excitedly within their sockets, looking up and down, back and forth, trying to take in what was suddenly happening all around them.*

All of the butterflies hanging in the room seemed to be coming "alive" all at once! The threads that formerly served to suspend them in midair now seemed to serve as "leashes" to prevent them from escaping as they flitted and twirled in a lively "animated" dance! About two minutes later, as if to remove all possible doubt from the minds of Matsuyama Saito's guests, each of their hand-held butterflies also came to life, obviously twitching and dancing to the same "universal tune" as the rest!

Suddenly, and much sooner than the observers wished, the spectacle came to an end. Each of the beautiful creatures returned to its original, seemingly inanimate state, and a calmness once again settled into the room. But in light of what they had just witnessed and experienced, "calm" was far from how the shihan felt inside their reeling minds!

Master Saito slowly opened his eyes and smiled at the others, saying, "Imagination is the creative-eye and the directing force of the universe. Anything you imagine sets creative life force in motion that always causes some degree of manifestation or synchronicity to occur! Likewise, anything you cannot imagine will never come into existence! Therefore the true warrior understands that his thoughts—and his alone—are responsible for the things and events, victories and defeats, that cross his destiny's path."

Master Saito then concluded by saying, "Take this truth, backed up by the memory of your experience, and with it begin a new era of creative responsibility and a higher level of warriorship. It is time now for you to continue your journey along the true Way of the warrior. And it is also time for you to take leave of me!" And with this simple dismissal, and knowing no additional words need be exchanged between them and the master, the six shihan got to their feet and quietly walked out the front door of the master's butterfly "sanctuary."

Within minutes they were descending the mountain trail that would eventually take them back to grandmaster Hatsumi's Bujinkan dojo. Each carried priceless new knowledge and understanding of okuden-sakki, "the secret teachings of the power of intent." And they also knew they would certainly not be lacking for conversation on their long trek back!

Imagine . . . Success Clearly with the Mind's-Eye!

This is the fourth maxim of the *Samurai* A.C.T.I.O.N. Plan. Unlike some of the other maxims, the message here is singular and straightforward. But again, as with so many things, it is easy to overlook or take for granted the amazing power at your disposal. The fact is that the powers of the imagination are undoubtedly incredible—incredibly creative and helpful or incredibly destructive and debilitating! Fortunately, it is strictly and solely up to *you* how the forces of the imagination affect your life. For that reason, a deeper look into this psychological miracle might prove invaluable to you and your warrior-trading efforts. It is my most sincere wish that I had you here, in person, because that way I could dramatically reduce your learning curve concerning this wonderfully potent mental process! But for now we must make due with the "correspondence" relationship we have.

They say a picture is worth a thousand words. For this reason, I *hesitantly* chose to share the somewhat *unbelievable* story of Matsuyama Saito with you—to hopefully evoke powerful "mind-pictures" of these amazing events through the force of your imagination. But even if I was successful in doing so, I italicized the critical words *hesitantly* and *unbelievable* in the last sentence for a good reason. Even though I can assure you from first-hand experience that the events described in the story are absolutely true, I am still aware of how hard it would be for the uninitiated person to even consider their possible authenticity.

I presented the story with a certain sense of hesitancy only because I would never want to impede your progress down the true Way of warriorship, especially by throwing an "unbelievable" stumbling block in your path. That's why I say that I wish I had you here in person. Again, if a picture is worth a thousand words, then a first-hand demonstration of the phenomenal powers of warrior-imagination (like those I present in my retreat programs) would surely be worth a million. But for now we'll just have to make do with words, mind-pictures, and, hopefully, your open-minded spirit of adventure!

Warrior Imagery and Its Three Levels of Physics

To begin our study of the potential capabilities of your mind's-eye, it would be helpful to once again apply the three levels of physics the *samurai* saw in all processes and things in nature. In this case it would mean that your mind is capable of (1) *simple physical imagination,* (2) *superphysical imagination,* and (3) *metaphysical imagination.* And even though all three levels of imagination unwittingly occur within the minds of everyone at one time or another, my objective is for you to develop the ability to *willfully* engage the powers of each level for your advantage and profit! After all, there has to be a reason why we tend to refer to the highly accomplished, successful people in this world as being "true visionaries" of their time!

SIMPLE PHYSICAL IMAGINATION

Simple physical imagination can be described as the normal thoughts and images that routinely flow through the mind every day. Most nonwarriors and many psychologists would say that simple physical thoughts are relatively harmless (and therefore presumably powerless) since they consist of "visual static" for the most part. But my experience causes me to take serious exception to the idea that simple images are altogether harmless or powerless.

It is important to remember that the subconscious mind *cannot* distinguish between fact and fantasy. If you entertain a thought or image long enough or with enough detail, the subconscious mind will automatically go to work on it. For example, try vividly imagining a nice yellow lemon sitting on a table in front of you. Now imagine slowly cutting the lemon in two, and, as you do, feel and smell the tart citrus juices that come dripping off both halves onto your fingers. Now imagine picking up one half and bringing it near your nose and mouth. Smell it . . . savor it! Now imagine biting deeply into the wet, dripping lemon, allowing its overwhelmingly sour juices to fill your mouth.

End of experiment!

If your mind works like mine does, you could begin to feel the sides of your tongue begin to tingle and your saliva glands begin to water. But common sense may say that such a reaction is not only stupid, but probably impossible. But nonetheless, the reactions were probably there—even though the lemon wasn't! Your subconscious mind, being the slave to your imagination that it is, had no choice but to go to work on what it "saw"! My point here, though, has nothing to do with slobbering over imaginary lemons (although I want to go back to this experience when we discuss *superphysical imagination*). What *is* important about this level of imagination to the warrior is that it is responsible for how you *feel*—in other words, your mood and demeanor!

You and I have both seen some people who always seem to be in a good mood—kind of optimistic, I guess you would say. On the other hand, we also know people who seem like a chronic thunderstorm waiting to happen, day in and day out. So what could cause such a diversity in mood and demeanor, especially between people working in the same job and in the same environment? The answer is *habitual* negative or positive imaging. For one reason or the other, one person will fall prey to thinking negative or pessimistic thoughts most of the time. Someone else in the same situation may exhibit the tendency to consistently think positive and optimistic thoughts, even when those thoughts are not necessarily warranted by the way things are currently going!

It is an absolute fact that pessimism breeds negative expectations, while optimism breeds positive expectations. And one of the most straightforward and consistent tenets of the *samurai's kyokushin* (laws of the universe, as we discuss in Chapter 14) is that "you get what you expect!" The bad news (and warning) here concerns the "habitual" aspect of this issue.

Exercising Positive Simple Physical Imagination   Surprising as it may seem, how you use the power of *simple-physical imagination* is often more a matter of habit than intent. When someone says they do something "habitually," they are usually providing themselves with a great excuse for denying responsibility for their life's outcome. When something causes you harm or doesn't serve to further your personal goals, then there is *no reason* for not setting about to change it. And the good news here is that bad habits *can* be broken and good habits *can* be created. So begin practicing *positive* simple physical imagination today, and before long it *will* become a habit, and the creation of optimistic moods and positive expectations will become second nature to you!

> *Surprising as it may seem, how you use the* power of simple-physical imagination *is often more a matter of* habit than intent.

SUPERPHYSICAL IMAGINATION

Superphysical imagination can be described as thoughts and images that set *direct* creative forces in motion. By "direct," I mean that what is created either occurs *within* the body or as a direct result of the body. A couple of simple, interesting examples might make this clearer for you.

There was a period when I was many years younger during which chronic migraine headaches often plagued me. If you've ever had one of those babies, you know what I mean when I say that they are unpleasant, to say the least. After their onset nothing seemed to help them other than spending the whole day in bed trying to sleep it off. As destiny and good fortune would have it, one such headache caused me to miss the second day of a three-day *kendo* (full-contact fencing) seminar being presented by a highly respected *kendo-ka shihan*.

It just so happened that the master was also a physician by profession, and upon hearing what had kept me away the day before, he offered to show me how to eliminate the onset of the headache. He proceeded to explain to me that a migraine was caused by a sudden "ballooning" of isolated blood vessels in the brain. As this ballooning first begins to occur, he explained, it often causes pressure on the optical centers of the brain, which creates the visual distortion I often experienced about 30 minutes before the throbbing pain began. He finished his explanation by telling me that the physical antidote to the headache was to simply send blood *away* from the brain and *into* the hands and feet. And that's where he lost me!

I asked, "How can you just send blood from one part of your body to another?" In response, he held out both of his hands, palms down, and said, "Like this . . . watch." As I watched his hands, one of them suddenly began to turn a deep crimson color, while the other hand turned a very pale white. Upon touching the crimson hand it felt really warm while the pale hand felt cold and clammy. He opened his eyes and looked at me with one of those characteristic Japanese looks that lets you know that you're supposed to be understanding something.

Even though I was fascinated, I didn't understand his point. He said, "Watch again . . . my forehead and hands!" This time his forehead became noticeably pale white, while *both* his hands became the same deep crimson color. When he opened his eyes, I decided it was the right time to verbalize my ignorance by asking, "So how did you do that, *shihan?*" His answer was pure and easy to apply, just like his *kendo* techniques, as he said, "Just *imagine* that your hands and feet are soaking in the hottest water you've ever felt, while someone is cooling your forehead with an icy-cold washcloth." I hardly ever had any more trouble with migraine headaches after beginning to use superphysical imagination, through which the images in my mind *di-*

rectly created a change and response in my body—even though there was no hot water and no cold washcloth!

The negative antithesis to my personal success story in defeating headaches can be found in every medical practice and hospital in the land. Just about any physician can provide you with an abundance of examples of patients who are "obviously" sick (based upon their alleged symptoms), but shouldn't be! People from all walks of life come to these physicians with a wide assortment of maladies, so-called diseases that often cannot be detected or verified through initial tests or examination. Upon being told, "There is nothing wrong with you," these people sometimes set out to prove the "stupid doctor" wrong!

With the passing of time and the combined power of *simple physical* pessimism (or is it misguided optimism?) and *superphysical* bodily manifestation, people can often develop the physical malady they so believed in, sometimes eventually dying from its effects. In other words, they become the fictitious hypochondriac who had his tombstone inscribed, "See, I told you I was sick!"

The principles inherent within these examples are now taught by a wide variety of self-help/self-control programs, including biofeedback clinics, self-hypnosis tapes, and stress management seminars to name a few. If you would like to experiment for yourself with a verifiable form of superphysical imagination, you might try the following exercise I like to have my retreat attendees perform.

An Exercise in Superphysical Imagination   Sitting down in a chair, take two ice cubes of nearly identical size, one in each hand. Hold your clenched hands, palm down, out in front of you. As you do this, imagine that your right hand is very hot and getting hotter all the time. You might find it easier to do this if you simply "remember" what it would feel like to have your hand immersed in steaming water. Whatever method or type of imagery works best for you is fine, but keep *all* of your attention on the "hot" hand.

The objective here is simple and revealing: *to make the right hand's ice cube melt faster than the left hand's.* If you have any problems accomplishing this, try making the left hand the "hot" hand instead of the right. The odds are that you will be able to make this work with either hand you choose, and I would hope that such results would make an impact on your belief system.

Conventional experts tend to think of these ideas and "skills" as break-through technology in the emerging field of psychosomatic medicine. But you and I can think of it as the centuries-old principles of *samurai* superphysical imagination at work. We'll let them call it whatever they want!

Also remember that you employ superphysical imagination when you visualize something you want to bring to reality *directly*—by way of your own hands or body. For example, a carpenter first designs a cabinet in his mind before starting to build it with his hands and tools. An artist first sees the images in his mind that he wishes to paint or sculpt before going to work with a brush or chisel. An architect sees his building in his mind before he commits it to a blueprint. An Olympic gymnast sees his floor routine being performed perfectly in his mind before actually competing. And in his morning meditation before the trading day actually begins, a warrior-trader clearly envisions attentively and intuitively watching his markets, and sees himself swiftly and confidently picking up the phone to place buy and sell orders as opportunities warrant.

All of these are examples of superphysical imagination, which in turn leads to *direct physical manifestation* through the forces of your own actions. And when you blend the forces of simple physical optimism, superphysical creative vision, and metaphysical synchronicity (which I'll discuss next), your warrior-imagination truly becomes a formidable power—or what the *samurai* called *okuden-sakki!*

The Power of Synchronicity

. . . to understand how all events and occurrences come to interconnect is beyond the scope of our limited perception.

The *samurai's okuden-sakki*, or "the secret teachings of the power of intent," predominantly revolve around the apparent interconnectedness of all events—or synchronicity. An idea such as this is, admittedly, so immense and so complex that it easily defies most human understanding. But that certainly doesn't mean in any way that it isn't true! It simply means that to understand *how* all events and occurrences come to inter-connect is beyond the scope of our limited perception. And add to this the natural skepticism that would accompany most people's limited three-dimensional definition of *reality*, which I discussed in the last chapter regarding intuition. But let's look at this from within the framework of something familiar that most people *do* believe in and accept.

What if a group of scientists, circa 1940, were to suddenly find a modern-day personal computer in their laboratory. And let's further imagine that this computer was accompanied by a complete set of operational instructions and a letter from the scientists who had teleported the device back through time, describing the computer's mind-boggling (and probably unbelievable) functions, including something called "screen-touch windows" capabilities. So they plug the thing into a wall socket, turn it on, and begin to experiment to see if they can make it work. Lo and behold, they discover that by following the written instructions and the internal tutorials, they *can* make it function as it was designed to do.

But that doesn't mean they understand *how* it's doing what it's doing. Even if they were a roomfull of Einsteins, they would still be unable to comprehend the technical *synchronicity* of it all. In fact, with their current level of technological understanding, all they *could* do would be to make use of the *results* produced by this "unbelievable" collection of interconnected energies functioning before their eyes.

Or on the other hand, since they couldn't possibly understand the particular functioning of microprocessing, capacitive discharge windows activation, and the like, I guess they *could* choose to put the computer in a closet, deny the computer's dazzling functions and capabilities they've just witnessed with their own eyes, and try to forget that they've ever even seen a "higher" way of getting things done. That way they could get back to what they were doing—trying to figure out a way to lengthen the life of the vacuum tubes in Motorola radios beyond their usual two-week life expectancy.

So I guess you could say that the universe is like an omnipotent computer, one possessing infinite layers of interactive software. And you could take this analogy a step (or many steps) further by saying that the prompts and instructions that make the software do what it does are the thoughts and

The Way of warrior metaphysical imagination *is simply recognizing your own responsibility for the events in your life, and through that recognition, taking intentional, willful control of the universal software to shape your own destiny program.*

images generated within the consciousness of mankind and nature. You do not have to be a software or hardware expert to make the universal computer work—it does so already, and it does it all by itself. And the good thing about the universal computer, to which we are all interconnected, is that it never crashes, experiences glitches, or goes into endless loops! Everything happens because of some kind of instructional input—either yours or someone or something else's. The Way of warrior *metaphysical imagination* is simply recognizing your own responsibility for the events in your life, and through that recognition, taking intentional, willful control of the universal software to shape your own destiny program.

METAPHYSICAL IMAGINATION

Since I don't have you here to demonstrate such things to you myself, perhaps I can help you gain some degree of experience with and belief in the powers of *metaphysical imagination* through some simple experiments you can do by yourself or with a partner. But as I describe these things, be sure to also keep in mind that examples of synchronistic occurrences can be observed all around you every day! You may think of someone, and later that day she calls you. You may discuss a favorite movie you once saw, only to discover later that it's on TV that very night. You may be wondering what you should do for an ailing azalea bush in your yard, and then two days later while scanning the radio stations for something besides commercials, you happen to come across a gardening talk show that happens to be about— you guessed it—caring for ailing azaleas!

Such "co-incidents" happen all the time, and they can involve events around the house, around the block, around the country, or around the globe—sometimes even beyond that! By becoming aware of the interconnectedness between your thoughts, comments, or needs and the "co-incidental" events that follow, your confidence and belief levels will definitely increase and solidify. But of course, what you ultimately want is to intentionally *cause* synchronistic events to occur, and you can begin by trying the following "synchronicity exercises" using metaphysical imagination.

An Exercise in Metaphysical Imagination This exercise, which I call "word/event association," is both fun and easy. It can set synchronicity forces in motion in less than two minutes, and for increased verifiability, is best done with a partner. The idea is to select a word, preferably a noun, randomly from your imagination. There are no rules or limits on the nature or specificness of the word. For example, in one of my favorite retreat stories (which I will elaborate on as I proceed), the retreat attendee who selected the "focus-word" first picked *bananas*, but then decided to make it "more difficult for the universal computer" by adding *Chiquita* to the word.

After selecting your focus word, close your eyes and clearly imagine everything about the word you possibly can. In my retreat example, we imagined the shape, color, and overall appearance of a Chiquita banana, including its little sticker. We imagined the way it would smell and taste as well as the way it would feel in our hands. We also spelled the word out loud, and then spelled it in our heads.

Once you have done this imaginative focusing, it is then time to "release" the word. This means that you just turn the word over to the forces that be, with *no* particular expectations other than to simply be "connected" to the word and any events that might evolve around or synchronize with it. It is crucial that you genuinely *let go* of the word and not bother to think or concern yourself with it any more. That way, when a synchronistic event *does* occur, it will kind of jump out at you. It's that simple!

Our Results Were Astounding

During the course of my example retreat, three profound synchronistic events occurred before my attendees went back home. The evening after we had done the focusing and releasing exercise, our group stopped by a local grocery store to pick up some fresh vegetables for the next day's demonstrations. As we were about to enter the store, we were forced to jump out of the way of a large, heavily loaded flatbed dolly that had gotten away from its owner. As it passed us, barely missing our toes, someone exclaimed, "Look, it's loaded with crates of Chiquita bananas!" And damn if it wasn't. Everyone got a good laugh (and verification) from the incident, and they assumed that this would be the end of it. But it was not to be!

My wife Lyndee, who had been in attendance that morning during the focus session, had to work that night at the retail store where she is the manager. Lyndee is a very competitive retailer, and that night was pushing hard to win a contest involving who had the largest number of credit card sign-ups in her district.

Just before closing at nine o'clock she was a mere one card short of victory, since she was currently tied with another manager in Memphis. Lyndee asked the last (and only) customer remaining in the store to please sign up for a credit card, explaining that it would help her win a contest if she did. However, for reasons unknown to Lyndee, she didn't seem to want to do it.

Not willing to let victory slip through her fingers, Lyndee asked her why she didn't want to apply. When the lady hesitantly explained, Lyndee smiled from both surprise and satisfaction. It turned out that the customer lived on a cul-de-sac named Chiquita Circle. It seemed that when she filled out an application for something, she was often teased about being the "Chiquita banana lady"! After this humorous disclosure, the customer went ahead and applied for the credit card and Lyndee won the contest. In fact, she was so excited she could hardly get the story out of her mouth fast enough when she rejoined the group later that night!

The next day when we were on the interstate enroute to practice *zazen* meditation under a nearby waterfall, everyone was having a grand old time talking about our two extraordinary Chiquita banana occurrences. Just as we were passing next to a large tractor-trailer rig, as if the driver didn't see us at all, the rig suddenly swerved into our lane causing me to abruptly brake and slow down. This instantly stopped all conversation as everyone looked to see what had happened.

The fellow who was riding up front with me in the van, and who had been turned around backwards talking with the others, suddenly exclaimed, "Damn, did you guys see that?" At first everyone, including myself, assumed he was referring to the discourtesy of the rig's driver. But upon following his pointing finger, we all suddenly saw the reason for his exclamation! There on the side of the trailer was a giant picture of a bunch of bananas—it was a Chiquita banana transport truck that had almost run us off the road!

My point in relating these true stories of evoked synchronicity is to give you some idea of the many ways words and events can interconnect. As you conduct your own experiments, be open to any and all possibilities, and don't put any time constraints on getting results. That way you won't be disappointed. If you want to narrow the parameters and reaction time of your experiments, try picking your focus-word, doing your concentration, and then let it go, just before you read the daily newspaper. See if the word comes up in relation to any articles, advertisements, or anything else in that particular issue of the paper. You'll be surprised at the unusually high percentage of "hits" you'll have, even when you narrow the synchronic possibilities to today's news only.

The fact is that there are many unique and interesting ways to "practice" metaphysical imagination. The exercises I have detailed herein are just intended to get you moving in the right direction and to strengthen your belief in the existence and power of synchronicity. But the point of the whole chapter is to give you the clearest possible understanding of why the *samurai* felt it was important to *"Imagine . . . victory clearly with the mind's-eye!"*

Like master Saito said in the opening story, "Imagination is the creative-eye and the directing force of the universe." If you can come to appreciate this truth, then we are continuing to accomplish our warrior-trading mission. Each and every action you take when you engage the markets should be initiated with a clear vision of what you want to accomplish, without exception. In this Way you will definitely enhance your wins-to-losses ratio, and at the same time you will be helping to eliminate the action-stopping fear experienced by so many nonwarrior traders—which is the subject of the next maxim and our next chapter!

True Tales of the Warrior-Trader

Inasmuch as I opened this very unique chapter with a rather unorthodox but true story that was very special to me, I may as well conclude with a special warrior-trader's story of a similarly unorthodox nature. And in an effort to spare this outstanding gentleman any potential ridicule or heckling from his peers, I have decided to call him J.D. (for John Doe) and not mention his city of residence.

What makes J.D.'s inclusion in this segment special is not only the outstanding way he uses metaphysical imagery in his institutional trading work for Prudential Securities, but the fact that he was one of the six participants in the so-called Chiquita banana retreat program I mentioned several times in this chapter. In fact, it was probably the fact he was so impressed by the synchronistic events of that particular program that his previously conservative mind (by his own admission) was opened and convinced enough to give meditative imaging and synchronicity a sincere try when he returned home.

J.D. explained to me that in the course of his work, it is important to make regular contact with his rather substantial list of clients. He further explained that he much more preferred to speak with them when they called him rather than the other way around. So, to get them to call him more regularly, he decided to conduct an experiment using the metaphysical imagination principles he learned during his training. J.D. jokingly refers to what he does as "signing on to the cosmic internet"—which is pretty close to the truth as far as I'm concerned!

Each morning before the sun comes up, and while there is still very little "psychic static" in the airwaves, as he puts it, J.D. sits and practices Budo-Zazen. During the introspective period of his meditation (see "I" in the S.T.I.L.L. meditation format discussed in Chapter 8), J.D. imagines the faces of three select clients. While he's doing this, he essentially "wills a connection" to form between him and them, with the intent that a thought of him will germinate in their minds later, hopefully resulting in their deciding to give him a call within a day or so of his making the "synchronistic connection."

Now it's possible that J.D. may be blowing wind up my skirt, but he tells me that he has been very impressed and excited about his results with this procedure. According to him, he has had at least a 50 percent connection rate with these select people, meaning that approximately half of them do indeed call him within one week of his meditation. He also tells me that his business with these clients has increased nearly 30 percent since, as he sees it, they are more inclined to place more money with him since they called him to begin with!

So regardless of what you might initially think about this approach or how the "magical" powers of warrior-imagery and synchronicity actually work, one thing is for sure. There is at least one warrior-trader out there putting them to work in his trading business—and doing so successfully! And the way I see it, if he can do it, so can you! At least it's worth a try, don't you think?

CHAPTER 11

The Way of Warrior Fear-Management

TRUE TALES OF THE BUDO

The official witnesses for the shogun *at Edo filed solemnly, one by one, into the* hondo, *or main hall, of the fortress of Lord Yoshinaka Kira, where the ritualistic ceremony would be performed. It was an imposing scene, indeed. The large hall, supported by large pillars of polished wood, was completely level except for an area front and center that was elevated several inches above the rest of the floor. From the ceiling hung several large unlit lamps. The elevated surface was completely covered by a beautiful white matting, and at the frontmost edge of the platform atop the pristine whiteness was laid a small thick rug of deep scarlet-red.*

Tall candles placed at regular intervals around the platform gave out a dim, mysterious light, just sufficient to let the proceedings be adequately seen. The eight witnesses took their places, four on the floor on the left side of the platform and four at the right. No other person was present.

After a period of several quiet minutes, Rinjiro Yamada was escorted into the hall, and up to the platform by three officers of Lord Kira's court. Yamada, one of Naganori Asano's 47 faithful samurai, *was a powerful figure of a warrior at 32 years of age. As he approached the platform he walked with grace and poise, wearing the traditional white attire for ceremonial* seppuku, *the ritual of honorable suicide. Besides the three officers of the court, Yamada was accompanied by his* kaishaku, *a swordsman of his choosing who would skillfully take his head at the exact moment dictated by the protocol of* seppuku.

With his kaishaku *at his left side, the condemned man first bowed politely to the witnesses kneeling to the right of the platform, and then turned and did likewise to those at the left. In each case the bow was ceremoniously returned. Yamada then assumed* seiza *(a kneeling position) in* the center of the scarlet-red rug facing out toward the darkness of the large hall. His kaishaku assumed iaigoshi, a half-seated/half-crouched position, five feet to his left side.

One of the three attendant officers then came forward, bearing a small four-legged wooden stand like those used in Buddhist temples for offerings. On the stand, its handle wrapped in white rice paper, was the ceremonial tanto, a finely crafted blade of approximately 10 inches, with a point and edge bearing a nearly mystical sharpness. Lifting the blade reverently from the stand, Rinjiro Yamada lifted it to his forehead with a slight bow and then placed it on the rug in front of himself with the glistening tip pointing toward the gap between his knees.

After a brief period of silent introspection, Yamada began to speak, his face and voice completely devoid of emotion or hesitancy, saying, "I am the faithful samurai of my fallen master, Naganori Asano. As leader of a group of 47, I orchestrated the plan of revenge that was carried out against Lord Yoshinaka Kira. I personally severed the head of Lord Kira and placed it at the tomb of my master. I will be the first of my loyal legion to pay the price for our actions by disemboweling myself in your presence. I beg you who are present to do me the honor of witnessing this act."

Upon completing his official statement of purpose, Rinjiro Yamada bowed once more and then allowed his upper garment to slip off his shoulders and to fall down around his waist. Naked from the waist up, according to tradition, he tucked his large sleeves under his knees to prevent him from falling backward—for a true samurai must always die falling forward! With a deliberate steady motion, he then picked up the tanto with both hands, bringing the glistening tip to the left side of his abdomen. As he looked down at the blade, he did so with almost a sense of reverence. He had trained all his life for the possibility of this very moment. He had envisioned this act in precise detail countless times in order that, in the event that his destiny deemed it necessary, he would possess the inner strength and power to carry it out to its honorable conclusion.

Lifting the gaze of his eyes once again out into the room's darkness, Yamada was well aware of the magnitude and meaning of what he was about to do. And even though he was physically, mentally, and spiritually prepared to begin the hara-kiri (belly-cut), for the first time since arriving in the room he noticed he was afraid—no, terrified! Thoughts and images passed rapidly through his mind. Thoughts of his life of service and warriorship . . . his family . . . the face of Lord Asano, for whom he was about lay down his life. And there were thoughts and questions of the hereafter, the next unknown phase of his existence. What would it be like? Would he still have consciousness of himself? These were questions for which there simply were no answers.

Rinjiro Yamada, his awareness suddenly coming back to the present moment, realized that retrospection and anticipation of the unknown was of no use to him. The time to act was now—now being the only moment a warrior could ever hope to control! And with this last cognitive thought, he breathed once more into his hara, summoning all of his life force into his hands and center. With a firm pull, the blade slid smoothly into the left side of his belly with such a sharpness Yamada felt no pain. Then, still gripping the blade, he cut across and through his own bowels, stopping four inches right of center, as an overwhelming awareness of sickening pain enveloped his consciousness. But before the pain could overtake his consciousness, Yamada turned the blade, and began cutting sharply upward to a point just beneath his ribs. As darkness overtook him, the brave warrior removed the bloody instrument of honor and lowered his head forward, thinking a final thought, Now it has been done as prescribed!

Upon seeing Rinjiro Yamada begin to droop forward, his kaishaku, who had been carefully watching the drama unfold, leapt up from his crouched position, drew his sword, and began to cut in one smooth motion. The kaishaku's blade cut cleanly through the dying warrior's neck, except for the last one inch, keeping his friend's head from separating from his body. This brought a swift end to any further suffering on Yamada's part and the end of the faithful and courageous service of one of Naganori Asano's 47 samurai!

Only . . . Exist in the Present Moment to Control Fear!

This is the fifth maxim of the *Samurai* A.C.T.I.O.N. Plan, and within it exists a very simple, yet powerfully functional truth. In reading of the various exploits and feats of daring by the *samurai*, it would be easy to assume that they were totally courageous—possessing no fear whatsoever. Nothing could be farther from the truth. The *samurai* did acknowledge and experience fear. This fact is reflected often in their many writings. The difference between a *samurai* and the average man, however, was that the *samurai* never let fear *stop* them from taking action. After all, that's what really mattered in the final analysis.

To Be Afraid Is to Be Human

Always remember that to experience fear is to simply be human. As far as I know, in the entire history of man there has never been a totally fearless person. Even Jesus Christ was said to have experienced overwhelming fear in the garden of Gethsemane as he faced his impending arrest and persecution.

Anyone who claims to be free of fear, in my opinion, is either a liar, a fool, or high on methamphetamine—any of which should warrant your quickly taking leave of him. So please take solace in the fact that to experience fear makes you no less of a person or a warrior!

All of the above is not to imply, however, that fear is not harmful or dangerous to you. Fear is a cunningly effective enemy that can eat you up quicker than a pit full of hungry alligators! In fact, if I were to arrange a list of the six most destructive human emotions (consisting of fear, anger, greed, guilt, lust, and envy), fear would have to top the list as being the most debilitating, especially to the warrior. So for the sake of efficiency, and to avoid giving the enemy too much "platform time," let's just look closely enough at this "emotional alligator" to figure out how to wrench its jaws open when it tries to get a grip on you.

The Three Instinctual Fears

In teaching students to understand and cope with this perfectly human emotion, I find it helpful to explain to them that there are three *instinctual fears: fear of loss, fear of pain,* and *fear of the unknown.* Any other fear experiences will always fall under one of these three headings, one way or the other. That would even include the greatest fear known to man—the fear of death!

> *... there are three instinctual fears:* fear of loss, fear of pain, *and* fear of the unknown.

When the issue of fearing death *is* raised by someone I'm training, I sometimes try to help the person see the three instinctual fears more clearly with an expansion of my alligator analogy. I explain that, if you were attacked by an alligator, it's not so much that you would be afraid of being *killed* as you would be (1) *afraid of the pain* you would experience while getting chewed up by the alligator's jaws, (2) *afraid of losing* your identity as you're digested in the alligator's stomach, and (3) *afraid of not knowing* where you'll end up two days later after passing through the alligator's guts.

In spite of my weak attempt at humor, my point here is that fear is not as big or as difficult an animal to tame when you break it down into its three basic *instinctual* types like I have here.

Fear Rarely Exists in the Present

The next thing that my *sempai* often find helpful in understanding and managing fear is to recognize that nearly all fear is either *anticipatory* or *reflective* in nature. This means that when fear is present (in any of its three types), the experiencer is either thinking back to *past* events, giving credence to his *present* fear, or prequalifying his present fear by thinking *ahead* to the potential outcome of some *future* event. Either way, he is using *simple physical imagination* (as detailed in the previous chapter) to create his problem.

After you come to recognize that the source of most fear sensations is either anticipatory or reflective, the next important truth to recognize is that fear tends to manifest itself in one of two levels of *intensity* and *duration*. I refer to these two levels as *chronic fear* and *acute fear.*

The Nature of Chronic Fear

Chronic fear is a relatively low intensity fear, but tends to be spread over a long period of time. Generally it is something that permeates your thoughts on an everyday basis. Back in Chapter 2, I described fear as being one of the insidious "motivation-eaters." It is actually *chronic fear* that is predominantly responsible for this problem.

During my years of private clinical practice, I would estimate that at least seven out of 10 cases I consulted on involving intense neurosis were actually the result or by-product of *chronic fear.* In the clinical world, *chronic fear* is referred to by another name, one that most everyone can identify with—worry! People worry about money. They worry about their jobs. They worry about their kids', their spouses', or their parents' well-being. They worry about the state of affairs in the world. I've even consulted with people who consume valuable emotional energy worrying about who's cheating on who in their favorite soap opera.

Now I don't mean to imply that these things are not important issues that need our attention. On the contrary, I know that they usually *are* (except for the soap opera)! But to render *repeated* attention to issues that are currently outside of our perimeter of control is a waste of life force and a distraction away from the situations we *do* have an element of control over in the present moment. And that's the point of our maxim—to focus your energies into what's going on *now*, because *now* is the only moment you can control.

It isn't too hard to notice when you've been feeling out of sorts emotionally for a while. When you do notice it, I suggest you simply dedicate a few moments to honest, objective introspection about the bottom-line root of the feeling(s). I bet that more often than not you will discover that the psychogenesis of the bad mood or feelings involves something in the past or pending in the future. Then make it a point to repeatedly redirect your emotional energies and attention back to the present moment and the immediate issues you are handling. This way you will break the *chronic* nature of your worry or fears. And when anticipatory or reflective thoughts *do* manage to creep into your mind, *use* their temporary presence in your consciousness to reaffirm or rearrange the priorities you are working on in the present.

The Nature of Acute Fear

For the warrior or warrior-trader whose primary concern is the initiation of effective action in the face of risky opportunity, it is the obstacle of *acute fear* that represents the greatest potential impediment. Acute fear is the kind of fear that is quite intensive, but is usually short-term in nature. It is the kind of fear that can make you feel paralyzed where you are and feel seemingly unable to act. And even though acute fear is felt very much in the present, don't be confused into thinking that it is *not* anticipatory or reflective in nature. I assure you that it *is!*

For example, if a knife-wielding mugger suddenly jumped out of an alley and demanded your wallet, you would likely experience instantaneous acute fear. But even though the event was sudden and unanticipated, the *present-tense* fear you feel is still motivated by the *anticipation* of possibly getting cut and/or losing your valuables. The fear might also be reinforced by the *reflective* memory of a previous mugging years ago, during which you *did* get cut and had your wallet taken. Even if you were fortunate enough to possess some level of self-defensive skill, in such a situation as this, you would likely find yourself unable to take appropriate defensive or offensive action until you refocused your attention to the present moment. Like it or not, this is a basic psychological fact of physical warriorship.

From a warrior-trading perspective, let's say that instead of a mugger jumping out of an alley, it is the market that suddenly makes a threatening or opportunistic move. For discussion purposes, we could assume that you are currently holding a position, and to *defend* your position from taking a loss as a result of this sudden move, you have to take prompt action. Or on the other hand, we could assume that you have no position but are waiting for the right conditions to materialize in order for you to *offensively* "engage" the market. Again prompt, immediate action is required.

Either way, when the moment of truth occurs, fear could suddenly enter your mind. This could be because you *anticipate* a possible negative outcome *or* because of serious drawdown you experienced last month during similar market conditions. In order for you to clear your mind of the potentially debilitating fear, just as in facing a mugger, it would be necessary to refocus your attention to the present moment in order to initiate the tactical action required!

The Warrior's Ways of Clearing Fear

So let me now remind you of the two physical processes through which the warrior clears his mind of fear, whether it be acute or chronic. I say "remind you" because we already covered both of these warrior techniques in Chapter 8, "The Way of Warrior Centering". They are *haragei* ("one-pointed centering") and *kokyu-kihara* ("breathing into the energy-center")! To employ these two techniques to control fear in any situation, you simply (1) *keep your body aligned,* (2) *maintain your one-point* by breathing deeply into your abdomen, *and* (3) *keep your weight underside!* It's that simple . . . that quick . . . and that effective!

So you see, it really doesn't matter if the fear you experience is the fear of loss, the fear of pain, or even the fear of the unknown. It doesn't matter if the fear was brought on by reflective or anticipatory thinking. And it doesn't matter if the fear has been hanging around for awhile and has become chronic, or if it comes on suddenly like an acute danger in the dark. To the true warrior, and certainly the warrior-trader, the solution remains constantly and perpetually the same! He and you must bring consciousness back to a centered sense of the present moment—or now—the only controllable moment in all of eternity.

This truth, combined with the rest of the *samurai* wisdom and insights you may ultimately come to understand and apply, will inevitably provide you with a noticeable advantage over the "enemy" you've been hoping for, and a much greater probability of success in the long run! And now all that remains to complete our study of the *samurai's* psychology of engagement is to look at the warrior's Way of commitment to his decisions *and* his actions. So let's move on and see what else you can discover and use to your advantage and profit!

True Tales of the Warrior-Trader

A great example of acute fear management comes to mind with the story of J.C. of Chicago, Illinois. J.C. works as a pit-trader at the Chicago Mercantile Exchange, where he has accumulated over 10 years of experience.

At the time of his first contact with me, it seems that J.C. had been experiencing increasingly frequent and severe anxiety episodes. As much as he had tried, J.C. could not determine a point of origin for these episodes, nor had he been able to establish any sense of control over them once they began. It was his hope that perhaps I could help him figure out why he was having them and, even more hopefully, develop an effective means to control them.

As with most people suffering from anxiety or panic disorders, J.C. experienced three predominant symptoms at the onset of these episodes. The first was the feeling that he was suddenly lost and that everything was caving in on him. The second (and usually the most frightening) was the feeling of suffocation—as if he couldn't take another breath. The third symptom—and one to be expected considering the circumstances—was the firm belief that he was going to die as a result of the episode.

When the time came for us to work together, the first thing I emphasized to J.C. was that it wasn't necessary to figure out how the attacks began, and that it was more important to gain some control over their onset. Fortunately (as you learned in Chapter 8) the primary method of warrior centering and fear management involves breathing abdominally. I further pointed out that when someone is beginning to experience panic, his instinct is to try and breathe into his chest, which unfortunately is the center of the anxiety-generated tension. Therefore we concentrated on his mastering kokyu-kihara *("breathing into the one-point").*

Secondarily, J.C. then learned to focus his entire attention to the air filling his abdomen, which would automatically tend to put his consciousness into the present moment and away from the attack itself. This combination of controlled breathing and focusing of his attention would serve to give him some degree of tactical control over the onset of the attack and, in time, would provide him with an important level of renewed confidence in his self-control potential.

Once J.C. returned to the Merc with his new psychophysical "armament," things progressed pretty much as I had expected. He had several more anxiety episodes, but as I had predicted to him, each was a little less intense and of shorter duration. Eventually he came to lose his anticipatory fear of their onset, which naturally lessened their likelihood of occurring altogether. I am pleased to report that as of my last communication with J.C., he had been totally free of any panic episodes for over six months, an accomplishment for which I sincerely and respectfully congratulated him!

As I have said many times in the past (and will probably say many times again), more often than not, our most dangerous enemies are those that can sometimes swell up inside of us. Following the true Way of warrior centering and fear-management will help guarantee that you will be able to slay these "emotional alligators" when and if they lift their ugly heads!

CHAPTER 12

The Way of Warrior Commitment

TRUE TALES OF THE BUDO

Before Mitsuyoshi Yagi's seigan *examination commenced, headmaster Yamaoka Tesshu presented a dissertation to those in attendance concerning the reasons and benefits of training in* kendo *(the Way of the sword). He first spoke of the "four poisons" of* kendo: *doubt, fear, surprise, and confusion. According to the master swordsman, these four deep-rooted emotional or intellectual problems represented the* kendoka's *greatest nemeses to victory in battle as well as to powerful, enlightened living.*

He went on to expound that the only way to neutralize these poisons and to develop true warriorship in these modern postfeudal times (circa 1885) was to confront a great number of opponents in a row with a grave and absolute resolution to survive, no matter how bad things got during such an extended series of matches! Tesshu Kenshi indicated that it was his belief and experience that only through the rigors of self-elected and self-administered shugyo *(the Way of austere physical discipline) could the modern warrior develop a true appreciation for warrior-commitment and a strong platform of emotional control.*

Indeed, Yamaoka Tesshu Kenshi was a living, breathing example of his own teachings. Tesshu was a samurai *who had found himself without an occupation at the age of 31, when the* shogunate *was superceded by the Meiji restoration of the emperor's authority in 1867. But his warrior reputation, political sentiments, and talents as a negotiator made him useful as an advisor to the emperor's court for a period of 10 years.*

Around 1871 he had set up his own school of swordsmanship, the Ito Shoden Muto Ryu. The primary martial discipline practiced in his dojo *was* kendo, *a ferocious but nonlethal emulation of the original fighting methods and tactics of the* samurai. *Rather than use the* samurai's *ominously lethal* katana, kendo *matches were carried out with a* shinai, *a slatted bamboo stave wrapped in leather. Each contestant wore a set of protective armor called* dogu, *which adequately protected the head, shoulders, chest, arms, and waist from serious injury.*

But this was not to say that such matches lacked for realism or seemingly life-threatening danger. Quite the contrary was true, especially at the dojo of Yamaoka Tesshu, who was known by his peers as Tesshu the Demon. The master's ability to render a kendo opponent unconscious with the sheer focus and intensity of his "cuts" was well known, and he expected no less from his students.

Very few had ever even passed his examination for intermediate certification, much less for advanced certification, and the reason for this was simple. Tesshu's "basic" examination was imposed after a course of practice of 1,000 consecutive days. The test consisted of 200 consecutive contests with other students of the Ito Shoden Muto Ryu—all held within one day! The second or intermediate examination—called seigan—consisted of 600 matches over a three-day period. The third and highest-level examination—which fewer than 50 students were said to have ever passed—was a seven-day ordeal with 1,400 matches.

Through his own education and experience as a samurai, master Tesshu felt that swordsmanship should lead to the heart of things, where one can confront life and death. As the number of matches accrued during his examinations, he felt that the ordeal eventually took on the authentic feeling and reality of a fight to the finish. Thus in order to survive it, his testing sempai would have to rely purely upon his commitment and warrior-spirit! Mitsuyoshi Yagi, who had been a student of master Tesshu for six years, was about to undertake just such an ordeal and discover for himself if his sensei's premise was valid—the time had come for his seigan to begin.

With the cry of "Hachime!" the first match began with a flurry, as he parried blows and dealt his own back to his opponent. Each match would last 5 to 10 minutes, with a rest period of approximately equal proportions following. There would be no points and no winner would be assessed at the end of the matches. The idea was to endure—no, to survive!

Mitsuyoshi was in top physical condition, so it took a couple of hours for the first signs of fatigue to set in. Stiffness in his legs and arms came first. Then the first waves of dizziness were felt, as his body tried to adapt to the duress of continual battle. Before long his cuts and blows lacked the snap and power they had possessed 10 matches earlier. That's when the first poison—doubt—began to creep into his mind. With his doubts came a new awareness. It seemed as if his opponent's blows were becoming 10 times stronger. He seemed to feel their shock all the way to his feet. As the hours and matches passed, the second poison—fear— began to work its dark magic on his psyche.

Mitsuyoshi soon began to flinch in fear when the tip of his opponent's shinai snapped toward his face, something he had not done since the earliest days of his training. But in spite of these obstacles, he continued to fight on, relying on the warrior philosophies he held dear to his heart to get him through the ordeal.

By the middle of the second day Mitsuyoshi Yagi felt like a numb mass of barely moving parts. Many times he felt himself to be on the brink of paralysis if not death. But something *deep down inside him—a magically powerful faith and a sense of commitment to surviving this experience—seemed to enable him to continue holding his weapon out in front of him and to present some semblance of an offense. But through the cloudy haze of what consciousness he had left, Mitsuyoshi was gradually confronted by two more nemeses he had never faced before. He found that he was becoming suspended in a kind of slow-motion surreality, and in this timeless state every move his opponents made overwhelmingly surprised and confused him. Remembering back to master Tesshu's dissertation, he recognized that his "poisoning" was complete, and he also knew that the master had been right about something else as well—he truly felt that this was now a fight to the finish, a matter of life or death!*

Sometime during the last 100 matches, something deep inside the beaten, woozy, and practically delirious Mitsuyoshi seemed to come alive—to be reborn! His mind began to clear, his techniques began to possess some of their original snap. In fact, some of his techniques became better than they ever had been before. Amazingly, a new power began to fill the mind and body of the dedicated warrior, enabling him to even begin backing his opponents up after parrying their attacks.

Even though his mind had become crystal clear, he seemed to give up on any perception of time, something he could not seem to help but think about two and a half days earlier. As he aggressively backed up yet another opponent, he came to the realization that he had astonishingly reached a point in his psyche—and his life—wherein he knew he could go on indefinitely and defeat any number of opponents if necessary! And as he stood ready and waiting for his next opponent to step in front of him, Mitsuyoshi Yagi became aware of an unfamiliar sound that greeted his mind and senses—applause! He had just completed—and survived—the 600th match!

Mitsuyoshi Yagi's undaunted dedication and commitment to his shugyo *had seen him through a "poisonous" nightmare of near failure and enabled him to awaken to a new dawn of warrior-power and possibilities!*

Never . . . Stop or Look Back Once Action Has Begun!

This is the sixth and final maxim of the *Samurai* A.C.T.I.O.N. Plan and one that deals with the all-important issue of dedication or commitment. As I've mentioned before as we studied the previous five, all of these maxims work together in an interrelated manner, each depending on the others to establish the warrior's overall action-psyche. This is particularly true of the sixth, which works in harmony with the first—*accept all possible losses before entering the battle!*

It seems like an almost poetic balance that the first and last maxims should reinforce each other the way they do. In order to make a truly effective commitment to a plan of action, it is first necessary to accept any possible downside to the plan. Likewise, before you could truly accept the potentially negative repercussions of a plan of action, it would be necessary to be firmly committed to it. In this case, acceptance is like arming and empowering the warhead of a missile. But the warhead is useless unless it is delivered to its intended target. Therefore, commitment becomes the missile and its guidance system that will take the warhead unerringly to its destination.

Morals, Ethics, and Commitment

It saddens me to say that this country has for some time been in a state of moral and ethical decline. Much of that decline has been due to a slow but steady erosion of personal commitment to the things that really matter most. The predominant slogan now seems to be, "I'll try so and so *unless* or *until* such and such happens." Obviously the operative words here are *unless* and *until*, both of which imply conditional commitment.

Evidence of this can be seen practically everywhere you look. Couples get married with the intent of staying together *unless* they have a fight or develop differences between them. Workers take jobs with the intent of staying with it *until* something better comes along. Men and women go on diets and exercise programs, intent on staying on them *unless* or *until* they become achy or hungry. These and many other examples simply indicate a general lack of understanding of what it means to truly commit or dedicate yourself to a plan of action.

This problem is even more evident in the arena of financial risk-taking, particularly trading. I have had the occasion to visit with hundreds of frustrated, soon-to-be extraders who seem to be convinced that no one can actually make money in the markets. But as I pry out more details from them,

I often discover that they've actually been "experimenting" with the markets on a part-time basis. They seem to have made no genuine commitment of time, money, or energy to learning what it takes to win in market war games. It usually turns out they were just looking for a quick buck, and had the initial attitude of "I'll try trading *unless* or *until* I lose some money." When they do lose some, their tendency is to quickly "divorce" themselves from trading and then bad-mouth it on the way out.

Commitment Equals Empowerment

The fact is, commitment is one of the most empowering forces in the human psyche, if not the entire universe! Commitment, combined with acceptance, centering, trusting, imagery, and living in the controllable present, *can* enable a warrior to move mountains. And it can certainly help *you* to consistently reap the profits you deserve from taking risks. But like any other warrior "skill," you must understand how to practice and apply it on a regular basis. So let me share with you some of the warrior's Ways and means to develop effective commitment that I and my *sempai* have found helpful over the years.

The Five Parameters of Commitment

It has long been my experience that the ability to make a genuine warrior commitment to something and to follow through to its reasonable conclusion depends upon five parameters, most of which are indirectly implied in the *Samurai* A.C.T.I.O.N. Plan maxim we are now studying. They are

1. *You must know what you want to accomplish!*
2. *You must possess a real desire to accomplish it!*
3. *You must develop a workable plan with which to accomplish it!*
4. *You must set a reasonable timeframe within which to accomplish it!*
5. *You must never second-guess yourself if you fail!*

Because each of these parameters is of critical importance to your ability to "never stop or look back once action has begun," let's take the time to briefly inspect some of the meaning and intent behind each.

1. YOU MUST KNOW WHAT YOU WANT TO ACCOMPLISH!

It may seem obvious to you and me that a target must first exist before we can take a shot at it. But surprisingly, this is not true for many people, including many traders. Reasonable and precise goal-setting and action parameters are a very important component in the method and life of any successful person. You cannot hope to have success in any endeavor if the parameters for achieving it are vague or wishy-washy. Planning is the real key here, and impatience and sloppiness are its primary enemies.

I've seen plenty of examples of this in my many years of casino gaming. The casinos make their livelihood from people with a wad of money in their pocket and an impatient desire to make a quick killing. Anyone with any experience at all knows that 99 percent of the time, the only thing that will get killed is their bankroll—and quickly! These wannabe gamblers don't seem to want to take the time to study and learn about money management and the statistical nuances of the (war)games they choose to play. And sometimes, even if they *do* have some rudimentary knowledge of how to play (and hopefully manage their money), they blow this to Hell by partaking of the "free" drinks constantly offered by the casino cuties.

The Value of Stop-Losses and Stop-Wins   The *samurai* didn't just think to himself, 'I want to be victorious in all my battles!' and then just go out there and start fighting someone. Quite the contrary. They were amazingly effective strategists, often planning well in advance of a battle their every move, countermove, and sometimes even possible countercountermoves. This way their victory tally accumulated one engagement at a time. Likewise, traders can't just jump into this or that market thinking, 'I want to make some money today!' Rather, they should know *how much* money they can *reasonably* expect to make—no less and no more—this theoretical figure being within practical reach.

Some people tend to disagree with the "no more" part of my last sentence. While I agree that there are times when you should let your winnings ride, for the most part I find it to be wiser and more effective to employ not only stop-losses in financial risk-taking but stop-*wins* as well. Otherwise, you will sail right on past your destination without knowing it, which would be considered poor judgment in the *samurai's* eyes. Knowing as close to exactly how far you must go to achieve your goal is essential to being able to apply the rest of the *Samurai* A.C.T.I.O.N. Plan and to being able to fully commit your mind and energies to the task at hand.

A great medical analogy to this is pain. If a patient is in severe pain, and he is told by his physician that the pain could be of an indefinite duration, the patient will likely give up on trying to endure it. On the other hand, if the physician had more wisely "predicted" that the pain would last one hour, one day, or even one week, the patient would far more likely be able to handle and tolerate it until the crisis were over. So, as you can see, no matter what arena one is fighting in, it is important to know what you plan to accomplish and to perhaps set a series of realistic (and thus attainable) goals in order to see them through to fruition. These goals, combined with the desire I will address next, will get you where you want to go.

2. You Must Possess a Real Desire to Accomplish It!

Nothing can weaken your resolve to follow through with a plan more than the lack of genuine desire to achieve the end result. This is again why it is important to think things through before taking action on anything. Desire, and the resultant commitment, was the only thing that got Mitsuyoshi Yagi through the 600 *kendo* matches in this chapter's opening story. As I've mentioned previously, possessing absolute resolve and intent creates a force in the mind of the warrior called *sakki*. The fighter who possesses *sakki* is truly formidable indeed.

You too can possess such formidability if you will only make up your mind that the plan of action (and the goal you will achieve through it) is something you truly desire and believe in. Without such desire and *sakki*, you will surely balk or completely stop at the first hint of trouble, which is *not* the Way of the warrior! So remember that desire, combined with these other parameters, will yield an indomitable spirit that is truly unstoppable. Then you will need a good plan to follow.

3. You Must Develop a Workable Plan with Which to Accomplish It!

Without such a plan, you can be assured that one or more of the four poisons of doubt, fear, confusion, and surprise will eventually infect your mind. Effective planning will always help to minimize (if not eliminate) these poisons. In Chapter 11 I discussed the nature of fear in detail, and you will recall that fear of the unknown was one of the three *instinctual* fears. That's where research and planning can help. The more you know about a situation or an opponent, the less likely you are to become fearful or doubtful.

Additionally, as I discussed in Chapter 10, the more planning and mental simulations you do of specific measures and possible countermeasures, the less likely you will be to become confused or surprised by any sudden changes or twists in the course of events. Proper planning enables you to concentrate on the fully committed execution of your plan, instead of you being distracted by trying to come up with countermeasures to changing events you didn't take the time or trouble to anticipate. Having the proper plan in mind, what you need next is a pre-set window of time to get it done.

4. You Must Set a Reasonable Timeframe within Which to Accomplish It!

It is very common for people to make two kinds of mistakes under this very important parameter. They tend to either give themselves an unrealistically *short* amount of time to fulfill a plan of action or fail to set a limit as to how *long* they will pursue a certain plan of action before changing or redirecting their efforts. Failure to set limits on either end of this spectrum can, and probably will, be devastating.

The key here is the word *reasonable.* You wouldn't expect to be able to have a house built in a week's time. In fact, I don't think you would want to live in it afterwards, even if you could. On the other hand, you wouldn't want to let the construction process linger on for years either, since your interest and enthusiasm in the house would inevitably wane after so much time had passed.

It is just a psychological fact of life that, in order to keep moving forward on a plan of action, there have to be established time parameters to work within. In spite of what the movies tend to portray, *samurai* conflicts and battles were very short in duration. The *samurai* knew that if he could not bring down his opponent with a reasonable number of attempted cuts, he would be wise to back off and rethink his situation and strategy. He also knew that if the battle lingered on too long, one of the four poisons would eventually get him defeated and killed.

So the lesson here is for you to be sure to allow yourself a reasonable amount of time to achieve your mission (which, as I said already, should be well-defined), while, on the other hand, you make sure that your mission does not drag on *too long*, thus avoiding a loss of psychological momentum, faith, and interest.

So hopefully you can see that *knowing what you want to achieve*, combined with *real desire, a workable plan,* and *a reasonable timeframe* to achieve it in, should empower you to move confidently forward, without stopping, toward the accomplishment of your mission. And in the unfortunate event that something *did* go wrong in your *current* mission, the final item of importance is to *not look back* after the fact!

You Must Never Second-Guess Yourself If You Fail!

It has often been said that hindsight is always 20/20. While this is certainly true, it can be either helpful or destructive, depending on how you use it. The *samurai* never looked back, thinking to himself, Maybe I could have tried this offensive technique or that defensive technique. He understood that the present moment was the only one he could control and that the future was all he could ever hope to shape. The past was done and gone, and whatever he *did* do was what he simply did—no questions asked and no second considerations given.

But that isn't to say that the *samurai* didn't learn from his mistakes. Every warrior knows that trial and error is our greatest (and often only) teacher. The only positive purpose in looking back on past events is to assess *future* courses and behavioral corrections. It is never to be used to beat yourself up over what you *could* have done in this or that situation. What's done is done, and that's that. Coming to truly understand this truth and adopting it as a living philosophy into your life could be the most transformational thing you could ever do for yourself.

The true warrior automatically assumes responsibility for his actions. But at the same time he understands that he cannot undo what has been done, and that there is opportunity in every situation that occurs. Thus he, and you, transform mistakes into opportunities for improvement and greater wisdom and insight. There simply isn't any better way to look at it, as I hope you would agree!

The Way of Commitment Conditioning

So now that we've looked at what I feel are the requisite parameters for making a resolved "don't stop and don't look back" commitment to a plan of action, let me tell you about the *samurai* method of "commitment conditioning," the Way of *shugyo!*

The word *shugyo* literally means "the Way of enlightenment through physical discipline." Most people who work out physically practice *shugyo* whether they know it or not. The most common hints to this can be detected in their comments concerning why they work out to begin with. These might include "I feel much more focused," "I do a better job at work," "I feel more peaceful inside," and "I seem to have more energy." The fact is, exercise *does* make you feel better. It's always easier to *do* well when you *feel* well. Besides, keeping the body fit is an important step toward maintaining the centering triangle we've talked so much about herein. But despite all of these fine benefits, the ultimate purpose of practicing *shugyo* regularly is really something much deeper—to develop a *conditioned* sense of commitment and inner discipline!

The first 30 minutes of every class I conduct at my *dojo* is always dedicated to *shugyo*. This may consist of anything from simply running in place to doing a taxing series of martial-art–related exercises. Regardless of what we do, the objective is the same—to go up against the infamous "wall" that every athlete is familiar with! This so-called wall is a point you reach when your body becomes overwhelmed by fatigue. When the students reach this point, they find themselves at a critical crossroad in their mind. Internally they are forced to ask themselves, Do I surrender to the fatigue, *or* do I push on and see what's on the other side? It is always my hope that they will choose to push on, because beyond that wall lies the miracle of the true martial Way. What they discover is that beyond fatigue is the next level of strength, courage, and discipline, a special "something" that comes from their spiritual center or one-point!

Commitment and the Three Levels of Warrior-Physics

I make it a point to constantly remind both my students of the martial arts *and* my warrior-trader *sempai* that commitment—like all other aspects of reality—manifests itself in one of the three levels of warrior-physics, and that it takes regular practice to elevate their commitment capability to the highest level! The *simple physics* of committing to something is to simply give it lip service. The *superphysics* of committing to something is to have it well planned and thought out, and to possess a firm mental commitment to executing it. Ahh . . . but the *metaphysics* of commitment . . . that's where the true empowerment enters the picture!

> A metaphysical commitment *is one in which body, mind, and spirit have been fully dedicated to the cause, leading it to take on the intensity of a life-or-death situation . . .*

A *metaphysical commitment* is one in which body, mind, and spirit have been fully dedicated to the cause, leading it to take on the intensity of a life-or-death situation—as in Mitsuyoshi Yagi's *seigan* examination at the *Ito Shoden Muto Ryu Dojo* of master Tesshu! Since my students know in advance that the *shugyo* period lasts exactly 30 minutes, they are assured that there is a definite "stop-loss" to their pain or discomfort should they choose to push on beyond the wall. Often knowing this is enough to get them to give it a try, and to not stop once they've begun. It can work for you in the same way.

The Everyday Practice of *Shugyo*

As I said, many people unintentionally practice *shugyo* daily. Perhaps you do too. It can be accomplished through *any* exercise medium. Running, walking, biking, climbing, aerobics—even meditating in extreme environments, such as cold or heat—all qualify as *shugyo*; any of these will teach you to make deep-level commitment to a plan of action. To qualify as *shugyo* it is only necessary that your activity be *continuous* and *physically and emotionally taxing*. I will be giving you more specific daily training guidelines and suggestions in Chapter 15, "The Way and Day of the Warrior-Trader," but perhaps for now you could be considering some of your regular activities that might serve this purpose.

The Section in Review

So this brings us now to the conclusion of our study of the *Samurai* A.C.T.I.O.N. Plan and the *Samurai's psychology of engagement*. Let me take this opportunity to recap what we've covered by describing another activity I regularly have my *sempai* participate in—one that I recommended you try earlier in our study. The activity is board breaking, and, as I have said before, it is more of a *psychologically intimidating* undertaking than it is a physical one, and for that reason it will serve my purpose of review.

In order to prepare to break the board, the students must first *"accept . . . all possible losses before entering the battle!"* The only possible losses that must be accepted here are the rare (but most formidable) possibilities of damaging their hand in the process and/or experiencing stinging pain. That's pretty much it.

Then they must *"center . . . themselves in body, mind, and spirit!"* This is accomplished by recognizing that there is more to breaking the board than just a hand striking wood. There are *simple physics, super physics,* and *metaphysics* (manifested as bodily, mental, and psychic strength) at their disposal. By breathing into their one-point, keeping their body aligned, and keeping their weight underside *(haragei)*, they will cause body, mind, and spirit to overlap and synergize in the "triangular zone," creating a powerfully confident mental and physical "stance" from which they can deliver the desired blow.

They must then *"trust . . . their warrior skills and intuition!"* Hopefully, through having seen board breaking done before by other people, their trust can evolve into something they can believe at the gut level—*faith*, the highest form of trust. By allowing themselves to get in touch with all that is—the universal song—they will just "know" that they can accomplish their mission!

Then they will employ the power of the mental focus by *"imagining . . . success clearly with their mind's-eye!"* Since the subconscious mind does not know the difference between fact and fantasy, seeing the action of breaking the board in advance of the real thing desensitizes the mind to fear and sets powerful creative forces in motion that will reinforce the force of the hand.

When the moment to strike grows imminent, they will *"only . . . exist in the present moment to control fear!"* They will recognize that all fear is either anticipatory or reflective and that neither is of value to the warrior. *Now* is the only moment over which they have control; therefore, they stay in the present by breathing firmly and attentively into the one-point to take on the strength, wisdom, and courage of 10 tigers!

And as the all-important blow is delivered with all the force and commitment that exists within them, they will *"never . . . stop or look back once action has begun!"* By completely and totally "following through" with their hand (and their plan of action), they are guaranteed a very high probability of success—and a broken board! And in the event that they misjudged the hardness of the board or the proper technique to have used, they will not look back and beat themselves up by saying, "I'm so stupid! I should have done it differently or picked a different board!" They will simply transform the stinging in their hand into an opportunity to improve their technique—and to practice the *samurai's psychology of recovery and resilience,* which is the subject of our next section and chapter!

True Tales of the Warrior-Trader

Some years ago I happened upon the opportunity to simultaneously compare, first-hand, the considerable attitudinal (and associated performance) differences between two traders: one who benefited from a true sense of commitment and one who genuinely suffered from a lack thereof! And interestingly, the reason I was originally retained by these two separate individuals (who lived on opposite ends of the country) was not for assistance with their trading performance, but rather to assist them in trying to quit smoking.

As coincidence (or was it synchronicity?) would have it, B.W., who lived in San Francisco, California, and D.L., who was from Boston, Massachusetts, were both referred to me by a common friend who had some years earlier managed to kick the smoking habit with the help of my clinical services. Both had great respect for this common friend—who was also an accomplished trader—and hoped to duplicate his victories over smoking and the markets, since my clients were also neophyte traders who were just getting started.

In my separate sessions with B.W. and D.L., I emphasized the same important truth to each of them—that their attitude and a sense of absolute commitment to giving up cigarettes was essential to their success. B.W. seemed to understand this. He took my message to heart and indicated a willingness to "do whatever it took" to remain smoke-free after our set-up session. D.L., on the other hand, immediately countered my comments with concerns over "any possible feelings of discomfort" he might experience "while he was quitting."

A side note at this point! A very important difference between these two candidates for new health and a new life should be immediately obvious—a difference that not only proved to affect their respective abilities to quit smoking, but also became apparent in their trading efforts! B.W. saw quitting as a total, "right now" deal. In his mind he was either a smoker or a nonsmoker—no gray area in between. He was ready to pay the price in terms of money, effort, and dedication—unconditionally! All he wanted from me was the necessary technical help in making the transition more efficiently.

D.L., however, was quite a different story. He saw quitting as a slow-motion process filled with gray areas. Instead of viewing himself as a smoker or a nonsmoker, he tended to view himself as a smoker painfully "trying to reform." From many of his initial comments there was also no doubt that he was simply looking for an easy way out. Essentially, he wanted to pay me to quit for him—something any exsmoker knows to be impossible!

About three months after I worked with B.W. and D.L., the common friend (and my former client) called unexpectedly and gave me an update on these guys. It seems that he had stayed in almost daily contact with both of them since our session because they were learning his trading system from him. And what he told me didn't surprise me a bit.

It turned out that B.W. (from San Francisco) had had a pretty rough time with physical withdrawal, but despite this he had remained smoke-free and seemed to have gotten over the worst of his problems. The friend also said B.W. indicated that he "knew he would never smoke again, no matter what happened!" But D.L. (from Boston), he informed me, had really blown it by constantly slipping and "requitting" dozens of times that he knew of. Naturally this made me feel happy for B.W. and sorry for D.L. But what I found extremely interesting (and the most pertinent point in this story) were his comments about their respective efforts with their trading!

Once he had mastered the basics of the trading system, it seems that B.W. jumped right in with both feet—and once again with absolute commitment and conviction. He had put forth the necessary money, time, attention, and dedication to do it well. And because he had, he was making increasingly consistent profits from his efforts.

But the friend went on to say that, by comparison, D.L. had unfortunately "lost his ass" by jumping in and out of his trading efforts. He also indicated that whenever D.L. took a hit in the markets—which were mostly due to his erratic attention to market conditions and activity—he would get "really pissed at their trading system" instead of looking at his own possible lack of focus and dedication to the trading day! It also turned out that not only was D.L. still smoking and losing his money in the markets, but he had also decided to divorce his wife of 12 years because "she just wasn't supportive enough of him."

So you see, it really doesn't matter if you're trying to quit smoking, stay happily married, or become a successful warrior-trader—the common denominators for success are still the same! And without a doubt, a sense of absolute, total commitment and dedication to your mission should be at the very top of your priority list! For like Miyamoto Musashi once said, "Without absolute commitment to the battle at hand, the warrior is already slain before the first blows are exchanged!"

PART THREE

---

*The Samurai's Psychology
of Recovery*

CHAPTER 13

The Way of Warrior Resilience

True Tales of the Budo

The heat and blazing light of the funeral pyre illuminated the face of Taku Nagato as he stood somberly watching. Two days had passed since the attack had been launched against his stronghold by enemies of the Tokugawa shogunate. Although he and his samurai had fought courageously and had managed to kill the majority of the invaders before they fled in retreat, their victory had not come without a considerable price. Nine of his loyal retainers had lost their lives in the battle, along with four nonmilitary residents of the fortress.

Sadly, one of these casualties had been Nagato's beloved wife Mariko. They had been married 17 years earlier in a Buddhist temple near Osaka, the union having been prearranged between his and another prominent bugei (samurai) family, as was the tradition of the times. More often than not, such marriages were a matter of convenience and societal conformity, and a way to bring one or more sons into the world to carry on the husband's family name. Love or romance rarely entered the picture. This had not been so in Nagato's case, however, inasmuch as he had come to truly love and cherish Mariko over their years together, and to appreciate her having given birth to his two sons and one daughter.

The flames he now watched were quickly consuming the beautiful but lifeless body of his Mariko, the smoke sending her earthly remains into the heavens where they would become re-united with the universe, as Buddhist tradition would have it. But just as intensely as the flames consumed her remains, the intense flame of grief seemed to consume Nagato's body, mind, and spirit. Even though his Zen training and samurai upbringing had taught him to avoid attachment to anything—including family members—he still found it hard to imagine going forward with his life of warriorship without his wife's company and affection.

But in spite of his current state of shock, deep down inside Taku Nagato knew he must—and would—come back to fight again soon, with a renewed warrior spirit and a powerful sense of centeredness. And he also knew that he would accomplish this through the practice of misogi—the samurai's traditional *Way* of physical, mental, and spiritual cleansing and purification!

In the days that followed, Nagato spent time in retreat, meditating upon and opening up to the feelings he experienced, as misogi tradition called for. He knew that before he could work through and thus free himself from the effects of his intense grief, he must first give full recognition to his emotions. To hide from them would be catastrophic.

He had already reflected on his initial feelings of disbelief upon hearing of his wife's demise, feelings that had seemed to quickly turn into anger. He also remembered the subsequent guilt he felt as he realized he had been angry at not only the murderous marauders who had taken Mariko's life, but surprisingly at Mariko herself for having gotten killed. This feeling had quickly been replaced with feeling of remorse over not having been able to do more to save her life, even though he had done all that could humanly be done at the time. Ultimately, his further reflections had then led Taku Nagato through a short phase of despondency during which he had even questioned his own worth as a person and his effectiveness as a samurai.

Once he had pulled all of these various emotions from the dark recesses of his mind, they had come to be exposed to the bright light of truth and universal law. One by one, all of Nagato's emotions born of his grief began to dissolve in the face of his warrior philosophy and understanding—dissolving like so much dried blood under the influence of the clove oil he had used to cleanse his own katana after the battle had ended. As he practiced the ritualistic misogi breathing exercises which were accompanied by the ringing of a hand-held bell, he once again came to recognize the transient nature of all things—power, wealth, status, and even family. He was once again spiritually reinforced by the realization that all things—even defeat—happen ultimately for the higher good.

Before long Taku Nagato was back in good form—recentered in body, mind, and spirit—and ready to return to the service of the Tokugawa shogunate. And even though he was once again prepared to do battle with the forces of oppression with a clear mind and a steady blade, he held a new truth within his heart—a very personal truth. Even though the emotionally destructive shadows of his loss had been flushed from his warrior-psyche, Nagato knew he had intentionally tucked away one memory he wished to carry with him to his death—that of the living and smiling face of his Mariko—who in life had been his wife and the mother of his children, and who now in death, had become the source of his new-found resilience and warrior strength!

Bad Things *Do* Happen to Everyone

"Shit happens!" a popular bumper sticker reads. And unfortunately, it happens to virtually everyone, good or bad, at one time or another. It just seems to happen to warriors and traders more often than anyone else. But the truth of it is that it just *seems* that way, the reason being that we are out there routinely putting money and personal well-being on the line—in other words, taking *risks!*

Taking risks, as I've said before, automatically involves the possibility—no, *inevitability*—of failure and defeat at some point or another. And it seems poetically just that we should address the issue of warrior resilience in Chapter 13, a number that many people associate with bad luck or misfortune. Perhaps then this is a turning point for this maligned number, since this chapter may very well bring you some much-needed insight on recovering from the defeats (no matter how devastating) we must all experience from time to time.

Getting Ready to Handle Defeat

The previous chapters have provided you with invaluable information about arming your psyche for entry into battle, whether it be against an armed assailant or the commoditiy or stock markets. Having the appropriate mindset going into battle often does a great deal to ward off the detrimental emotional effects of possible defeat from the onset. Nonetheless, it would be additionally helpful in developing warrior-trader resilience for you and me to look closer at the most common psychological side effect of defeat—grief—from the perspective of both the historical *samurai* and conventional behavioral psychology.

Behavioral scientists tell us that grief is a universal experience throughout the animal kingdom. Even dogs, cats, and parakeets experience it. But the difference between animals and people is their memory capability and level of mental functioning. Animals' experiences with this are limited to what is called *short-term grief*, due to their limited memory and their capacity for adapting to change.

On the other hand, humans are highly susceptible to *long-term grief* due to their expansive and complex memory ability as well as their higher level of mental functioning. Unfortunately, this same higher mental functioning affords humans a much greater number of potential grief experiences than animals. It is commonly believed by these same behavioral scientists that grief is experienced as the result of *any* unfortunate or unpleasurable event. Sometimes it is so brief and of such low intensity that we may not notice it, but it is there just the same.

Short-Term versus Long-Term Grief

It has been my experience that, although grief is a natural reaction to loss, the intensity and duration of that grief are directly dependent upon the perceptions and mental discipline of the experiencer. Even if someone has "accepted all possible losses before entering the battle," he will still most likely experience some degree of grief over a loss. And that's not necessarily bad. But there is a *big* difference between *short-term* and *long-term grief*. And one of the major problems I have observed among many traders is their tendency to transform what could have (and should have) been short-term grief into a much more intensive and debilitating long-term grief.

Many traders tend to dwell on their losses—even masochistically embrace them—until the inevitable grief that results becomes a real problem for them in ways and for reasons I am about to cover. So let's take for granted that, like losses, grief is going to occur from time to time. But it will help if you understand this emotional predator a little better, so you can tame it more efficiently when it rears up its uncomfortably ugly head.

> *Many traders tend to dwell on their losses— even masochistically embrace them. . .*

Handling the Five Phases of Grief (or Loss)

The first important rule of thumb regarding the handling of grief (or any loss) is to acknowledge it and give it some recognition. As in Taku Nagato's opening story to this chapter, it is important to pull grief out of the dark recesses of the mind where it can lurk, and bring it out into the bright light of objective reality where it can be inspected and dealt with. Once grief is out in the open, it is important to understand that it usually evolves through five distinct phases, one or all of which may occur very quickly or very slowly, depending on the philosophical and psychological makeups of the individual. These five phases are: (1) *denial*, (2) *anger*, (3) *guilt*, (4) *depression* or *despondency*, and finally (5) *acceptance*.

PHASE 1: DENIAL OF LOSS

Denial is when you refuse to admit that something bad has happened. Psychologists say that this is an instinctive, self-protective suppressive mechanism in the brain attempting to protect you from the truth. Such denial of reality can only lead to ulcers, mental breakdowns, or worse! I have seen traders who tried to act as if nothing had happened after they lost a major chunk of their trading account. The *samurai* would say that this is foolish and dangerous. They would say that losses are losses—whether they have been accepted in advance or not—and they *must* be accounted for. If they are not appropriately accounted for, then their reality will then manifest in your mind in the form of anger.

PHASE 2: ANGER OVER LOSS

Anger, as it relates to grief, is almost always misguided. The tendency here is to be mad at just about anything and everything—except yourself. For example, let's say you were to suddenly lose a considerable sum of money while trading several S&P contracts. Let's further say that the actual reason you lost the money is because you didn't follow your trading system as you should have. Instead of recognizing, Hey, I just lost my money! you instead find yourself furious with the markets, the guy who sold you the trading system, and maybe even your long-deceased grandfather who used to trade stocks in the old days and who helped shape your interest in trading to begin with.

Obviously, all of these targets for your anger are inappropriate, and the anger is just a way of directing yourself away from the truth—that *you* are responsible for what happened. Once that realization does come forward in your mind, guilt makes its appearance on the grief scene.

PHASE 3: GUILT OVER LOSS

Guilt that is motivated by grief usually appears in the form of self-criticism. You begin to look overly hard at what you *could* have or *should* have done differently, a fallacious tendency that we discussed in the last chapter. You may find yourself doubting your potential as a trader altogether and may even swear off ever taking another trade to avoid feeling this way again. And because you are a natural risk-taker at heart and because you really do love the trading game, you would likely then begin to feel depressed or despondent.

PHASE 4: DEPRESSION OR DESPONDENCY OVER LOSS

Depression or *despondency*, as hard as it is on you, is even *harder* on those around you. What first began in you as grief will quickly transform itself into much more noxious and less identifiable characteristics. These could include irritability, short-temperedness, sleeplessness, fatigue, health problems, loss of concentration and motivation, or an overall lack of interest in what's going on around you, just to name a few. But with the passing of enough time, a lot of luck, and hopefully a lot of support from the people around you, you would eventually reach the final phase of grief—which is not actually a part of grief at all, but a *lack* of it—*acceptance!*

PHASE 5: ACCEPTANCE OF THE LOSS

Obviously, ultimately, the goal of warrior resilience is to possess the inner constitution or ability to accept those defeats or losses that *do* occur in battle and life. But don't feel badly if at first it takes longer than you hoped to accomplish this! Just remember that, all things considered, only the strongest of our species—the most battle-tested warriors—tend to possess the ability and propensity to circumvent the first four phases and move straight to this final and most hoped-for condition of conclusive acceptance. I am absolutely confident that soon, by applying the *samurai* mind-sets and philosophies we are studying together, your own experiences with the occasional defeat or loss will bear out that it *can* be done!

So as you can see, grief can really get out of hand if you let it. But it is certainly not the Way of the *samurai*—or the warrior-trader—to do so. So how can you avoid the pitfalls of such a natural occurrence as guilt, and develop the resilience you want and need to become an indomitable warrior-trader? Well, the answers are simple, and most of them we've already covered in one way or another in previous lessons. But for the sake of clarity and understanding on your part, let me redefine and reframe them again here. As I do, be sure to keep in mind that your day-to-day practice of the warrior Ways may very well downgrade what the average person might experience as grief into a simpler and easier-to-handle sense of mild disappointment—a feeling that would normally pass quickly from the mind of a *samurai* without the need for specific intervention. But when time for intervention did arise, fortunately the *samurai* had a specific Way of doing so!

Misogi—The *Samurai* Way to Emotional Resilience

Please never forget that it is my belief that self-discipline is the Way to mastery. Thus, I further believe it is healthiest to practice traditional *samurai misogi* (literally meaning "cleansing and purification of the warrior-psyche") after each and *every* substantial disappointment or loss you might incur in the course of business *and* life. In fact, the last 10 minutes of every class I conduct at my *dojo* are always dedicated to the three steps of *misogi*, the reason being that I want all my students to develop the habit of "cleansing" their psyches of any emotional leftovers they may have accumulated during the past two to three hours of training.

The reason that there are *three* steps to *samurai misogi* (and thus warrior-resilience) is likely to have become apparent to you by now. Since experiencing loss or defeat tends to throw you off-center, then restoring your centeredness would naturally require a balanced attention to *body (simple physics)*, *mind (superphysics)*, and *spirit (metaphysics)*.

The Three Steps of *Samurai Misogi*

What I would like to describe is the basic *misogi* routine I tend to use whenever I experience a disappointment and need to quickly bounce back to a peak-performance mind-set. This same routine would apply whether I have been training at the *dojo*, playing blackjack or poker at a casino, or trading the markets from my office at home. And again I want to point out that the only difference between these cleansing and recentering methods and those you would use before entry into battle is their purpose. In advance of the battle, centering is intended to *prepare* your psyche to fight. After the battle, *misogi* recentering is intended to cleanse and rebalance the psyche and restore you to original form (resilience).

MISOGI EXERCISES FOR THE BODY

For the body, I like to take a simple walk. As I walk I first concentrate on keeping my body aligned. I allow my feet to blend smoothly with the ground in harmony with my breathing. (See the discussion of *aiki*, in Chapter 6.) With each step, I propel myself with gentle "pulses" of energy from my one-point, keeping my motion smooth and level, rather than up and down. (See the discussion of *kiai* in Chapter 6.) As I breathe, I do so deeply into the spiritual "center" (see *kokyu-kihara* in Chapter 8), thus renewing my *ki* ("life force").

MISOGI EXERCISES FOR THE MIND

For the mind, I am first attentive to my breathing and the vital role it plays in my overall centeredness. After a short period of this mindfulness (see Chapter 4), I begin to introspect on the *kyokushin* or "universal laws" (which I will cover in Chapter 14) that apply to the situation that resulted in my loss, and remind myself of the absolute truth they hold. I then briefly look for any apparent lessons to be found in my defeat, and resolve to make any necessary behavioral corrections that may improve my performance and my chances for victory in the future.

After contemplating these things, I then simply "allow" my observations to be committed to my "inner computer" for future unconscious reference. Then as I continue my *misogi* walk, I begin to allow all internal dialog to quiet down and then cease altogether, entering a state of mindlessness (See *mushin* in Chapter 5.)

MISOGI EXERCISES FOR THE SPIRIT

For the spirit, I continue to walk peacefully but steadily, my mind still free of thought or specific intent, as I allow the "intuitive one-mind" of the universe to fill my consciousness and psyche. This can often render messages and lessons of a much higher order, as I begin to mindlessly enjoy a feeling of faith that all things, including my loss or defeat, occur for the higher good. (See Chapter 9.) By this time, usually no more than 15 to 30 minutes, I can be back to the starting point of my *misogi* walk—and back to my old self again. I usually feel recentered, refreshed, and reasonably ready to re-engage the "enemy" when opportunity again presents itself.

Please remember that this description of my particular method of renewal is in no way intended to crimp your style. You may find variations on this that suit you far better than what I do, and I encourage you to try them out for yourself! And for conditioning and practice sake, keep in mind that the exact same procedures can be employed to *prepare* for risk-taking. This means that everyday, whether you win or lose, you should be practicing some variation of these centering (or recentering) principles to maximize your warrior-trader performance. In Chapter 15, I will be providing you with several daily "warrior-trader training" formats from which to choose. This will serve to bring together everything you've learned into some concise, easy-to-use formats you can depend on in a clinch.

But before we can get involved at looking at a day in the life of the warrior-trader, there is one more category of *samurai* understanding and insight we absolutely *must* delve into. For it is here in this final (and ultimate) realm of warrior wisdom—the realm of universal truths and laws—that the reason and purpose for every action, reaction, event, situation, and outcome can be found! So let's not waste another minute; let's move on.

True Tales of the Warrior-Trader

Sometimes the best stories come from the actual words of the warrior-traders themselves. This is particularly true in the case of one very special female trader who found herself needing the benefits of warrior resilience more than we would have expected when we first trained together. The following is an excerpt from a letter we received from her at the dojo:

> *There is no doubt that my pursuit and study of the Way of the warrior mind and spirit has been a fruitful and profitable one—and in a way I never would have expected, it may have even saved my life!*
>
> *As you may remember, when I came to the dojo to study with you, my main problem was my fear of taking a loss in the markets. You may also remember that*

whenever I did take a loss, I would inevitably go into a depression that could sometimes take weeks to get through. I had begun to think that I just didn't have what it took to be a trader. But thanks to my warrior training and philosophies (and to the events I am about to relate), I am pleased to say that I no longer have any fear of taking losses in my trading.

You see, approximately six months after attending your training program, a lump was found in my left breast. My physician did an immediate biopsy, which confirmed my greatest fear—that it was indeed cancerous. I was advised that a mastectomy followed by radiation treatments was my only choice—and hope—for survival! There simply are no words to describe the magnitude of fear and distress that I experienced at this point, facing the pure, unmitigated fact of my mortality—and the inevitable loss I was about to incur!

But then, as the four days before the surgery agonizingly passed, something inside of me sort of "snapped." Maybe it was some kind of emotional overload or something, but instead of becoming increasingly more afraid (which I don't think was possible anyway), I began to think about all the things I had learned in the course of my warrior training, particularly about the psychology of the samurai. In some weird way, I think I came to understand what it must have been like to be an actual samurai—facing his mortality and the risk of incalculable loss every day of his existence!

Then, the day before I went into the hospital, I did something that really surprised me. I traded! In fact, I traded better than I ever had before in my life—I was alert, focused, fearless, and aggressive. After all, what did I have to lose that could be worse than the danger I already faced? Money? I suddenly realized (was this satori?) that you can always recover from the loss of money (or anything else for that matter, except your life), if you just maintain your warrior balance and fighting spirit—even if you experience loss again, and again, and again if need be!

I carried the thoughts of my exhilarating (and very profitable) trading day into the darkness of the anesthesia as the surgery began the next morning. When I awoke hours later, my doctor informed me that everything had gone well, and that only a partial mastectomy had been necessary to remove the malignancy. I was naturally ecstatic over this news, and felt not only relief and joy, but also kind of "reborn" at the same time—a feeling that has not left me to this day, some six months later!

So today, which is the one-year anniversary of my training at the Bushinkai dojo, I felt it was only appropriate to write and share with all of you my wonderful triumph over not only the cancer, but my former fear of loss as well! I also hope that, perhaps someday, my personal story will serve to inspire and motivate someone else who may face a similar fear and crisis as I did.

Best wishes to my dojo family, and may your victories be as sweet and meaningful as my own!

So as I said at the beginning of this segment, some stories are best told in the words of the participants. I know for sure that my rendering would surely have been inadequate! But to this courageous and very wise warrior, I do wish to extend my personal congratulations—and to let her know that "someday" she mentioned could very well be today!

CHAPTER 14

The Way of Universal Law and Truth

TRUE TALES OF THE BUDO

Taisen Deshimaru Roshi was delivering a lesson and dissertation on Budo-Zen *to a small group of students at his* zendo, *or training hall of Zen. Specifically, the* roshi *was expounding on the importance of the* kyokushin—*the Way of universal law and truth. As he concluded, one of the students asked, "Master, why is it important for us to learn of these laws and truths you speak of?" The insightful* roshi, *knowing that the student's question was a practical one, decided to respond in kind with an equally practical Zen fable. This way the student would hopefully deduce his own answer from between the lines of the story, as the Way of Zen would properly have it.*

Deshimaru Roshi began, "Once upon a time there was a very special village nestled comfortably along the shores of a very large and beautiful lake that was fed by the distant mountain streams. Life was peaceful and good for residents of this village, and had been for countless generations. One of the things that made this village special was that no one had ever lacked for food or sustenance. While at first glance this may not seem to be something unusual or outstanding, a closer look at the lives of the villagers revealed that the source of their abundance was extraordinary indeed!

"As legend had it, every day just before high noon the residents of the village, young and old alike, formed a long line approximately 400 feet from the shore of the lake and stretching almost a half a mile in length. Each villager also held a small cane basket in his or her hands. The reason for this noon time ritual was truly remarkable. It seemed that every day at exactly 12 o'clock, a mysterious gigantuan foot, bigger than three houses, materialized high in the sky over the center of the lake. Exactly 10 seconds after the foot appeared, with absolutely unerring regularity, it would always come down in a singular

tremendous stomp into the center of the lake, after which it would lift right back up into the sky and disappear again."

"What's more, the thunderous stomp of the giant foot would always set off a series of huge waves that would come crashing onto the shore, bringing with them a considerable number of live fish that would be left flopping on the ground near the villagers after the wave subsided. All that was required of the villagers was to hurriedly gather up the fish into their baskets, and thus enough to eat was always had by all!"

After the roshi had finished telling this tale, he stood and announced that the training session was ended, and began to leave the room. But before he could exit, the inquiring student, now more curious than ever, called out to to his teacher, "Master Deshimaru, please wait a moment. While your story was certainly interesting, I don't see what it had to do with the kyokushin. What is the lesson to be learned from this tale? Please tell us!"

Hearing this, the roshi stopped and turned, and for some time looked quietly into the eyes of the student. Soon a twinkle appeared in the master's eyes and the hint of a smile appeared at the corners of his mouth as he said, "The fable contains three simple messages that encompass all of the other laws and truths of the universe. The first is that all things happen for the higher good! The second is that the laws and truths of the universe affect everyone equally, whether they are aware of them or not!" Having said this, the master then turned and walked toward the door.

"But master, what about the third lesson in the story?" the student quickly asked before the roshi disappeared through the doorway. Looking over his shoulder but still leaving, the master replied, "Foolish boy, can you not figure out something so obvious as that for yourself?" His voice now coming from down the hallway, the roshi concluded, "The third lesson is don't be on the lake at high noon, of course!"

The Facts of Life We Are All Subject To

The idea of studying a list of "laws" may at first seem a little uncomfortable to some people, particularly those who are independent-minded. Conformity to pre-set rules tends to run against their grains. Another possible cause for concern could be that they *already* have a set of laws or commandments they live by, and they don't wish for any *new* laws to conflict with them. If either of these two sentiments have come to your mind, let me set you at ease!

The kind of laws that I am about to discuss are not man-made laws or rules of any kind. Rather, they are simply observable facts of life that universally affect everyone, without exception—whether they know of them or not.

As you have learned, the legendary *samurai* were very observant about the way things were, and equally objective about the way they operated within the framework of what they observed. They believed in moving in harmony, as much as possible, with the apparent laws of nature to which they were subject. It should be equally obvious that this should be true of traders as well. Many less-than-enlightened traders seem to operate under the notion that the markets should conform to *their* belief systems, whereas common sense dictates that their belief systems about the markets *should* be formulated by what they observe to be true! The latter is the true Way of the warrior-trader, to be sure.

In addition to the observable laws of the markets, there are a number of other natural laws and truths that ultimately determine the eventual success or failure of traders or other financial risk-takers. It seems only logical that to know something of these other laws should be desirable, and that it should bring about a sense of comfort and reassurance to anyone trying to operate under their influence. If you were to step off the edge of a tall building, whether or not you knew about the natural law of gravity—or whether or not you agreed with it—that natural law (at least on this planet) would quickly reduce you to a pile of slop on the sidewalk below in a matter of seconds. But obviously, you say, no one in his right mind is going to do such a thing! Well, why not? Because *knowledge* of and *experience* with the law of gravity have taught them that such a step would likely bring about disastrous results.

If You're Going to Be Destroyed, at Least Know Why

Yet every day, traders and other financial risk-takers take uncertain steps that could bring about equally disastrous results, yet more often than not, they haven't got a clue as to why. And that's the reason why it's important to at least be exposed to the *samurai's kyokushin*, the Way of universal laws and truth! This way, you at least afford yourself a greater fighting chance at

Yet every day, traders and other financial risk-takers take uncertain steps that could bring about equally disastrous results, yet more often than not, they haven't got a clue as to why.

success, not to mention a little peace of mind to boot. It may be that as I present and comment on these universal laws, you may find yourself occasionally thinking, Oh, I already knew that—that's not something new! In this case, consider it an important reminder. But whatever you do, please do not lessen your appreciation of the role that particular law or truth plays in the overall scheme of things. *All* of the laws matter… all of the laws are urgently important to the warrior—especially the warrior-trader!

The 10 Laws of Warrior-Trader *Kyokushin*

Although I could dedicate an entire book to the subject and contents of the *kyokushin*, I have narrowed the focus of our study to the 10 laws that have the greatest relevance to trading and financial risk-taking. You can pursue a more expansive knowledge of universal laws by reading the many classical works on warriorship such as *The Book of 5 Rings* (Musashi Miyamoto) and *The Art of War* (Sun Tsu). But for our purposes, the 10 laws of warrior-trader *kyokushin* are

1. *The Law of Duality.*
2. *The Law of Cycles.*
3. *The Law of Evolution.*
4. *The Law of Choices.*
5. *The Law of Responsibility.*
6. *The Law of Inertia.*
7. *The Law of Momentum.*
8. *The Law of Synchronicity.*
9. *The Law of Manifestation.*
10. *The Law of Process and Action.*

You will discover that these universal laws—like the maxims in the *Samurai* A.C.T.I.O.N. Plan—work in an interactive way with each other, yet each renders its own unique influence upon the grand scheme of things. So to aid you in your study and appreciation for these laws, I would like to briefly comment on each one separately in order to possibly shed a brighter light of understanding on their respective truths.

1. THE WARRIOR'S LAW OF DUALITY

The Judeo-Christian tradition holds that, "In the beginning there was the Word, and the Word became light. And the heavens were thus separated into two opposing parts: lightness and darkness." From the time of this primordial beginning up until the present moment, everything that has come into being owes its very existence to the nature of duality and opposition. It is an absolute truth that nothing can exist without its antithetical counterpart. So in a sense you could also think of this as the "Law of Relativity" if Einstein hadn't already coined the term. Night cannot exist without day. Good cannot exist without evil. Forward cannot exist without backward. Push cannot exist without pull. And according to the *samurai's kyokushin, in* (positive) cannot exist without *yo* (negative).

So what important message does this hold for the warrior-trader? It's simple. Short positions cannot exist without long positions. Profits cannot exist without losses. Good luck cannot exist without bad luck. Success cannot exist without failure. And perhaps even more fundamental to your cause, market rises cannot exist without market falls. And without the dualistic principle of rising and falling, the markets would cease to exist altogether. So the next time the market rises or falls against your position, rather than be uselessly angry, it might be more appropriate to think, Thank God! The market still exists! Now I'll be able to get back in there again when I'm ready!

2. THE WARRIOR'S LAW OF CYCLES

Once duality and opposition came to exist, everything was set into motion in the form of oscillation or vibration. Consistent with this natural law, all events and conditions are therefore predictably cyclical. This truth represents good news to all of us. Providing we move in reasonable concert with the other natural laws, the *Law of Cycles* guarantees us that after a period of bad luck we are naturally due

> *Once duality and opposition came to exist, everything was set into motion in the form of oscillation or vibration.*

a period of good luck. It further guarantees that after a market drop, there will be a market rise. And I'm sure you could come up with several other examples along this same line of thinking.

But it is important to remember that the *Law of Cycles* applies to *all* events and conditions—including you and your emotions! After a period of fear, there should soon follow a period of courage. A period of depression will naturally be followed by an offsetting period of hope and optimism. Realizing the existence of such internal cycles can be very helpful to you in the philosophical sense. Most people who feel their lives represent a cesspool of lousy circumstances tend to focus exclusively on the negative cycles and fail to see the likely shorter positive cycles in their existence. And this is unfortunate.

The real value of recognizing the reality—and dependability—of cycles to the warrior-trader is knowing that he should plan appropriately for holding on tight during the predictable hard times, and then be prepared to move like hell in the good times. This reminds me of a person on a slow-moving merry-go-round that passes by a basket of money once a month. As he passes by the basket on each monthly cycle, he has only 10 precious minutes to grab all the money he can before the basket is out of reach again.

The nonwarrior simply sits back on his butt complaining about his poverty and lot in life. When the money basket suddenly appears around the curve, he is taken by surprise and only has time to take a few reckless grabs at the money. But the warrior-trader knows that the money (and all other positive, desirable things) will be coming back within reach eventually. He has carefully conserved his energy and resources in preparation for the eventual return of his financial gathering opportunity. And—thanks to the Laws of Responsibility, Synchronicity, and Manifestation—the more ready and vigilant he is, the *faster* the merry-go-round turns and the quicker the money basket comes around! Not a bad deal, huh!

3. THE WARRIOR'S LAW OF EVOLUTION

This is a law that is easily overlooked by the nonwarrior. Once they reach a certain point of comfort in their situation, most people see no harm in simply becoming complacent where or as they are. While there is certainly nothing wrong with enjoying such comfort for a while, to allow it to become stagnant is contrary to the universal *Law of Evolution*. The oscillatory (and thus cyclical) nature of all things, situations, and events demands that all of creation (reality) is in a constantly evolving state of *change!* Thus it is imperative that you understand that, within the *Law of Evolution*, there exist two antithetical sublaws that have a *dramatic* effect on your existence: the *Law of Progression* and its "evil" counterpart, the *Law of Regression*.

While the *Law of Evolution* says that all things *must* evolve or change, its sublaws state that things or situations either *progress* as a result of direct intervention or attention (*Law of Progression*) or, in the *absence* of attention or direct intervention all things or situations will *regress!* And the seemingly unfair advantage the *Law of Regression* has over the *Law of Progression* can be observed in the fact that regression can work its universal magic *twice* as fast as progression—which in turn means that warriors have to be *doubly* careful and vigilant of their current situation and evolutionary status.

Some Examples of Progression and Regression Three simple examples of these truths come to my mind, examples you will likely be able to identify with personally. The first has to do with the nature of fitness. The second has to do with gardening. And the third deals with interpersonal relationships—particularly marriage.

It has always irked Lyndee and me to observe that it can take two to three weeks to really get back into shape after a *one*-week layoff from exercise. It doesn't seem fair or equitable to us at all, but like it or not, that's the way it is. Natural law dictates that either we must work to improve our bodies constantly, or they will automatically deteriorate right before our eyes. In other words, as some great sage once said, "Ya gotta use it or ya'll lose it!"

Have you ever planted a vegetable garden? If so, you have watched the *Laws of Progression* and *Regression* duel for supremacy right in your backyard. In order for your garden to produce the healthy vegetables you want, you must constantly be on guard for the insidious marauders of your agricultural efforts. Bugs, birds, drought, fungus—and let's not forget *weeds*, the number-one nemesis of every gardener—are always out to take control of your project. Let it go unattended for a week and you could easily need two to three weeks to get your garden back in productive shape again.

And marriages (or any other relationships) are no different than our bodies or gardens. Two people originally get married because of common interests and a mutual sense of love and respect for the people they are marrying as they are *right then*. But the *Law of Evolution* calls out for each of us to grow as human beings and to experience numerous metamorphoses. While this is individually good, it can be disastrous for the marriage if it too doesn't evolve along with the two individual parties involved. Sometimes one spouse will experience *progression* while the other may try to stay the same—or possibly experience *regression*—thus pulling them farther and farther away from their original commonality with each other. Before they know it, their lack of recognition of the *Law of Evolution* sadly results in an all-too-common visit to a divorce court.

> It is essential that, while holding firmly to the foundation of your trading knowledge, you should always be open to the possibility of new ideas and new methods.

To the warrior-trader, the *Law of Evolution* imparts an important message. It is essential that, while holding firmly to the foundation of your trading knowledge, you should always be open to the possibility of new ideas and new methods. No one is perfect, particularly not financial risk-takers. By always assuming that there is room for improvement—in both yourself and your methods—you will more likely progress toward success than regress toward failure.

4. THE WARRIOR'S LAW OF CHOICES

The majority of what happens in your life is the direct result of the choices you make. You are both burdened and blessed by the responsibility of free will. Many people fall prey to feeling trapped by their circumstances, and subsequently resign themselves to their situation or lot in life. The *samurai* understood that life was a do-it-to-themselves affair and that, regardless of their situation, there were *always* choices that could be made.

I have counseled with countless clients and students who think they are powerless to change their lives.

I have listened to people who claim to be trapped in a bad marriage. When I sometimes suggest to them that they could choose to get a divorce, their knee-jerk reaction to this was often, "Ohhh no! I couldn't do that to him [or her]!"

I have visited with people who were hooked on drugs, yet chose to live in the seediest, most drug-infested neighborhoods in the city. When I suggested that they could move elsewhere and remove themselves from the influence of their destructive surroundings, they would often respond, "How could I do that? That's where I've always lived!"

And I have also talked with traders who have repeatedly lost money in a particular market or with a particular trading system. When I suggested that maybe they need to consider a different market or a new trading methodology, more than once I have heard them say, "But that's the market I like" or "I've invested too much time and money in this system not to use it!" For better or for worse, all of these people have to live with the results of their choices—just like you and I do.

As a warrior-trader, once you begin to recognize and honor the universal *Law of Choices*, you can begin to live and trade with a sense of clarity and intention. You are no longer a victim. You take full advantage of each day and opportunity by choice—as the true Way of the warrior would dictate. And even though you cannot control the circumstances that affect your life, you *do* have the power to choose your particular response to whatever may arise. And even if you occasionally become intoxicated by this personal power you possess, and end up making a few bad choices here or there, at least it is still you who is at the control panel of your destiny! In these cases, all that matters is that you assume responsibility for your choices and then move on.

5. THE WARRIOR'S LAW OF RESPONSIBILITY

It is my hope that by this point in our journey together down the path of warriorship, not a whole lot needs to be said about the importance of responsibility. The *Law of Responsibility* is the logical universal follow-up to the *Law of Choices*. As a warrior you must *always* be willing to pay the price for your decisions and actions. I've been telling students this for decades, just as I was continually told by my mentors.

If you choose to drop out of training for a while, you must be prepared to endure the greater-than-normal pain of being out of shape when you come back. If you choose to stuff yourself on Thanksgiving Day, you must be willing to diet and exercise like hell to offset your indulgence. If you choose to have an affair, you must be ready to face the inevitable hurt and anguish when your deceit is eventually discovered. And of course, if you invest the majority of your trading account in a "sure thing," only to see the bottom fall out of that market, you must accept responsibility for your choice and be ready to have to rebuild your assets to get back on your feet.

As I have mentioned a couple of times earlier in this book, I have observed a serious lack of willingness or ability to accept responsiblity for what happens among many traders I've visited with over the years. I'm sure you would agree that such denial can only be counterproductive and ultimately destructive in the long run. In such cases, making these people wake up to their responsibility for their own actions is my first wish for them and my first objective in steering them down the true path of success. In the event that *you* need such a wake-up call, I hope the *Law of Responsibility* will speak loudly and clearly to your new warrior consciousness as well!

6. THE WARRIOR'S LAW OF INERTIA

In the field of mechanical physics the *Law of Inertia* states that, "An object at rest tends to stay at rest." In the *samurai kyokushin*, this law refers more to apathy, laziness, and emotional resignation. Like the guy on the merry-go-round we talked about under the *Law of Cycles*, nonwarriors tend to want to just sit on their butts and complain about the way things are. And according to this law, the longer you sit there in this static condition, the easier it becomes to keep on doing the same thing—which is nothing. Therefore the *Law of Inertia* really serves as a reminder and a warning. It warns that procrastination is dangerous and that lost time will *never* be found again.

The true Way of the *samurai* recovery from defeat is one of action and assertion against the situational and emotional inertia it tends to cause. And to begin asserting your action-oriented will to get back into the battle, we can again borrow information from the field of mechanical physics.

It is a fact that, in order to push a wagon loaded with bricks a distance of 12 feet, it takes 90 percent more energy to push the wagon the first 12 *inches* than it takes to cover the last 11 feet! Why is this? Because once the wagon gets moving, thus having overcome the effects of the Law of Inertia, the benefits of it's antithetical counterpart, the *Law of Momentum*, begin to take effect, which is good news for the warrior indeed!

7. The Warrior's Law of Momentum

"An object in motion tends to stay in motion." This is how mechanical physics defines the *Law of Momentum*. But in the *samurai's kyokushin*, it means that, "A warrior in progress tends to make *more* progress!" Emotional and situational momentum is the universal reward for having dedicated the short-term burst of focused energy toward overcoming the dampening effects of inertia to begin with. The hardest part about beginning an exercise program is getting to the gym the first day (inertia). But once you get started, it gets easier and easier to keep at it (momentum). The hardest thing about writing this book was getting started on the introduction. After that it got easier and easier—and more enjoyable as well.

In times of defeat, the Law of Momentum offers you reassurance that things will look, feel, and be better once you get started back on the right path again.

In times of defeat, the *Law of Momentum* offers you reassurance that things will look, feel, and *be* better once you get started back on the right path again. This helps to provide the necessary motivation and impetus to put forth that necessary burst of effort and energy to get you started back—and moving in harmony with the rest of the universe, as set forth in the *Law of Synchronicity*.

8. The Warrior's Law of Synchronicity

Because of their limited three-dimensional perceptions of reality, nonwarriors can easily view themselves as being separate and apart from the rest of everything. But by now I am hopeful that my numerous stories, examples, experiments, and lessons have helped you, the budding warrior-trader, to see everything differently. To view yourself as separate from the universe is to limit yourself to strictly being a powerless pawn or puppet in the game of life and trading. But on the other hand, to see yourself as an integral, inseparable, and mindful part of the machinery we call reality is to enable yourself to reclaim your natural and indisputable role as the "center" of everything going on around you!

One of the most dramatic transformations I tend to see in the traders that go through my retreat program occurs within the realm of the *Law of*

Synchronicity (or unity). I'll never forget one trader who was a very stoic and pragmatic kind of guy and was also a third-generation cotton farmer and cotton futures trader. I gathered from his many conversations with me and the other traders in attendance with him that weekend, that over the years his family (including his father, grandfather, and great-grandfather) had successfully dealt with every level of the cotton markets, from growing, harvesting, and ginning it to trading it at the international level.

But even though he had been so closely involved with this commodity, this guy never really felt "connected" with it in the "unified" sense. But I watched with interest as the rather cool pragmatism about his relationship with the cotton markets gradually dissolved as his mind opened and his experiences grew throughout the three days he was with me.

The climactic moment seemed to occur for "the cotton man," as we fondly came to call him, as he sat meditating under a rushing waterfall, which was one of the final "challenges" on our training itinerary. As he emerged from the continuous flow of the falls, this formerly stoic, pragmatic trader made his way over to where I was sitting on a rock taking it all in. As he sat down, he hesitantly began to tell me that he had had a kind "vision" or *satori* (sudden enlightenment) while in the water. He went on to explain that in order to tolerate the weight and roar of the falls (which, by the way, really isn't that big, but just seems to be when you're under it!), he had found it necessary to become "unified" with it, just as I had predicted before he had gotten in.

But the thing that surprised him was that during his "unification experience," his mind had suddenly become filled with a myriad of thoughts, images, and feelings about—of all things—the cotton markets! He said that for the first time in his life, he recognized that the market was "a living, breathing thing" and that he was inseparable from it! Needless to say, "Mr. Cotton" has since done quite well for his family in the cotton markets.

To recognize and honor the *Law of Synchronicity* is to see the unity and harmony between all things, events, and situations. As you open up your mind and perceptions to this truth, you will find it harder and harder to call synchronistic happenings "luck" or "coincidence." And even though the limited capacities of your human mind cannot fully understand how such events come to be interconnected, you nonetheless *know* that there are omnipotent forces at work, constantly creating the reality that you experience and, more often than not, that *you* helped to create—by way of the *Law of Manifestation!*

9. THE WARRIOR'S LAW OF MANIFESTATION

The message contained in this powerful universal law is quite simple yet easily overwhelming to the uninitiated mind. We are taught from early childhood to believe that the creative force of the universe is "out there" somewhere. But nothing could be farther from the truth. As I have pointed out before, every ancient spiritual teaching known to man (including Judeo-Christian teachings) expounds that the "kingdom is within you" and that "you will create or become what you think of the most." (See Chapter 10.) Therefore the truth within the *Law of Manifestation* can be summed up in this simple advisory that we have all heard at one time or another: *"Be careful about what you wish for—you'll probably get it!"*

The *samurai* knew that his thoughts and imagination possessed a power and potential that was every bit as tangible as the razor-sharp edge of his *katana*. He also recognized that the metaphysical level of his imaginative powers were an integral part of the creative force of the universe. Because he knew from many validating experiences that this was true, he was always careful to habitually direct his thoughts in the direction he wanted his destiny to go, rather than to inadvertently use his manifestory powers to bring about "bad luck" and possibly his own demise.

> *He also recognized that the metaphysical level of his imaginative powers were an integeral part of the creative force of the universe.*

And it should be just the same for you too, the warrior-trader. By using the incredible potential implied by the Law of Manifestation, it is possible for you to intentionally (but effortlessly) attract or create the various things, events, circumstances, and opportunities you need to make your life rich and fulfilling—especially if you do so in an orderly, proactive manner, as prescribed in the final *Law of Process and Action*.

10. THE WARRIOR'S LAW OF PROCESS AND ACTION

This is the most practical of the 10 laws I have chosen to present, and is certainly one that applies to everything else I have presented in the scope of our study together. The reason I say this is because the *Law of Process and Action* is a commonsense directive about how to get things done and the importance of actually *doing* something with your potential, rather than just pondering the possibilities.

The word *process* refers to taking a large task and breaking it down into smaller, more manageable parts. Referring back to an analogy I have previously used, no one could hope to just jump in and build a building in a week. Such a project takes planning and careful execution over a prescribed period of time, to be sure. Likewise, you cannot expect to become a good trader (and especially a warrior-trader) overnight. Such an undertaking also takes introspective study, careful planning, diligent practice, and, of course, a reasonable amount of time to see your goal come to fruition.

The first half of the *Law of Process and Action* dictates that every worthwhile endeavor, particularly following the true Way of the warrior-trader, be viewed as a journey. And likewise, the law further encourages you to recognize and remember that every journey is made up of a series of steps, and through the action of each sequential step you will inevitably arrive, sooner or later, at your intended destination—a place we'll call "mastery" and success!

And that brings us to a postscript message in this final universal law. The legendary *samurai* of feudal Japan powerfully demonstrated that progressive action is the only way to dependably benefit from knowledge. An old Budo-Zen addage says, *"Knowledge without action is impotent! Knowledge combined with action is wisdom!"* So I encourage you to take this saying to heart, and take the collective knowledge contained in these 10 laws, and the rest of this book as well, and begin to progressively transform it into warrior-wisdom through your daily actions and experiences—and there is no better time to start than *now!*

True Tales of the Warrior-Trader

There is no doubt that the universal laws of the kyokushin, *like gravity, affect all of us in one way or another. Therefore, to relate a personal story about each of the laws I have presented herein would probably warrant writing a separate book to do them justice. However, let me tell you about one fellow with whom I had a day-to-day relationship over a period of two years. His story may summarily help to put the reality and importance of the* kyokushin *into perspective for you.*

I originally met C.K. in the men's restroom, where I learned that he was an investment banker working for the firm located next to my office. And it was in the course of our many "urinal consultations" (as he called them) that I learned what an unhappy guy he really was. In fact, his favorite philosophical statement was, "Life sucks and then you die!" So after hearing this come from his mouth who knows how many times, I decided I would begin a little strategic intervention—just to see if it would make any difference—and I decided to simply introduce him, little by little, to the samurai's kyokushin.

Over the months that followed, it gradually became apparent that C.K. was responding to the many samurai sayings and bits of wisdom I used to "parry" his grumblings and complaints. In fact, he began to intentionally try to catch me whenever I might make an occasional pit stop between clients. And what I saw in and heard from him was indeed interesting.

The first thing I noticed was that he began to say, "What goes up has to come down some time" or "What goes down has to come up eventually," depending on whether the markets had treated him well or badly that day. He was beginning to recognize the Laws of Duality and Cycles.

Then C.K. began to intermittently speak of "getting out of the junk bond racket" and "maybe going back to school so I can do something more worthwhile and less stressful with my life." He was beginning to catch on to the Laws of Evolution, Choices, and Responsibility. And it was also becoming very obvious that his original unhappiness and sense of hopelessness were breaking down in the process.

Finally, with a bit of consistent prodding from Lyndee and me both, C.K. started working out physically with us two or three times a week, which in turn gave me more quality time with him. Not long after we began working out together, K.C. even enrolled in night courses at the local university to pursue a degree in business finance. He told me a few weeks later that it had been "hard as hell at first to get back into the exercise and studying thing," but that "it was getting easier and easier to stick with it!" C.K. had discovered the truth and inevitability of the Laws of Inertia and Momentum.

Needless to say, C.K. and I became fairly good friends, and in our quieter times together he began to tell me about the way his luck was changing for the better! Not only had his business contacts and opportunities expanded and improved, but he had even found himself in a satisfying relationship that hadn't "crashed and burned in a month" like countless others had before. He also timidly told me that he somehow felt he was "inexplicably attracting good things and good people" into his life in a way he never had before. Lo and behold, C.K. was experiencing first-hand the wonders and dependable powers of the Laws of Synchronicity and Manifestation!

Eventually, C.K. did in fact quit his bond trading job, married the woman he had manifested into his life, and moved to London (where his wife was from) to trade gold futures for a reputable company there. And to be perfectly honest, I have no idea how he is doing today since we lost touch with each other after his big move. But as an experienced sensei *to countless students just like C.K., my intuition tells me he is doing fine now. And I am also confident that the final Law of Process and Action has since become equally obvious to C.K., especially in those moments when he reflects upon the Ways and means that brought him the happiness, satisfaction, and success he probably enjoys today—those being the universal truths and laws of the warrior-trader's* kyokushin!

CHAPTER 15

The Way and Day of the Warrior-Trader

TRUE TALES OF THE BUDO

I wish to put down in writing for the first time the Way in which I have been disciplining myself for many years, and which path I have given the name of Nito Ichiryu—*"The Way of Two-Swords-as-One School." I am Shinmen Musashi Miyamoto no Kami Fujiwara no Genshi, born a* bushi *of the domain of Harima, on the main island of Nippon, or Honshu. I have reached the age of 60.*

I have devoted myself to the Way of the warrior since my youth, and had my first battle at the age of 13. Subsequent to many victories, after the age of 30 I began to reflect on the road I had been traveling and came to the realization that my conquests had not been the result of my having attained the full secrets of swordsmanship. Rather, they were the result of having attained a deeper understanding of the true Way as a result of disciplining myself day in and day out. Thus, at the age of 50, I came face to face with an ultimate realization (satori) *of the true Way of warriorship—the* Heiho *of Bushido!*

Heiho *is the Way of the warrior class. However, in today's world, there are few warriors who exhibit the discipline or dedication to attain an understanding of the true path of* Heiho. *In speaking of paths, there are many. There is the path of Buddha, by which people might save their souls. There is the path of Confucianism, by which people might be intellectually enlightened. There is the path of the physician by which people's bodies can be made well. And there are the paths of archers, musicians, poets, teamen, merchants, and practitioners of the other arts and skills. But there are few who are willing to dedicate themselves to the true path of* Heiho.

It is generally accepted that the Way of the warrior is the resolute acceptance of the possibility of loss and the inevitability of death. To the warrior it is only a matter of when and how. But the Way of such acceptance is not limited only to warriors. Priests, women, or anyone who practices a trade can also find power in surrendering to the inevitable. They too may even choose to die if obligation or avoidance of dishonor calls them to do so.

In order for a warrior, regardless of his occupation, to follow the path of Heiho, *it is necessary to keep in mind that the essence of* Heiho *is to build an indomitable spirit and an iron will, and to take complete control of his mind. Warriors must believe that they cannot fail in doing anything they set their mind to. The warrior must be able to win in one-on-one combat and in battles involving several opponents at once in order to win fame for his* daimyo *and honor for himself. This is accomplished by virtue of the* Heiho *of Bushido.*

There are those who say that even if you master the Way of the warrior, it will be of no use in practical matters. I am here to attest that the true path of Heiho *is such that it applies at any time, in any situation, and to any endeavor!*

Miyamoto Musashi, circa 1640

The Way of the Warrior-Trader in a Nutshell

In the course of speaking at numerous trading conferences and symposiums, I have often been asked to summarize the Way of the warrior-trader into a nutshell. My pat answer has always been that it is "to live and trade with the holistic discipline, patience, acceptance, and uncomplicated mentality of the *samurai.*" My response is often met with polite head nods and "Hmmms," but I always know deep down inside that these people really do not understand. After all, how *could* they possibly know from the brief glimpse I was able to convey in the typical 30 to 60 minutes allotted to speakers at such gatherings. Nonetheless, their questions *are* sincere, and they really do want to learn more about the true Way of warrior trading.

Besides wanting to provide an educational medium through which my retreat attendees could better prepare for their personal training experience with me, my other motivation for writing this book is to be able to comprehensively answer those sincere queries from conference attendees. In the future, when they come up to me with curious, hopeful looks in their eyes, I will be able to warmly shake their hands, congratulate them for their open-mindedness, hand them a copy of this book, and with complete confidence say, "*This* is the Way of the warrior-trader!" Even Miyamoto Musashi, the most respected and famous *samurai* in Japanese history, believed that the Way of the warrior was applicable to any situation or profession—even trading—as you read in the excerpt from his *Gorin-No-Sho* (Book of Five Rings), which opened this, our final chapter. And the way I see it, if the Way worked for Musashi, it can unquestionably work for us too!

Some Daily Structure for the Warrior-Trader

So the time has come now to help you develop some daily structure for applying what you have learned and hopefully will continue to learn. To accomplish this, it seems only right that I should provide you with a glimpse of a day in the life of someone whom I feel lives and trades the Way of the warrior-trader. And what better example could I pick than that of my trader friend whom I mentioned in the introduction of this book.

You may recall that this friend, whom I will call R.K., was originally responsible for introducing me to the challenging and stimulating business of helping stocks, futures, and commodities traders—something for which I am deeply grateful! I am pleased to present this overview of R.K.'s routine, not only for the sake of your benefit, but also as a way of acknowledging and commending him for his dutiful (*and* profitable!) application of the warrior Ways we have worked on in the course of our studies together.

Early to Bed, Early to Rise

The typical trading day starts early for R.K., usually long before the sun has come up. Right after awakening, he gets up and goes to a special place in his home he has set aside for meditation work. Sitting appropriately, R.K. proceeds to practice his "centering" breathing exercises (*kokyu-kihara*). After a couple of minutes of this he then reflects on the potential opportunity this trading day represents, and he reminds himself that trading is an "art form" and that it *must* be executed from this perspective. He also reminds himself that profits are only the *by-product* of his Way of trading, and that each trading "technique" he might execute that day must be done purely for the sake of "artistic perfection" and nothing more!

After his meditation period, R.K. will usually do some form of exercise—sometimes jogging, sometimes walking on his treadmill—all the while keeping his body aligned, maintaining his one-point, and keeping his weight underside (*haragei*). Regardless of what type of exercise he employs, it is always cardiovascular in nature in order to get his heart (and spirit) into high gear. Although his exercise periods vary in duration depending on what he has chosen to do that day, he generally dedicates about 30 minutes to it on an average.

Proper Fuel for Proper Performance

After his physical workout and a cool-down period, R.K. usually eats a light breakfast of fruit and high-protein/high-fiber cereal. He has come to recognize that, if he is going to expect peak performance from himself, then it is *essential* that he provide his body with the appropriate peak-performance fuel. And this should hold true for any meal of the day.

As he eats, he makes it a point to practice mindfulness and relaxed, regular breathing, which allows him to experience the true flavors and textures of his food. After eating, Rick goes back to his meditation area and practices *zazen* meditation (with his focus upon breathing and clearing his mind of unnecessary static) for approximately 15 to 20 more minutes.

Reviewing the "Battle Plan"

By 6 A.M., R.K. is out in his trading office, which is located in a kind of mother-in-law quarters adjacent to his home. I have a great deal of respect for the way he has set up his trading environment, whose importance I believe too many traders overlook. R.K. learned while studying at my *dojo* that a *shibumi* environment ("pristine and uncomplicated simplicity") is best suited for preparing the warrior's mind and spirit for the rigors and challenges of battle.

For the first 45 minutes to an hour his priority is to review his charts and records of the previous day's market and trading activity, while allowing his natural intuition (backed up by his trading skills and experience) to "feel" what direction things might take once the market opens.

Hajime! (Let the Engagement Begin)

At market open, R.K. sits in front of his three monitors, erect and centered in his chair, taking in everything that is happening. The environment in his office is intentionally quiet and serene, the way R.K. wants his mind to be. Behind his computer trade-station, on the wall where he can always see it, is a razor-sharp *samurai* sword he received from me during his training at my *dojo*.

I always make it a point to present each of my personal warrior-trader *sempai* with some type of *samurai* memorabilia, such as an authentic sword, as a reminder of the seriousness and reality of the war game they are engaged in. However, R.K. takes it a step further by also having a *bonsai* tree on a shelf next to his sword, as a reminder of the Zen nature of true warriorship. He recognizes the absolute need for warrior patience and inner calm to subdue his action-oriented mentality until a potentially profitable opportunity presents itself.

Recentering for Clearing and Renewed Focus

About once per hour, R.K. makes it a point to stand up and move around for a minute or two to avoid psychological and physical fatigue brought on by sedentariness. When he sits back down, he always repeats his practice of *kokyu-kihara* and *haragei* by breathing deeply into his one-point and recentering himself in his chair. Then, sometime during the middle of the trading day, he makes it a point to do *zazen* meditation again for about 10 minutes. R.K. says that this helps him to "clear away any psychological or emotional clutter" from his morning trading session.

Recovering in the Event of Losses

In the event that he incurs any substantial losses in the course of his trading day, R.K. tells me that he always makes it a point to close out his positions and leave his trading office for a while. Amid this break he takes a walk, during which he undergoes emotional and spiritual cleansing and rejuvenation by practicing *misogi*, the traditional *samurai* inner-cleansing and rejuvenation process detailed in Chapter 13. Nine times out of 10, he tells me, he is usually ready to go back and "take another swing at it" within 30 minutes.

The Sun Sets on the Warrior-Trader

At the end of his trading day—whether it was profitable or not—R.K. concludes by making appropriate notations about the day's events and prints out the charts necessary for the next day's consideration and review. He then leaves his trading office and goes back inside his house for 15 to 30 more minutes of *zazen* in his special meditation area. When he is through with his meditation, R.K. makes it a point to completely "let go" of whatever happened today. This way he is genuinely able to spend some quality time with his lovely wife and enjoy his evening (and his life!) doing whatever the two of them might find appealing.

Before retiring to bed for the night, R.K. makes it a point to review his notes concerning his trading day. Then he practices three to five minutes of *kokyo-kihara* deep-breathing, this time to relax and prepare his mind and body for restful and rejuvenating sleep. R.K. finds that many times, reviewing his notes followed by deep breathing allows his unconscious mind, while he sleeps, to work out solutions for some problem or dilemma he may be working to resolve.

In addition to his daily warrior-trader routine, once a week R.K. rereads a section of his Zen-mind retreat training manual (which in your case would be this book) to remind himself of the appropriate Way of looking at such warrior issues as motivation, self-perception, and life purpose. This also helps him to more deeply commit to memory the inner truths contained in the *Samurai* A.C.T.I.O.N. Plan and the universal laws of the *kyokushin.*

Some Final Comments and a Farewell Wish

So there you have it. A look at a day in the life of a person who I feel successfully lives and trades the Way of the warrior-trader. I realize that in the course of our study together I have presented you with a considerable volume of information, concepts, and ideas to sort through. But I am confident that after a period of time and with a little dedicated practice and experience, you will find, as our example warrior-trader has, that the true Way of the *samurai* was really quite simple and uncluttered. But it is up to you to push forward and discover how this all fits into *your* scheme of things—something I sincerely hope you will take the time and effort to do! And as one final token of wisdom to aid you in this very important pursuit, I would like to close with a short Zen story that I have always been fond of.

Once upon a time a curious young fish asked a wise old fish, "Where is the 'Great Ocean' the elders so often speak of?"

"Why, it is everywhere, in every breath you take, constantly renewing your life force!" the old fish replied.

"Then why is it I've never seen something as great as this?" asked the young fish.

To this the wise old fish responded, "Because it is so close to you ... so much a part of you ... it seems to some to be invisible, even though the proof of its existence is all around you!"

"Oh, I sea!" said the enlightened young fish.

The true *Way of the Warrior-Trader* is a path of holistic discipline, patience, acceptance, and uncomplicated mentality—and it is not always an easy one to follow. But you now have in your possession an ocean of knowledge and information that can get you where you want to be if you will simply see—with the open eyes and mind of a warrior—that which is invisible to the less-informed or less-enlightened! So I leave you for now, with a smile and a hope, and the heartfelt wish often extended by Obi-Wan Kinobi, the futuristic *samurai* of the *Star Wars* saga, to his aspiring *sempai* Luke Skywalker, "*May the Force be with you!*"

GLOSSARY OF TERMS

action blocks— (1) overanalysis, (2) self-doubt, (3) hesitation.

action catalysts— (1) well-grounded stance, (2) a "harmonize, then enter" tactical philosophy, (3) dependable psychology of action.

ai— when used as a prefix, literally means "blending"; when used as a suffix, literally means "focusing" or "sending."

aiki— literally means "blending with oncoming energy"; the *samurai* predominantly used this concept defensively when "receiving" or parrying an attacker's blow.

aikido— literally means "the Way of energetic harmony."

analysis paralysis— the way overanalysis tends to be experienced by traders.

batto-jutsu— literally means "combative cutting skills," which refers to cutting with the *samurai* long sword (*katana*).

biofeedback— any process or device designed to give an individual information about normally unperceivable internal bodily activity, changes, or conditions.

bu— literally means "war"; more accurately interpreted to mean "to make peace."

Buddha— literally means "the enlightened one."

Budo— literally means "the Way of war"; more accurately interpreted to mean "the Way of making peace."

Budo-kansuru— literally means "the *samurai* Way of trust and intuition."

Budo-zazen— generally refers to Zen meditation as practiced by the *samurai* to prepare himself for the rigors of warriorship.

Budo-Zen— generally refers to Zen practices and applications unique to the *samurai*.

bugei— the classical war arts of feudal Japan.

bugeisha— a practitioner of the classical war arts of Japan.

Bujin-san— literally means "honorable (or Mr.) warrior spirit."

bushi— a member of the warrior class of feudal Japan; a *samurai.*

bushido— literally means "the Way of the *samurai.*"

Bushinkai— literally means "the society of mental (or internal) warriors."

center one-point— a point approximately three inches below the navel; also called *hara.*

centering— refers to aligning and organizing mind, body, and spirit for the purposes of action and/or stability.

chado— literally means "the Way of tea"; usually refers to the practice of the ancient Japanese tea ceremony.

chadoshi— literally means "a master of the Way of tea (or tea ceremony)."

chiburi— the process of "flicking" blood from the cutting edge of a *samurai* sword after executing a killing blow.

chudan-no-kamai— a face-high defensive posture used by the *samurai* and *kendoka* when facing off with an opponent.

Confucianism— the body of knowledge and philosophy revolving around the works and thought of the Chinese sage Confucius, usually dealing with the ideal of establishing harmony between all things within the universe.

conscious competency— the third of four phases one passes through when learning any skill; refers to the ability to perform a task correctly when conscious thought is dedicated to the task.

conscious incompetence— the second of four phases one passes through when learning any skill; refers to the point wherein the practitioner recognizes for himself that a task is being performed incorrectly.

daimyo— literally means "great name"; refers to a war lord or head of a province who lived in the castle of that province. These powerful lords retained large numbers of *samurai*, who swore to them their allegiance.

Do— literally means "the Way of Path"; refers to any type of practice or discipline that results in the enhancement of the practitioner's physical, mental, and spiritual balance and well-being.

dogu— the name of the head, arms, chest, and waist armor worn by modern-day practitioners of *kendo* (fencing). It is designed to protect combatants from injury that could result from full-contact strikes with the *shinai* (bamboo sword).

dojo— literally means "a training hall of the Way"; usually refers to formal training halls of traditional martial arts.

empty mind— refers to Zen mind state in which there is no noticeable thought or internal dialogue taking place; also called *mu-shin*.

entrainment— the process of repetitively rehearsing mental functions in order to produce a predictable behavioral outcome.

esthetics— to collectively respond keenly to the inner beauty and inner nature of some thing, act, or event.

evolved faith— the type of faith or trust that is produced by a history of personal experience with that which is believed in.

following your breath— a Zen term that refers to placing one's complete attention onto the process of inhaling deeply into and out of the abdominal area; usually a precursor to Zen meditation (*zazen*).

full lotus position— a meditative position accomplished by the meditator placing the right foot's instep atop the left thigh, then the left foot's instep atop the right thigh, in an interlocking manner; combined with proper elevation of the buttocks by a cushion (*zafu*), this position is considered the nominal position for achieving physical, mental, and spiritual centering.

gaijin— literally means "someone from the outside"; a term usually used by the Japanese to refer to a foreign visitor.

godan— a fifth-degree black belt in a traditional Japanese martial art.

great void— the term used in Buddhist, Shintoist, Taoist, and Confucian philosophies that refers to the universe as a whole, which in its final essence is actually made up of "nothing."

gut level— refers to the highest order of feelings and intuition emanating from the center or one-point of the experiencer.

hajime— literally means "Let the engagement begin"; this command is used to begin all contests in the modern-day traditional Japanese martial arts.

hakama **pants**— an article of clothing worn predominantly by practitioners of the classical war arts of Japan; the original apparel of the *samurai*, this garment is still also worn by many Japanese cultural traditionalists.

half-lotus position— a cross-legged meditation position identified by the right folded leg being placed atop the left folded leg, but not interlocked as in the full lotus position.

hanko— the official "signature and seal" stamp usually used by high-ranking officials in signing documents; it is commonly hand-etched into bone or stone and dipped into a thick, blood-red ink paste.

hanshi-dai—literally means "the designated successor to the master"; generally refers to the person who is second in command of a traditional *dojo* of Japanese martial arts.

hara— literally means "ocean of energy"; refers to the spot two to three inches below the navel; also called "center one-point."

haragei— literally means "to align the energies"; refers to the process of keeping the body straight and aligned from head to lower back, maintaining an awareness of the lower abdominal area, and keeping the lower body (waist and legs) slightly flexed and "heavy."

hara-kiri— literally means "to cut open the seat of the soul"; refers to the specific type of cut utilized by someone committing ritualistic suicide (*seppuku*).

hasso-gamai— a preparatory posture assumed by a swordsman in which the sword is held high and to the right of the head.

hasso-no-kamai— interchangeable with the term *hasso-gamai*.

Heiho— the name given to *kenjutsu* (sword skills) by Ito Ittosai. This was done to point out that the Way of the sword must be more than mere techniques, but must contain a mind that is pure and calm. Only in this way can one take advantage of the opponent's weaknesses and movements.

higher power— that which transcends the measurable and definable powers and forces of three-dimensional reality; interchangeable with *metaphysics.*

holistic— to treat all parts with equal consideration in order to create harmony of function and existence between them all.

hombu— literally means "the official war seat"; usually refers to the home *dojo* of grandmaster (*soke*) of traditional Japanese martial art.

hondo— literally means "place of assembly"; refers to the largest and central-most room in a traditional *dojo* of the martial arts.

iaido— literally means "the Way of harmonious drawing and cutting" with a *samurai katana* (long sword).

iaigoshi— a crouched, semiseated posture used by the *samurai* when resting, which afforded them swift, unhindered access to their sword in case of attack.

in (and *yo*)— literally means "negative and positive"; the Japanese equivalent of Chinese *yin* and *yang;* refers to the dualistic nature of the universe, which is composed of opposite and opposing forces that in turn give rise to reality as we know it.

inner vision— a psychic-level capability that enables one to "see" or "sense" events remotely, without direct contact with them; interchangeable with *mind-vision.*

isagi-yoku— literally means "the art of dying with dignity."

is-shin— literally means "one mind"; refers to a state of intense concentration and focus, used by the *samurai* when initiating and then following through with an attack.

itten— literally means "the one-point"; interchangeable with *hara.*

judo— literally means "the soft Way"; refers to the traditional Japanese martial art and sport that specializes in throws and holds.

kai— literally means "society or organization."

kaishaku— a friend or trusted associate of someone committing ritual suicide (*seppuku*) whose job it is to sever the dying person's head by cutting 95 percent of the way through the neck in order to expedite death, minimize suffering, but keep the head from rolling away from the body.

kanji— ancient Japanese calligraphic characters used in *shodo* (the Way of the brush).

kansuru— literally means "trust and intuition."

karate-do— literally means "the Way of the empty hand"; refers to the Japanese martial art and sport specializing in kicks and strikes.

karma— a person's personal fate or destiny, which has been determined and shaped by past actions of the individual in his or her current or previous life.

katana— the devastatingly sharp long-sword of the *samurai.*

kendo— literally means "the Way of the sword."

kendoka— a practitioner of *kendo.*

kenjutsu— literally means "skills of the sword."

kenshi— literally means "master of the sword."

ki— literally means "life force"; refers to the ultimate spiritual essence of the universe of which all things and events are a part.

kiai— literally means "to send or focus energy"; although actually conceptual in nature, it is usually associated with the "spirit shout" used by martial artists when they launch and attack.

kokoro— literally means "to bring all inner resources together as one"; interchangeable with *synergy.*

kokoro-shinjutsu— literally means "to bring together all the forces of the mind, body, and spirit into one action."

kokyu-kihara— literally means "to breathe into the energy center"; one of the *samurai's* principal ways of achieving "center" and controlling fear.

kumite— literally means "crossing of the hands"; refers to a controlled sparring session between *karate-do* contestants.

kyokushin— literally means "universal laws and truths"; refers to the *samurai's* understanding of the way the universal scheme affects everything.

kyudo— literally means "the Way of the bow"; refers to the discipline of Budo-Zen archery.

learning phases— refers to the four phases of learning that everyone passes through when learning and acquiring a new skill; the four phases are (1) unconscious incompetency, (2) conscious incompetency, (3) conscious competency, and (4) unconscious competency.

life force— the essence of the total universe at its most infinite level, and the basis for all creation and reality; also called *ki.*

metaphysics— literally means "transcendent physics"; refers to the study of that part of reality that is unmeasurable yet nonetheless obvious and real; psychic.

microcosmic— a point of view that holds that even the smallest sampling of the universe (i.e., the atom) contains a complete and total representation of the rest of the universe.

mind-vision— a psychic-level capability that enables one to "see" or "sense" events remotely, without direct contact with them; interchangeable with *inner vision.*

misogi— the *samurai's* traditional methods of purifying the spirit and psyche, and recovering from physical and emotional losses.

mu-shin— literally means "empty mind"; the ultimate objective of *zazen* meditation; one of the most desirable states of mind to the *samurai* for instantaneous defense response; used in conjunction with *aiki.*

ninjutsu— literally means "skills of adaptability or flexibility."

ninjutsuka— a practitioner of *ninjutsu*.

nito ichiryu— literally means "the one school of two swords"; the name given to his philosophy and style of sword fighting by the famous *samurai* Miyamoto Musashi.

okuden-sakki— literally means "the secret teachings of the power of intent"; considered the highest order of study in the esoteric aspects of the traditional Japanese martial disciplines.

one-point centering— the process of achieving a balance of emotional, physical, and spiritual harmony through a combination of *kokyu-kihara* (breathing), *haragei* (physical alignment), and "*Budo-zazen*" (seated meditation).

presumed faith— a relatively "superficial" belief based principally upon what one is told by others; also blind faith.

psyche— a collective term for the joint relationship of mind and spirit.

psychosomatic— literally means "mind over body"; refers not only to the mind's ability to make the body ill, but also its ability to control its typically autonomic functions.

ronin— an unretained or masterless *samurai* who holds allegiance to no one.

sakki— the absolute, unswerving intent to carry through with a particular action.

samurai— literally means "one who serves"; specifically refers to the highest-ranked members of the warrior class in the caste system of feudal-era Japan.

san-chin— literally means "three spirit-breaths" and sometimes called the "three breaths of Zen"; refers to the initial slow, deep breaths traditionally taken at the onset of *zazen* meditation; one breath is for the mind, one for the body, and one for the spirit.

satori— literally means "sudden enlightenment"; often the result of studying and practicing Zen and *zazen* meditation.

saya— the scabbard of a *katana* (*samurai* long sword).

seigan— a horribly intensive test of warrior spirit, usually associated with the awarding of high-level ranks or accreditations in traditional *kenjutsu* or *kendo* (sword fighting).

seiza— the traditional Japanese kneeling/sitting position commonly used in some meditative practice and by traditional martial artists to open and close training sessions, and while resting.

sempai— literally means "special or selected student."

sensei— literally means "honorable teacher."

seppuku— the act of ritualistic suicide through self-disembowelment with a *tanto* (short sword).

shakuhachi— a two- to three-foot-long, handcrafted bamboo flute played by many Zen practitioners due to the breath and emotional control required to play it.

shibumi— refers to a simple, understated elegance.

shihan— literally means "respected master instructor."

shin— literally means "mind," "heart," or "feelings," depending upon the context in which it is used; from the martial perspective, "mind" is the most appropriate interpretation.

shinai— an artificial sword made of four slats of bamboo, which is designed to emulate the general length, weight, and feel of an actual *katana* (*samurai* long sword) and which is used to deliver full-impact strikes to vital targets in *kendo* matches.

shinjutsu— literally means "skills of the mind and heart"; generally refers to the *samurai*'s overall mental abilities and controls.

shogun— the "supreme general designate" of the ruling emperor, the shogun's responsibility was to oversee the actions of all *daimyo* throughout the land.

shogunate— the general term for the ruling domain of a *shogun.*

shugendo— literally means "to achieve enlightenment by means of facing fear and physical challenges"; the three most common *shugendo* practices are (1) firewalking, (2) prolonged meditation in pools or waterfalls, and (3) hanging upside down from ropes or vines from great heights.

shugyo— literally means "to achieve enlightenment and spiritual transcendence through the rigors of disciplined physical training."

simple physics— the most elementary and most obvious level of natural physics, where actions and events are caused by the simple interaction between one physical object and another.

simple-sensory— what is perceived by the average, unenhanced sensitivity of the five human senses of vision, hearing, taste, touch, and smell.

soke— literally means "founder" or "grandmaster"; refers to the highest-ranked living leader of a martial art or *dojo.*

sosho— an older, more traditional form of *kanji* than that used by contemporary Japanese, and more closely related to the original Chinese ideograms from which they evolved.

suki— the principle of taking immediate and decisive action against an opponent's weak point, loss of concentration, or opening in his defensive posture.

superphysics— the result of enhanced simple physics as the result of greater physical and psychological efficiency.

supersensory— refers to an enhanced functioning or sensitivity of any or all of the five senses, beyond the normal range of human capability. The *samurai* accomplished this through the dedicated practice of Zen mindfulness.

synchronicity— the interreactive natural relationship of all forces and powers within the entire universe, especially the causal relationship between seemingly unrelated thoughts, events, and objects.

synergy— an overall effect greater than the sum of all the individual parts, brought about by the harmonious co-existence and cofunctioning of those parts; interchangeable with *kokoro*.

tai— literally means "the physical body."

tai-shin-ki-kokoro— literally means "to bring body, mind, and spirit together as one force"; also interchangeable with *synergy*.

tamishi-giri— literally means "testing one's mastery of the cut"; usually refers to the *kenjutsu* or *iaido* practice of cutting large stalks of green bamboo or rolled straw to test the effectiveness of a particular cutting technique. In feudal times in Japan, this practice was conducted by placing two to five condemned criminals front to back in a row and then simultaneously executing them with a single cut of a *katana* to test its sharpness and quality.

tanto— literally means "short sword"; refers to the dagger-length blade often carried by the *samurai* while in the castle or fortress of a *daimyo* or *shogun*, where the long *katana* was not allowed; also the blade used to commit *seppuku* (ritual suicide).

tatami— a tightly woven hemplike floor surface commonly found in traditional *dojos* of Japanese martial arts and in some traditional Japanese homes.

tentative entry— refers to a half-hearted, fearful, or hesitant tactical move toward an opponent, which nearly always results in defeat.

three-breaths of Zen— interchangeable with *san-chin;* refers to the opening breathing sequence generally beginning a *zazen* meditation session, wherein there is one breath each for physical stability and centering, mental clearing and serenity, and spiritual renewal and balancing.

Togakure Ryu— an ancient *ninjutsu* family lineage (style) originating in the Togakushi village in the Iga mountains of central Japan, and which is now headed by Masaaki Hatsumi Soke.

transcendental— refers to that which goes beyond the normal physical, three-dimensional limitations of human functioning, perception, and existence.

transpiritual— refers to any concept, principle, or ideal that is viewed as common to all spiritual teachings or faiths.

triangular zone— referring to the "centering triangle" illustration contained in this book, this term refers to the condition when the body, mind, and spirit "circles" have overlapped onto each other within the confines of the triangle; interchangeable with being in the "peak-performance zone," described by many athletes and others.

twilight state— refers to a calm semisleep state characterized by the higher levels of theta waves produced by the brain; considered the most transcendental state by most meditators.

unconscious competency— refers to the fourth of four learning phases experienced when learning any new skill, and characterized by the ability of the performer to utilize the skill without conscious thought to it.

unconscious incompetency— refers to the first of four learning phases experienced when learning any new skill, and characterized by the performer not having any idea that he is doing something incorrectly or inefficiently.

underside— refers to that part of the body from the waist and lower.

yamabushi— literally means "mountain warriors"; refers to an elite offshoot of the *samurai* class that secluded themselves in the mountainous region of Japan to study and practice metaphysics, mysticism, and applied spirituality.

yin **(and** *yang***)**— Chinese term(s) for "negative" (and "positive"); refers to the dualistic nature of the universe; interchangeable with "*in* (and *yo*)."

yo **(and** *in***)**— Japanese term(s) for "negative" and "positive"; refers to the dualistic nature of the universe; interchangeable with *yin* and *yang.*

yodansha— refers to a fourth-degree black belt practitioner of a traditional Japanese martial art.

yudansha— a collective term for all black-belt–rank practitioners in a traditional Japanese martial art.

zafu— literally means "seat cushion"; refers to a firm cushion, usually filled with seed husks, used during *zazen* meditation to elevate the buttocks and hips into a position higher than the knees for proper centering.

zazen— literally means "seated meditation"; refers to the most common type of meditation utilized in the traditional practice of Zen.

Zen— literally means "meditation."

zendo— literally means "Zen Way"; more accurately refers to a formal training facility for the practice of Zen meditation; a Zen *dojo*.

A Personal Postscript and Invitation to My *Sempai*

I genuinely appreciate the opportunity to have shared this book's valuable information with you. Further, I realize that it is possible (perhaps even likely) that you may eventually have some questions about the information and ideas presented herein. For that reason I am pleased to extend to you a sincere invitation to personally communicate with me. You may do so care of

Zen•Mind International, Inc.

Dr. Richard McCall, Shihan

Toll-free-800-336-7061

For details about my personal *Zen • Mind Challenge*™ training retreats, call the number above or check our Internet home page at

http:// www.Zen-Mind.com

I look forward to the opportunity to visit with you and address your questions or concerns. Until then, best wishes for success with your training and your trading, and a heart-felt *Sayanara!*